Mary Lou

P9-CDD-836

GLIMPSES OF GRACE

GLIMPSES OF GRACE

DAILY THOUGHTS AND REFLECTIONS

Madeleine L'Engle
with Carole F. Chase

❈ ❈

HarperSanFrancisco
An Imprint of HarperCollinsPublishers

FIRST EDITION

Book design by Claudia Smelser
Set in Sabon and Trajan

Library of Congress Cataloging-in-Publication Data

L'Engle, Madeleine.
    Glimpses of grace : daily thoughts and reflections /
Madeleine L'Engle ; with Carol Chase. — 1st ed.
    Includes bibliographical references and index.
    ISBN 0–06–065280–2 (cloth)
    ISBN 0–06–065281–0 (pbk.)
    1. Meditations. 2. Devotional calendars. I. Chase,
Carole F.
II. Title.
BV4832.2.L445 1996
242'.2—dc20
95-50088

96 97 98 99 00 ❖ RRD(H) 10 9 8 7 6 5 4 3 2

CONTENTS

INTRODUCTION

When I read Carole Chase's lovingly chosen selections from my books, spanning more than a quarter of a century, I was amazed at how she had articulated my theology, fitting my many questions and rare answers neatly together. I wouldn't change much of what I have said.

What I would change, and am changing, is the way in which I have said it. When I was in grammar school I was taught that *he* and *his* were generic words that included *she* and *he*, and were less formal and no more sexist than *one*. When I wrote, "When a child builds a sand castle, *he* is completely . . ." it never occurred to me that *she* was excluded.

But language changes, or it dies, and language has changed radically since my first novel was published in 1945. Punctuation has changed. We use far less. And sensitivity to the personal pronoun has made us aware that not everybody assumes that *he* includes *she*. Now I frequently use the plural, *we*.

Perhaps the most difficult personal pronoun is that which refers to God. *He* is offensive to many people. I find *she* equally sexist. So when I wrote *And It Was Good* I went back to the earliest word the ancient Hebrew used for God, *el*, and I use it with a lowercase *e*. I find it slides easily into sentences, does not call attention to itself. It is, for me, felicitous.

I'm also interested that my understanding of God's power is more and more God's rejecting power, not because el is powerless, but because the greatest exercise of power is refusing power. We, too, like language, move, change, grow—or we slide backward, diminishing into rigidity.

It is my hope that the choices Carole has made from my writings will help me, and all of us, to be more open, willing to change, to live joyfully with the unanswerable questions, and to rejoice in the Creator, who transcends all our sexisms and who is constantly calling us into life, and life abundant.

—Madeleine L'Engle

ABOUT THIS BOOK

Glimpses of Grace is an appropriate name for this book of three hundred sixty-six readings drawn from Madeleine L'Engle's extensive writings. The clarion call of Madeleine L'Engle's faith is visible in both her fiction and nonfiction. All of her writings bear witness to her devotion to a gracious God of love she believes is the creator and sustainer of all the shining galaxies and each particular star as well as every butterfly and beetle.

Madeleine's faith in a God of wonder and love and openness is communicated powerfully and plainly in her writings, which reach beyond even the narrow confines of a particular denomination of Christendom and beyond Christianity itself. She believes that the Logos, the Christ, always has been and is part of all human searches for meaning and hope and for spiritual understanding. She writes to ask the unanswerable questions about the meaning of human existence and to seek answers or, perhaps, deeper questions.

While many people know Madeleine through one kind of book or genre it is likely that few are aware of the rich variety of the body of her work. Readers of this small volume will be exposed to excerpts from Madeleine's fiction, autobiography, personal commentary on scripture, and poetry, which span five decades.

Although her nonfiction, particularly the personal commentaries on scripture, is the best source of material with an overtly spiritual quality, I have intentionally sought to glean from selected novels those bright and shining gems that focus readers' attention on matters of the heart and spirit. Because it cannot be assumed that readers are familiar with each novel quoted, I have provided a few words to set the context of the story.

In her autobiographical writing, Madeleine has shared the joys and sorrows of her life with readers. *The Summer of the Great-Grandmother* describes the last summer of her mother's life. *Two-Part Invention: The Story of a Marriage* includes both the joyful years of her life with her husband, Hugh Franklin, and the moving account of his last illness and death.

The fantasies (*A Wrinkle in Time, A Wind in the Door, A Swiftly Tilting Planet, Many Waters,* and *An Acceptable Time*), Madeleine claims, are where the theology lies. These are indeed filled with Madeleine's beliefs about God, the nature of human being, and humanity's struggle with evil. While the attentive reader can find Madeleine's religious beliefs in every one of her books, the most obvious demonstration of her spirituality and her religion is in her Genesis Trilogy (*And It Was Good, A Stone for a Pillow,* and *Sold into Egypt*).

Madeleine L'Engle has the ability to translate ultimate concepts into graspable ideas for her readers. Better than any author I know, she opens windows in her writing on the things of God. Words are the paints on Madeleine's palette. Her imagination and intellect provide the brush strokes and patterns. She catches the light with her images and symbols.

Preparing the manuscript for this book has been for me a labor of love. I am grateful to Madeleine for the confidence and trust in me that she has demonstrated by asking me to edit this book.

Readers of these pages are invited to consider the daily selections as finely cut pieces of colored glass which when taken together form a stained glass window, a window through which we can glimpse God's grace from the perspective of one of the most spiritually alive and theologically articulate storytellers of this century.

—*Carole F. Chase*

JANUARY

FIRST GLIMPSE OF GOD'S GLORY

But we rebel against the impossible. I sense a wish in some professional religion-mongers to make God possible, to make him comprehensible to the naked intellect, domesticate him so that he's easy to believe in. Every century the Church makes a fresh attempt to make Christianity acceptable. But an acceptable Christianity is not Christian; a comprehensible God is no more than an idol.

I don't want that kind of God.

What kind of God, then?

One time, when I was little more than a baby, I was taken to visit my grandmother, who was living in a cottage on a nearly uninhabited stretch of beach in northern Florida. All I remember of this visit is being picked up from my crib in what seemed the middle of the night and carried from my bedroom and out of doors, where I had my first look at the stars.

It must have been an unusually clear and beautiful night for someone to have said, "Let's wake the baby and show her the stars." The night sky, the constant rolling of breakers against the shore, the stupendous light of the stars, all made an indelible impression on me. I was intuitively aware not only of a beauty I had never seen before but also that the world was far greater than the protected limits of the small child's world which was all that I had known thus far. I had a total, if not very conscious, moment of revelation; I saw creation bursting the bounds of daily restriction, and stretching out from dimension to dimension, beyond any human comprehension.

I had been taught to say my prayers at night: Our Father, and a long string of God-blesses, and it was that first showing of the galaxies which gave me an awareness that the God I spoke to at bedtime was extraordinary and not just a bigger and better combination of the grownup powers of my mother and father.

This early experience was freeing, rather than daunting, and since it was the first, it has been the foundation for all other such glimpses of glory. And it is probably why the sound of the ocean and the sight of the stars give me more healing, more whole-ing, than anything else.

CREATION—GOD'S CANVAS

It is an extraordinary and beautiful thing that God, in creation, uses precisely the same tools and rules as the artist; he works with the beauty of matter; the reality of things; the discoveries of the senses, all five of them; so that we, in turn, may hear the grass growing; see a face springing to life in love and laughter; feel another human hand or the velvet of a puppy's ear; taste food prepared and offered in love; smell—oh, so many things: food, sewers, each other, flowers, books, new-mown grass, dirt . . .

Here, in the offerings of creation, the oblations of story and song, are our glimpses of truth.

JANUARY 2

WINTER SOLSTICE

A new year can begin only because the old year ends. In northern climates this is especially apparent. As rain turns to snow, puddles to ice, the sun rises later and sets earlier; and each day it climbs less high in the sky. One time when I went

JANUARY 3

with my children to the planetarium I was fascinated to hear the lecturer say that the primitive people used to watch the sun drop lower on the horizon in great terror, because they were afraid that one day it was going to go so low that it would never rise again; they would be left in unremitting night. There would be weeping and wailing and gnashing of teeth, and a terror of great darkness would fall upon them. And then, just as it seemed that there would never be another dawn, the sun would start to come back; each day it would rise higher, set later.

Somewhere in the depths of our unconsciousness we share that primordial fear, and when there is the first indication that the days are going to lengthen, our hearts, too, lift with relief. The end has not come: joy! and so a new year makes its birth known.

THE MYSTERY OF
THE WORD MADE FLESH I

JANUARY 4   There is no more beautiful witness to the mystery of the word made flesh than a baby's naked body. I remember with sensory clarity sitting with one of my babies on my lap and running my hand over the incredibly pure smoothness of the bare back and thinking that any mother, holding her child thus, must have at least an echo of what it is like to be Mary; that in touching the particular created matter, flesh, of our child, we are touching the Incarnation. Alan, holding his daughter on his lap, running his hand over her bare back with the same tactile appreciation with which I had touched my children, made a similar remark.

Once, when I was in the hospital, the smooth and beautiful white back of the woman in the bed next to mine, a young woman dying of cancer, was a stabbing and bitter reminder of the ultimate end of all matter.

But not just our human bodies: all matter: the stars in their courses: everything: the end of time.

THE MYSTERY OF THE WORD MADE FLESH II

How marvelous is the ritual of the Holy Mysteries, the Eucharist, where we joyfully eat Love! For me, one of the most potent phrases in the Episcopal Book of Common Prayer is "in the mystery of the Word made flesh . . ." It is a mystery that cannot be understood in terms of provable fact or the jargon of the media. Mystery, unlike magic, can be understood only mythically. JANUARY 5

When we lose our myths we lose our place in the universe.

STARRY SKIES—ICON FOR EPIPHANY

When Descartes said, "I think, therefore I am," he did us no favor, but further fragmented us, making us limit ourselves to the cognitive at the expense of the imaginative and the intuitive. But each time we read the gospels we are offered anew this healing reconciliation and, if we will, we can accept the most wondrous gift of the magi. JANUARY 6

My icon for Epiphany is the glory of the heavens at night, a cold, clear night when the stars are more brilliant than diamonds. The wise men looked at the stars, and what they saw

called them away from their comfortable dwellings and toward Bethlehem. When I look at the stars I see God's glory in
the wonder of creation.

The stars can become idols when we look to them for counsel, which should come only from God. For the magi, astron-
omy and astrology were one science, and it is probably a very
sad thing that they ever became separated.

That is yet another schism which looks for healing, and we
have not been as wise as the three magi who came from their
far corners of the world, seeking the new king, the king who
was merely a child.

Surely if the world is as interdependent as the discoveries of
particle physics imply, then what happens among the stars
does make a difference to our daily lives. But the stars will
not and should not tell us the future. They are not to be worshiped. Like the wise men, we no longer bring presents to the
moon and the stars, for this child made the moon and the
stars. Alleluia!

SONNET, TRINITY 18

JANUARY 7

Peace is the centre of the atom, the core
   Of quiet within the storm. It is not
A cessation, a nothingness; more
The lightning in reverse is what
Reveals the light. It is the law that binds
The atom's structure, ordering the dance
Of proton and electron, and that finds
Within the midst of flame and wind, the glance
In the still eye of the vast hurricane.

Peace is not placidity: peace is
The power to endure the megatron of pain
With joy, the silent thunder of release,
The ordering of Love. Peace is the atom's start,
The primal image: God within the heart.

A GLIMPSE OF GLORY

After her mother's ninetieth birthday in the spring of 1971, Madeleine flew to England to be with her daughter Josephine and son-in-law, Alan, and their daughters in Lincoln and London. Josephine and her family picked Madeleine up at the airport, and they drove to Lincoln while granddaughter Charlotte sat on her lap. Madeleine was exhausted; she had come from her mother's birthday emotionally, physically, and spiritually tired. She wrote the following to give an example of an experience she calls an "intimation" of a life beyond this one.

JANUARY 8

Josephine and I began to sing to the little girls, trying to lull them into sleep, taking turns in singing the old nursery and folk songs, many of which had come to us from my mother.

Then, suddenly, the world unfolded, and I moved into an indescribable place of many dimensions where colors were more brilliant and more varied than those of the everyday world. The unfolding continued; everything deepened and opened, and I glimpsed relationships in which the truth of love was fully revealed.

It was ineffably glorious, and then it became frightening because I knew that unless I returned to the self which was still singing to the sleeping baby it would be—at the least—madness, and for Josephine and Alan's sake I had to come back from the radiance. . . .

Was this no more than hallucination caused by fatigue and hunger? That may have been part of it, but only part. I offer no explanation for this vision of something far more beautiful and strange than any of the great beauties I have seen on earth. I only know that it happened to me, and I am grateful.

A STONE FOR A PILLOW

JANUARY 9   A stone for a pillow. It sounds odd to us, until we remember that very few people on this planet go to bed at night on soft pillows. In Japan the head-rest is often made of wood. In some countries it is simply the ground. I've tried a stone, not in bed, but late on a hot afternoon, when I call the dogs, and walk across the fields to the woods. Placed under the neck in just the right way, a stone can help me relax after a morning of typing—though I wouldn't want it for a whole night. But for a time to rest, to think, to let go and be, a warm, rounded stone can be a good pillow, reminding me that I am indeed in the house of God, that wherever I call upon my maker is always God's house.

OUT OF TIME

JANUARY 10   For all our mechanical and electronic sophistication, our thinking about ourselves and our maker is often unimaginative, egocentric, and childish. We need to do a great deal of growing up in order to reach out and adore a God who loves all of us with unqualified love.

But all those thousands of years ago when our forbears lived in the desert of an underpopulated and largely unexplored planet, the God of Jacob was definitely a masculine God, the Father God of the Patriarchs. So, when I am within Jacob's frame of reference, I'll return, for his story, to the masculine pronoun.

But when I am lying on the rock in the late afternoon I am not in Jacob's time, or indeed not in any chronologic time at all, but in *kairos*, God's time, which touches on eternity.

I lie there quietly, lapped in peace, the blue of sky the ceiling, the stone under me the foundation, the trees forming arches rather than walls. The breeze is gentle, the sun not too hot; the stone is sun-warm and firm beneath me. Sometimes after dinner I go out to the rock known as the star-watching rock and wait for the stars to come out. There I can see all of Creation as the house of God, with the glory of the stars reminding me of the Creator's immensity, diversity, magnificence.

STARRY, STARRY NIGHT

The stars are often referred to in Genesis. El Shaddai took Jacob's grandfather, Abraham, out into the desert night to show him the stars and to make incredible promises. How glorious those stars must have been all those centuries ago when the planet was not circled by a corona of light from all our cities, by smog from our internal combustion engines. Jacob, lying on the ground, the stone under his head, would have

JANUARY 11

9

seen the stars as we cannot see them today. Perhaps we have thrown up a smoke screen between ourselves and the angels.

But Jacob would not have been blinded to the glory of the stars as part of the interdependence of the desert, the human being, the smallest insects, all part of Creation.

SEPARATED FROM THE STARS

JANUARY 12

If we look at the makeup of the word disaster, dis-aster, we see *dis*, which means separation, and *aster*, which means star. So dis-aster is separation from the stars. Such separation is disaster indeed. When we are separated from the stars, the sea, each other, we are in danger of being separated from God.

Sometimes the very walls of our churches separate us from God and each other. In our various naves and sanctuaries we are safely separated from those outside, from other denominations, other religions, separated from the poor, the ugly, the dying. I'm not advocating pulling down the walls of our churches, though during the activist sixties I used to think it might be a good idea if we got rid of all churches which seat more than two hundred. But then I think of the huge cathedral which is my second home in New York, and how its great stone arms welcome a multitude of different people, from the important and affluent to waifs and strays and the little lost ones of a great, overcrowded city. We need to remember that the house of God is not limited to a building that we usually visit for only a few hours on Sunday. The house of God is not a safe place. It is a cross where time and eternity meet, and where we are—or should be—challenged to live more vulnera-

bly, more interdependently. Where, even with the light streaming in rainbow colours through the windows, we can listen to
the stars.

A CARING GOD WITHIN THE STORY

*Madeleine rejects the forensic idea of a God who is associ-
ated with crime, like a judge in a courtroom.*

The God of the Patriarchs belonged to a people, rather than
to a place. El Shaddai, their God, was one god among many JANUARY 13
gods, the varied and various deities of the surrounding tribes.
Throughout the Old Testament, there are numerous refer-
ences to other gods, and to "our" God as the greatest of these.
Whose God is like our God? There is no other God like our
God. "Who is he among the gods, that shall be like unto the
Lord?" asks the psalmist.

The chief difference between the God of Abraham, Isaac, and
Jacob, and the gods of the other tribes, was that El Shaddai
cared for, loved his people, and did not stand apart from them
and demand constant blood sacrifices. It was the other gods
who were forensic. Jacob's God was the God who was *in* the
story. It is only slowly, as we move through Scripture, that this
God among many gods becomes the God who is One, the God
who is All. The human being's attempt to understand the Creator is never static; it is constantly in motion. If we let our
concept of God become static, and we have done so over and
over again throughout history, we inevitably blunder into a
forensic interpretation, and that does not work.

THE JOYOUS DANCE OF CREATION

The first day. The beginning of time. Time, which, like matter, was created in that first great shouting of joy, of making nothing into something; time, a part of nature, which, like space, like all creation, will have an end. (All created things die. Before the seed can grow, it must be planted in the earth, and so die to itself before it can become a tree. Or a wave. Or a flying fish.)

But in the beginning, when all things were first shown forth, the light and the dark danced together; in the fullness of their time they comprehended each other; they knew each other, and it was good. It was very good.

God created. God *made*.

Night and day—that first flashing rhythm which marked the birth of time. Water and land. Galaxies and suns and planets and moons, all moving in the joyous dance of creation. Matter and time making music together.

God made. Fish and sea animals and birds. Land and land animals, every kind of living creature, ants and auks and aardvarks. Dromedaries and dragons and dinosaurs.

CALLED TO CO-CREATE

God created, and it was joy: time, space, matter. There *is*, and we are part of that is-ness, part of that becoming. That is our calling: co-creation. Every single one of us, without exception, is called to co-create with God. No one is too unimportant to have a share in the making or unmaking of the final showing-forth. Everything that we do either draws the Kingdom of love closer, or pushes it further off. That is a fearful responsibility, but when God made "man in our image, male and female," responsibility went with it. Too often we want to let somebody else do it, the preacher, or the teacher, or the government agency. But if we are to continue to grow in God's image, then we have to accept the responsibility.

God's image! How much of God may be seen in me, may I see in others? Try as we may, we cannot hide it completely.

A young reader knowing of my love of new words, sent me a beautiful one: namasté: I salute the God within you.

GOD'S POWER

We live in a world which has become too complex to unravel; there is nothing we can do about it, we little people who don't have big government posts or positions of importance. But I believe that the Kingdom is built on the little things that all of us do. I remember my grandmother was fond of reciting:

JANUARY 16

> Little drops of water,
> Little grains of sand
> Make the mighty ocean
> And the pleasant land.

A single drop can't make even a puddle, but together, all our little drops and God's planning can make not only a mighty ocean but a mighty difference. Alone, there's not much we can do, but when Peter healed a cripple it was made very clear that it was not by his own power, but by the power of Christ, the creating Word, that the healing was accomplished.

This power is available to all of us. Indeed, with everything we do, we either use or reject it, for we do nothing in isolation. As the physicists who study the microcosm are discovering, *nothing* happens in isolation; nothing *exists* in isolation. Quanta, the tiny subatomic particles being studied in quantum mechanics, cannot exist alone; there cannot be *a* quantum, for quanta exist only in relationship to each other. And they can never be studied objectively, because even to observe them is to change them. And, like the stars, they appear to be able to communicate with each other without sound or speech; *there is neither speech nor language; but their voices are heard among them,* sings the psalmist.

EL—THE LORD

JANUARY 17   One of the early words by which the ancient Hebrews knew God was El. El—the Lord. Beth-el, for instance, means the house of God. So I find it helpful, wherever and whenever possible, to call God El, or el, rather than using the masculine or feminine pronoun, because the name *el* lifts the Creator beyond all our sexisms and chauvinisms and anthropomorphisms.

We human creatures, made in the image of God, in church as well as out, too often reject instead of affirming the Word which has proven to be the cornerstone. And we worry, too often, about peripheral things. (Like baptism: is dunking more valid than sprinkling?) And we are continuing to worry about sexist words to the point where we are coming close to destroying language. To call God either him or her, he or she, is in both cases to miss the wholeness of the Creator. And so we lose all sense of proportion, and try to clamp God once again within our own broken image.

And so I return to the reality of our trinitarian God of creation, el.

El. That power of love. That holy thing. Do we believe that it was a power of love which created everything and saw it was good? Is creation purposeful? Or is it some kind of cosmic accident? Do our fragments of lives have meaning? Or are we poor human beings no more than a skin disease on the face of an unfortunate planet? Can we see the pattern and beauty which is an affirmation of the value of all creation?

ACTORS IN THE DRAMA OF CREATION

I f new evidence should prove that evolution is not how it all happened, that won't do anything to change the nature of God, any more than Galileo's discoveries changed the nature of God. Nor would it shatter my faith. The Lord of Creation makes as el chooses, and only el knows how. "I will be what I will be," God replied to Moses when asked about his name. The options are all open, free. Free of all the restrictions we human beings try to impose on our Maker. Free to offer us an example of freedom which we hardly dare contemplate.

Creation continues lavishly, and we are part of it. Not only are stars and people and fireflies born, not only do they die,

JANUARY 18

but what we as creatures do during our lifespan makes a difference. We are not just passive, acted upon; we are also actors in the great drama of creation. As to the passionate arguers about creationism versus evolutionism, I still think they're missing the point. The more hotly they argue, the more widely do they miss the point. The more zealous they grow in defending their cause (like the church establishment of Galileo's day) the less are they able to sit back calmly and observe the evidence and say, "This, too, is the Lord's."

RECEIVING THE BODY OF GOD

I'm not sure where the idea came from that all of creation is God's body, but if we must have an analogy, it is not a bad one.

When I look at the galaxies on a clear night—when I look at the incredible brilliance of creation, and think that this is what God is like, then, instead of feeling intimidated and diminished by it, I am enlarged—I rejoice that I am part of it, I, you, all of us—part of this glory. And so, when we go to the altar to receive the bread and wine, we are taking into our own bodies all of creation, all of the galaxies. And our total interdependence is an astounding glory.

We are whatever we eat—junk foods, well-balanced meals, the books we ingest, the people we listen to—but most marvellously we are the eternally loving power of creativity. Does it sound incredible to say that when we receive Communion we are eating the entire universe? Of course it does, but it is also incredibly possible, and I rejoice in it.

ECSTASY!

The concentration of a small child at play is analogous to the concentration of the artist of any discipline. In real play, which is real concentration, the child is not only outside time, he is outside *himself*. He has thrown himself completely into whatever it is that he is doing. A child playing a game, building a sand castle, painting a picture, is completely *in* what he is doing. His *self*-consciousness is gone; his consciousness is wholly focused outside himself.

JANUARY 20

I had just witnessed this in Crosswicks, observing an eighteen-month-old lying on her stomach on the grass watching a colony of ants, watching with total, spontaneous concentration. And I had played ring-around-a-rosy with her; we skipped around in a circle, grandparents, parents, assorted teenagers, wholly outside ourselves, holding hands, falling in abandon onto the lawn, joining in the child's shrieks of delighted laughter.

And with her we were outside self and outside time.

REFUSE NOT THE QUESTIONS

But children want to know, and perhaps it is our desire not to let them down that has led us into the mistake of teaching them only the answerables. This *is* a mistake, and we mustn't refuse to allow them to ask the unanswerables just because we can't provide tidy little answers. In our fear of the unprovable we mustn't forget that they can learn from *The Tempest* as well as social studies; that they can learn from Aesop as well as the

JANUARY 21

new math; that *The Ugly Duckling* need not be discarded in favor of driver education. There is a violent kind of truth in the most primitive myths, a truth we need today, because probably the most important thing those first storytellers did for their listeners back in the dim past in their tales of gods and giants and fabulous beasts was to affirm that the gods are not irrational, that there is structure and meaning in the universe, that God is responsible to his creation.

Truth happens in these myths. That is why they have lasted. If they weren't expressions of truth they would long have been forgotten. One of the great historical pieces of evidence is the Bible, both the Old and New Testaments. Many books which were once in the Bible have dropped out of sight through the centuries. Those that have stayed with us are those that contain truth that speaks to us in our daily living, right where we are now.

THE PRAYER OF A LITTLE BOY

JANUARY 22

Small children do not yet have a sense of chronology and therefore live in eternity; they are far more willing to accept death than we are. When his dearly loved grandfather died, our young son shut up like a clam. It seemed to his older sisters that he didn't care. We said, Wait. That night during his prayers he reached the point in his "God bless" prayer when it was time to name his grandfather, and stopped. He started over, came to the same point, and stopped again. Started once more, and finally said, "And God, please take care of Grandfather wherever you want him to be, another star or wherever you think, and make him be all right, and we love him. Amen."

NEW PERSPECTIVES ON TIME

On a small ship the ability to be aware of our tiny, yet significant part in the interdependence of all of God's creation returns, and one's mind naturally turns to cosmic questions, rather than answers. Seeing the glory of the unpolluted horizon, the brilliance of the Southern Cross against the black velvet sky, opened up questions about creation and the Creator.

JANUARY 23

And laughter, too, for though we cannot take ourselves seriously enough, we can also take ourselves far too seriously.

One of the sailors remarked casually as he was swabbing down the deck, "It's a short walk from the womb to the tomb," and jolted us back from cosmic time to mortal time.

But mortal time is part of cosmic time, and during that short walk we are given glimpses of eternity, eternity which was before time began, and will be after time ends. The Word, who moved into time for us and lived with us, lives, as Christ, in eternity; so, when we live in Christ, when Christ lives in us we, too, are free from time and alive in eternity.

THE ELASTICITY OF TIME

Since we live in time, it is almost impossible for us to understand that eternity is not a time concept, that it has nothing to do with the passage of time. The astrophysicist's concept of time has changed radically in the past half century. Time is not, as the old hymn suggests, a never-ending stream. Time, like the rest of us creatures, is complex and paradoxical and full of quirks and surprises.

JANUARY 24

Sandol Stoddard in *The Hospice Movement,* quotes Dr. Cicely Saunders: "We learn, for example, that time has no fixed meaning as such. An hour at the dentist seems like forever, but an hour with someone you love flies past. And yet, wait a little and look back on it. The hour of discomfort and anxiety is totally forgotten. What we remember forever is the hour of love."

The hour of love is the hour when God's creature, time, and el's human creatures, like us, collaborate with each other.

MEG'S GIFTS

A Wrinkle in Time is a fantasy. In this excerpt, Meg Murry, the protagonist, prepares to leave Ixchel and go to Camazotz to rescue her brother, Charles Wallace. Three angelic beings, Mrs. Who, Mrs. Whatsit, and Mrs. Which, arm her for the journey with their gifts.

Mrs. Whatsit held up her hand. "We gave you gifts the last time we took you to Camazotz. We will not let you go empty handed this time. But what we can give you now is nothing you can touch with your hands. I give you my love, Meg. Never forget that. My love always."

Mrs. Who, eyes shining behind spectacles, beamed at Meg. Meg felt in her blazer pocket and handed back the spectacles she had used on Camazotz.

"Your father is right," Mrs. Who took the spectacles and hid them somewhere in the folds of her robes. "The virtue is gone from them. And what I have to give you this time you must try to understand not word by word, but in a flash, as you understand the tesseract. Listen, Meg. Listen well. *The* foolishness of God is wiser than men; and the weakness of God is stronger than men. For ye see your calling, brethren, how that not many wise men after the flesh, not many mighty, not many noble, are called, but God hath chosen the foolish things of the world to confound the wise; and God hath chosen the weak things of the world to confound the things which are mighty. And base things of the world, and things which are despised, hath God chosen, yea, and things which are not, to bring to nought things that are." She paused, and then she said, "May the right prevail."

Meg is tessered (transported) to Camazotz and though she cannot see Mrs. Which, she hears her voice. The evil being she encounters is a naked brain called IT.

"I hhave nnott ggivenn yyou mmyy ggifftt. *Yyou hhave ssomethinngg thatt* ITT *hhass nnott.* Thiss ssomethinngg iss yyourr onlly wweapponn. Bbutt yyou mmusstt ffinndd itt fforr yyourrsellff." Then the voice ceased, and Meg knew that she was alone.

LOVE IS THE KEY

Meg reaches Charles Wallace, who is in a puppetlike trance, having been brainwashed by IT. *She felt "the revolting rhythm of* IT." *And she saw her brother a repulsive, non–Charles Wallace creature. She could feel* IT *speaking through Charles Wallace, trying to take over her mind.*

JANUARY 26

Her body trembled with the strength of her hatred and the strength of IT.

With the last vestige of consciousness she jerked her mind and body. Hate was nothing that IT didn't have. IT knew all about hate.

"You are lying about that, and you were lying about Mrs. Whatsit!" she screamed.

"Mrs. Whatsit hates you," Charles Wallace said.

And that was where IT made ITs fatal mistake, for as Meg said, automatically, "Mrs. Whatsit loves me; that's what she told me, that she loves me," suddenly she knew.

She knew!

Love.

That was what she had that IT did not have.

She had Mrs. Whatsit's love, and her father's, and her mother's, and the real Charles Wallace's love, and the twins', and Aunt Beast's.

And she had her love for them.

But how could she use it? What was she meant to do?

If she could give love to IT perhaps it would shrivel up and die, for she was sure that IT could not withstand love. But she, in all her weakness and foolishness and baseness and nothingness, was incapable of loving IT. Perhaps it was not too much to ask of her, but she could not do it.

But she could love Charles Wallace.

She could stand there and she could love Charles Wallace.

Her own Charles Wallace, the real Charles Wallace, the child for whom she had come back to Camazotz, to IT, the baby who was so much more than she was, and who was yet so utterly vulnerable.

She could love Charles Wallace.

Charles. Charles, I love you. My baby brother who always takes care of me. Come back to me, Charles Wallace, come away from IT, come back, come home. I love you, Charles. Oh, Charles Wallace, I love you.

Tears were streaming down her cheeks, but she was unaware of them.

Now she was even able to look at him, at this animated thing that was not her own Charles Wallace at all. She was able to look and love.

I love you. Charles Wallace, you are my darling and my dear and the light of my life and the treasure of my heart. I love you. I love you. I love you.

Slowly his mouth closed. Slowly his eyes stopped their twirling. The tic in the forehead ceased its revolting twitch. Slowly he advanced toward her.

"I love you!" she cried. "I love you, Charles! I love you!"

Then suddenly he was running, pelting, he was in her arms, he was shrieking with sobs. "Meg! Meg! Meg!"

"I love you, Charles!" she cried again, her sobs almost as loud as his, her tears mingling with his. "I love you! I love you! I love you!"

CONSUMER IDENTITY REJECTED

Madeleine writes of the forties, the early years of her marriage with Hugh Franklin.

Our surroundings were not yet as unreal as they were to become. In the world of the theatre we touched on reality itself, and were shocked as the world around us seemed to reach out for the unreal. Planned obsolescence was just coming in, objects made with less than excellence, built to destroy themselves or to wear out. Plastic and synthetics were just

JANUARY 27

becoming available to the public. The word *synthetics* is enough: *unreal*.

Today we live in a society that seems to be less and less concerned with reality. We drink instant coffee and reconstituted orange juice. We buy our vegetables on cardboard trays covered with plastic. But perhaps the most dehumanizing thing of all is that we have allowed the media to call us consumers— ugly. No! I don't want to be a consumer. Anger consumes. Forest fires consume. Cancer consumes.

CARING, ONE PERSON AT A TIME

JANUARY 28 We may be a global village, but instant communication often isolates us from each other rather than uniting us. When I am bombarded on the evening news with earthquake, flood, fire, it is too much for me. There is a mechanism, a safety valve, which cuts off our response to overexposure to suffering.

But when a high-school student comes to me and cries because the two- and three-year-olds on her block are becoming addicted to hard drugs; when the gentle man who cleans the building in which the Cathedral library is located talks to me about his family in Guatemala, rejoicing because they are alive although their house has been destroyed by earthquake; when a goddaughter of mine in Luxembourg writes me about the hungry children of the immigrant Portuguese family with whom she is living, then in this particularity my heart burns within me, and I am more able to learn what it is that I can and ought to do, even if this seems, and is, inadequate.

But neither was Jesus adequate to the situation. He did not feed all the poor, only a few. He did not heal all the lepers, or give sight to all the blind, or drive out all the unclean spirits. Satan wanted him to do all this, but he didn't.

That helps me. If I felt that I had to conquer all the ills of the world I'd likely sit back and do nothing at all. But if my job is to feed one stranger, then the money I give to world relief will be dug down deeper from my pocket than it would if I felt I had to succeed in feeding the entire world.

THE MARRED GARDEN

In this fantasy, Many Waters, *the twins Sandy and Dennys Murry have been transported to the biblical time of Noah. They encounter the people from that time, unicorns, seraphim, and evil angelic beings called nephilim. Alarid is one of the seraphim.*

JANUARY 29

You come from a far time, and yet you speak the Old Language?"

"The what?"

"The Old Language, the language of creation, of the time when the stars were made, and the heavens and the waters and all creatures. It was the language which was spoken in the Garden—"

"What garden?"

"The Garden of Eden, before the story was bent. It is the language which is still, and will be, spoken by all the stars which carry the light."

"Then," Dennys said flatly, "I don't know why I speak it."

"And speak it with ease," Alarid said.

"Does Sandy speak it, too?" Dennys asked.

Alarid nodded. "You were both speaking it when you met Japheth and Higgaion in the desert, were you not?"

"We certainly didn't realize it," Dennys said. "We thought we were speaking our own language."

Alarid smiled. "It *is* your own language, so perhaps it is best that you didn't realize it. Do others of your time and place speak the Old Language?"

"I don't know. Sandy and I aren't any good at languages."

"How can you say that," Alarid demanded, "when you have the gift of the original tongue?"

"Hey, I don't know. Sandy and I are the squares of the family. Our older sister and our little brother are the special ones. We're just the ordinary—"

Alarid interrupted him. "Because that is how you are, or because that is how you choose to be?"

Dennys looked at the seraph, his eyes widening. "What happened to the Old Language?"

"It was broken at Babel."

"Babel?"

"The tower of human pride and arrogance. It has not happened yet, in this time you are in now. You do not know the story?"

Dennys blinked. "I think I remember something. People built a big tower, and for some reason they all began to speak in different languages, and couldn't understand each other anymore. It was in, oh, pre-history, and it's a story to, sort of, explain why there are so many different languages in the world."

"But underneath them all," Alarid said, "is the original language, the old tongue, still in communion with the ancient harmonies. It is a privilege to meet one who still has the under-hearing."

"Hey," Dennys said. "Listen. I guess because we got here so unexpectedly and everything was so strange, and we didn't have time to think, and when we met Japheth it just seemed natural to speak to him—"

"It is a special gift," Alarid told him.

"We're not special, neither Sandy nor I. We're just the sort of ordinary kid who gets along without making waves."

"Where in the future," Alarid asked him abruptly, "do you come from?"

"A long, long way," Dennys said. "We live at the end of the twentieth century."

Alarid closed his eyes. "A time of many wars."

"Yes."

"And the heart of the atom has been revealed."

"Yes."

"You have soiled your waters and your air."

"Yes."

QUESTION DEFINITIONS BOLDLY

Each time an unexpected discovery is made in the world of knowledge, it shakes the religious establishment of the day. Now, we are often taught that it is unfaithful to question traditional religious beliefs, but I believe that we must question them continually—not God, not Christ, who are at the center of our lives as believers and creators—but what human beings say *about* God and about Christ; otherwise, like those of the

JANUARY 30

church establishment of Galileo's day, we truly become God's frozen people. Galileo's discoveries did nothing whatsoever to change the nature of God; they threatened only man's rigid ideas of the nature of God. We must constantly be open to new revelation, which is another way of hearing God, with loving obedience.

DOUBT IS A DOORWAY TO TRUTH

The great metaphysical poet, John Donne, writes, "To come to a doubt, and to a debatement of any religious duty, is the voice of God in our conscience: Would you know the truth? Doubt, and then you will inquire."

If my religion is true, it will stand up to all my questioning; there is no need to fear. But if it is not true, if it is man imposing strictures on God (as did the men of the Christian establishment of Galileo's day) then I want to be open to God, not to what man says about God. I want to be open to revelation, to new life, to new birth, to new light.

Revelation. Listening. Humility.

Remember—the root word of humble and human is the same: humus: earth. We are dust. We are created; it is God who made us and not we ourselves. But we were made to be co-creators with our maker.

FEBRUARY

THE PURE FLAME
WITHIN—OUR ESSENCE

In Love Letters, *Charlotte Clement, the protagonist, is remembering an incident from the past when she had gone downstairs to say goodnight to her widowed father, James Clement, a writer who can't get his most recent books published.*

He wasn't in bed reading as she had thought he would be. He hadn't even started to undress. He was sitting on the side of his bed. Just sitting. Not gone off to wherever it was he went. Just sitting.

But he smiled when he saw her. "Ready so soon, Cotty?"

"It's been an hour, Father."

"Oh. Time can be deceptive. And I'm tired. I'm so tired, Cotty. There is nothing more physically exhausting than a sense of failure."

"But you're not a failure, Father," she said.

"Oh, Cotty, let's not fool each other any longer. Why do I go on groping in the dark? Why can't I accept the absurdity of existence and laugh, as the absurd ought to be laughed at? Why can't I face the fact that it's all an accident, that man is an unattractive skin eruption on an improbable planet, that what came gurgling up from the void will die down again into darkness." He stood up. "Why does all of me reject this, Cotty? Why must there be beauty and meaning when everything that has happened to me teaches me that there is none?"

Her throat was tight and it was difficult to say, "But there is."

He clasped her tightly in his arms. "Why do I do this to you, Cotty? Why do I try to drag you into the pit with me?"

"You don't," she said. "You don't, Father. And there isn't anybody for you to talk with, and I'm glad I'm the one, truly I am."

"Cotty, sweet, sweet, go on up to bed and don't worry."

"I don't want to leave you when you're feeling this way."

"I'm all right."

"You're not feeling all right about your writing."

"That will pass, too. Do you know how applejack is made?"

For a moment she thought that he must have made himself another drink. "No."

"You put apple juice in a keg and leave it outdoors all winter and let it freeze. Almost all of it will turn to ice, but there's a tiny core of liquid inside, of pure flame. I have that core of faith in myself. There's always that small searing drop that doesn't freeze. Don't worry about me, my darling. I'm all right. And you must get some sleep."

BEYOND ANTHROPOMORPHISMS

It is impossible for us human beings not to keep coming up with anthropomorphic gods. The righteous Lord of the Old Testament is an analogy of human righteousness as it was understood then. The gods we make today are equally anthropomorphic, God in our own image, because it's inevitable with finite human nature. Occasionally we are given the grace to turn away from our own image and toward God's image in us, and we have the model for this image in Jesus. He may have

FEBRUARY 2

been fully man, but he was most unlike us, or we are most unlike him, in that his Father was not an anthropomorphic God, but a Being entirely new, so new that we still can't understand the glorious Father Jesus showed us in everything he did and said and was.

PARTICIPATING IN THE IMAGE OF CHRIST

FEBRUARY 3 A young friend told me of an East Indian Christian who had suggested to her that we are not called to be Christians; we are called to be Christs. I find this both challenging and freeing when I am confused by all the things which Christians are doing all over the planet, in the name of Christ, which seem incompatible with all that Jesus taught.

I distrust the word *Christian* as an adjective; it has become less an adjective than a label, separating those who call themselves Christian from the rest of the world. How can those who would follow Christ assume that they are more beloved of the Creator than any other part of his creation, when God created *everything,* and saw that it was good? And if God created man in his own image, male and female, then all, *all* of humankind is part of that image, known or unknown, served or betrayed, accepted or denied. God loves every man, sings the psalmist. Perhaps it is more blessed to be aware of our part in the Image than not, but Jesus made it very clear that sometimes it is those who are least aware of it who serve the image best. It is truer to that image to be like the publican, aware of his unworthiness, than like the pharisee who was puffed up with the pride of his own virtue; it is truer to the image to say, "Lord, I believe; help thou my unbelief," than to dismiss the crucifixion by saying, "It is good for one man to die for the sake of the nation."

SIZE MAKES NO NEVER MIND

As for size—as the old southern phrase has it, size makes no never mind. Those two sources of radio emission, sending their messages across millions of light years, are as close together as the eyes in a beloved face. A grain of sand commands as much respect as a galaxy. A flower is as bright as the sun. But all, all are part of creation. So, as there is nothing we can do that does not affect someone else (we can never truthfully say "it's my own business"), there is nothing we can do that does not affect God. This is an awesome responsibility, and one which we offer and accept whenever we receive Communion, asking that we may dwell in God and he in us.

FEBRUARY 4

THE QUALIFICATIONS FOR GOD'S WORK

Slowly I have realized that I do not have to be qualified to do what I am asked to do, that I just have to go ahead and do it, even if I can't do it as well as I think it ought to be done. This is one of the most liberating lessons of my life.

FEBRUARY 5

The qualifications needed for God's work are very different from those of the world. In fact, when we begin to think we are qualified, we have already fallen for the tempter's wiles. Not one of us has to be qualified in order to employ lesson, meditation, and orison; to read, think, and pray over Scripture. We do not need to have gone to a theological seminary, or to have taken courses in Bible in or out of college. We do have to be willing to open ourselves to the power of the living Word. And sometimes that can be frightening.

HEALTHY AGNOSTICISM

FEBRUARY 6

At a church conference recently someone asked, "You have referred to your agnostic period. What happened to get you out of it?"

And I reply, joyfully, that I am still an agnostic, but then I was an unhappy one, seeking finite answers, and now I am a happy one, rejoicing in paradox. *Agnostic* means only that we do not *know*, and we finite creatures cannot know, in any intellectual or ultimate way, the infinite Lord, the undivided Trinity. Now I am able to accept my not-knowing—and yet, in a completely different way, in the old biblical way, I also know what I do not understand, and that is what my agnosticism means to me now. It does not mean that I do not believe; it is an acceptance that I am created, that I am asked to bear the light, knowing that this is the most wonderful of all vocations.

THE MYSTERY OF THE INCARNATION

FEBRUARY 7

In Jerusalem, inside the old city, I went to the great gold mosque which the devout Jew cannot enter because the mosque is built over the place where the temple stood and no one knows exactly where the Holy of Holies was placed. The Holy of Holies is so sacred that the place where it stood so long ago may not be stepped on, even inadvertently. I went in, with my shoes off, feeling deep awe (Moses took his shoes off before the burning bush, and so must we when we approach God's holy places), and I stood in front of a great spreading rock, the rock where Abraham laid Isaac and raised his knife to kill his son, and my skin prickled. In my bare feet I stood there, lost in wonder at the magnificent incomprehensibility of the Creator, who loves us so much that he came to live with us and be part of us and die for us and rise again for us and send the Holy Spirit to comfort us. And I was, somehow, comforted by the very incomprehensibility of all that makes life creative and worth living.

HUMAN BEINGS, NOT PUPPETS

My friend Dana and I talk about how we want to make everything all right for those we love, and cannot. Her mother died of pancreatic cancer only a few months ago. We say to each other that if we were God we would make everything all right, and then we stop. Look at each other. Because we suddenly see that making everything all right would *not* make everything all right. We would not be human beings. We would then be no more than puppets obeying the strings of the master puppeteer. We agree sadly that it is a good thing that we are not God; we do not have to understand God's ways, or the suffering and brokenness and pain that sooner or later come to us all.

But we do have to know in the very depths of our being that the ultimate end of the story, no matter how many aeons it takes, is going to be all right.

FEBRUARY 8

35

MATTERING TO OURSELVES

FEBRUARY 9 I suppose the perfect *is*ness of anything would be frightening without the hope of God. An oak tree is, and it doesn't matter to it—at least Sartre thinks it doesn't; it is not a thinking oak. Man is; it matters to him; this is terrifying unless it matters to God, too, because this is the only possible reason we can matter to ourselves: not because we are sufficient unto ourselves—I am not: my husband, my family, my friends give me my meaning and, in a sense, my being, so that I know that I, like the burning bush, or the oak tree, am ontological: essential: real.

WOUNDED HEALERS

FEBRUARY 10 Would I really be able to worship a God who was simply implacable power, and who was invulnerable? If I am hurt, I don't turn for strength and help to someone who has never been hurt, but to someone who has, and who can therefore understand a little of what I am going through. The people I know who are the most invulnerable also tend to show the least compassion.

The kind of person I turn to is someone who has been strong enough to face pain when it comes—and it does come. Someone who faces it, endures it, and tries as hard as possible to go through it and come out on the other side. Someone whose urge for health is strong enough to hold on to wholeness even in the midst of suffering. And someone who manages to retain a sense of humour, who has the gift of laughter.

As these are the qualities I look for in another human being when I am in need of healing, so these are the qualities I look for in God.

IMPRISONED SPLENDOR

Look! Here I am, caught up in this fragment of chronology, in this bit of bone and flesh and water which makes up my mortal body, and yet I am also part of that which is not imprisoned in time or mortality. Partaker simultaneously of the finite and the infinite, I do not find the infinite by repudiating my finiteness, but by being fully in it, in this *me* who is more than I know. This *me,* like all of creation, lives in a glorious dance of communion with all the universe. In isolation we die; in interdependence we live.

FEBRUARY 11

UNIQUE AND UNITED

God made us all unique, each one different, no two alike, just as there are no two maple leaves exactly alike, and no two snowflakes exactly alike. We need to learn to glory in both our similarities and our differences. A maple leaf is a maple leaf and not a snowflake, and we are human creatures, each one sharing in our humanness, but each one also uniquely different. As Christians we are alike in being people of the Resurrection, but we are also different in our ways of glorifying God. I grew up in the Episcopal Church with its liturgy and stained-glass windows and formal, beautiful language, and my husband grew up in the Southern Baptist Church with its gospel

FEBRUARY 12

singing and spontaneous praying, and we both learned from each other's treasures. By God's grace it did not separate us, but forged a deeper bond between us, and that is for me a wonderful example, an affirmation that we can be one despite our differences.

LINES AFTER SIR THOMAS BROWNE

FEBRUARY 13

If thou couldst empty self of selfishness
And then with love reach out in wide embrace
Then might God come this purer self to bless;
So might thou feel the wisdom of His Grace,
And see, thereby, the radiance of His face.

But selfishness turns inwards, miry, black,
Refuses stars, sees only clouded night,
Too full, too dark, cannot confess a lack,
Turns from God's face, blest, holy, bright,
Is blinded by the presence of the Light.

ONE THING IN PARTICULAR

FEBRUARY 14

Love Letters is set in Portugal, in two time frames. Charlotte Napier, an American, lives in the twentieth century. Mariana, a young nun, lives in the seventeenth century. She has watched the Portuguese cavalry pass by the convent. A handsome French soldier riding with them has been noticed.

Beatriz moved to Joaquina. "Why were you so busy watching Mariana instead of the parade?"

Joaquina's voice trembled. "Maybe I was afraid, which is something you and Mariana never seem to be."

"Afraid of what? That they'd come leaping over the convent wall to drag us off with them?"

"Stop it," Joaquina cried, all control broken by anger. "It was obvious that Sister Mariana was looking at one French soldier in particular."

Mariana moved to the fountain—to where Sister Maria da Assunçao and Mother Escolastica were standing. "Oh, Sisters, you all know that I always look at one person or one thing in particular. Joaquina's quite right. I look at one blossom on the bough. One little lizard sunning itself on the wall. One orange. One drop of rain as it slides down the windowpane. When I look at one more carefully, then I know all better."

Joaquina stepped out of the shadows towards the silver of the fountain. "Does eating rain make you understand it better?"

Beatriz was amused. "What are you talking about?"

"I've seen Mariana *eat* rain. I saw her stand out on the balcony one afternoon during a shower, and I saw her holding out her hand and catching rain and tasting it."

Mariana laughed. "It was wonderful."

"And I've seen her taking the petal of a flower and sucking it."

"I just wanted to see what the bees were after."

Beatriz looked affectionately at Mariana's laughing face. "We'd all like to get as much pleasure out of things as she does."

Joaquina tightened her lips. The happiness of the other sisters seemed to choke her. "I didn't think our lives were supposed to be spent in the pursuit of pleasure."

Mariana spoke earnestly and with joy. "Surely, Sister, we aren't meant to deny the wonderful things around us that are just asking to be marveled at."

TRUE TEMPTATION

The discussion among the nuns in the convent continues.

FEBRUARY 15

Now Mother Escolastica said, thoughtfully, directing the warmth of her smile first to Sister Maria da Assunçao, then to Joaquina, "The devil tempts us most subtly with the things that are in themselves good and pure and true. We can see that the bad and sinful things are bad and sinful, and, although because we are human and fallen and miserable sinners we do the bad and sinful things over and over again, they are not the real temptations. The real temptations are the good things, and not only the more obvious ones, like icon to idol, sacrament to superstition, but the less tangible ones. We cannot be too serious about our vocations," here she held Joaquina's sullen hazel eyes, "but if we let our seriousness preclude joy, then indeed we err. One of the requisites for sainthood is joyfulness, you know. I really find it hard to understand how St. Jerome ever became a saint."

Her smile bathed Joaquina again; then the old nun continued, turning to Beatriz. "Intellect. Using the brain God has given us. It would be sinful not to, but pride of intellect is a grave danger." Beatriz bowed her head submissively and Mother Escolastica nodded approval, then looked directly at Mariana. "Love. Loving. This is probably the most insidious and terrible temptation of all. You, child, do love a great many people, and most joyfully, but your very love sometimes clouds your judgment. I do not mean, as St. John of the Cross sometimes tells us, that you must stop loving people in order not to have your love of people come between you and your love of God. What I'm asking of you is far more difficult than that. There are always in our lives, even in the lives of Religious, a few people who are deepest and dearest in our hearts. And we must love God so much that even when these people are taken from us, by death or daemon, our love remains unchanged, because we love them only in and through God. I am not denying grief, for that would be sacrilegious. Nor am I even suggesting that we remove human love, for if we removed human love we would be completely safe, and we would have no need ever to grieve, and we would, I fear, forget to love our Lord. No, it is not a removal, but a different way of affirmation. To love so deeply that we are always in God, in Love, no matter what happens."

LOVE CHANGES THINGS

We do not love each other without changing each other. We do not observe the world around us without in some way changing it, and being changed ourselves. To listen to the news on radio or television is to be part of what is going on, and to be modified by it. But how on earth—or heaven—can that be reciprocal? *We* are changed by war and rumour of war, but how can we in turn change what changes us?

FEBRUARY 16

There are some obvious, small ways. We can join, if we are female, the League of Women voters. We can do volunteer work (despite a nine-to-five job) in the hospice movement. We can write our senators and congressmen. . . .

Those are a few of the obviously active ways. But there are less obvious ones that are equally important. I was asked how we could pray for our planet, with the devastating wars which are tearing it apart, with greed fouling the air we breathe and the water we drink. And I replied that the only way I know how to pray for the body of our planet is to see it as God meant it to be, to see the sky as we sometimes see it in the country in wintertime, crisp with stars, or to see the land with spring moving across it, the fruit trees flowering and the grass greening, and at night hearing the peepers calling back and forth, and the high sweet singing of the bats.

BEING AND SEEING

FEBRUARY 17

Meg has been seriously injured due to a faulty tesseract. Her father and Calvin seem unable to help her. A strange beast, native of the planet Ixchel, has carried her away from them in order to make her well. Meg and the creature, whom she has named Aunt Beast, have a conversation about light and sight.

Why is it so dark in here?" Meg asked. She tried to look around, but all she could see was shadows. Nevertheless there was a sense of openness, a feel of a gentle breeze moving lightly about, that kept the darkness from being oppressive.

Perplexity came to her from the beast. "What is this dark? What is this light? We do not understand. Your father and the boy, Calvin, have asked this, too. They say that it is night now on our planet, and that they cannot see. They have told us that our atmosphere is what they call opaque, so that the stars are not visible, and then they were surprised that we know stars, that we know their music and the movements of their dance far better than beings like you who spend hours studying them through what you call telescopes. We do not understand what this means, *to see*."

"Well, it's what things look like," Meg said helplessly.

"We do not know what things *look* like, as you say," the beast said. "We know what things *are* like. It must be a very limiting thing, this seeing."

"Oh, no!" Meg cried. "It's—it's the most wonderful thing in the world!"

"What a very strange world yours must be!" the beast said, "that such a peculiar-seeming thing should be of such importance. Try to tell me, what is this thing called *light* that you are able to do so little without?"

"Well, we can't see without it," Meg said, realizing that she was completely unable to explain vision and light and dark. How can you explain sight on a world where no one has ever seen and where there is no need of eyes? "Well, on this planet," she fumbled, "you have a sun, don't you?"

"A most wonderful sun, from which comes our warmth, and the rays which give us our flowers, our food, our music, and all the things which make life and growth."

"Well," Meg said, "when we are turned toward the sun— our earth, our planet, I mean, toward our sun—we receive its light. And when we're turned away from it, it is night. And if we want to see we have to use artificial lights."

"Artificial lights," the beast sighed. "How very complicated life on your planet must be. Later on you must try to explain some more to me."

"All right," Meg promised, and yet she knew that to try to explain anything that could be seen with the eyes would be impossible, because the beasts in some way saw, knew, understood, far more completely than she, or her parents, or Calvin, or even Charles Wallace.

CALLED AND CHOSEN

Meg asks Aunt Beast to sing to her while she is resting.

FEBRUARY 18

If it was impossible to describe sight to Aunt Beast, it would be even more impossible to describe the singing of Aunt Beast to a human being. It was a music even more glorious than the music of the singing creatures on Uriel. It was a music more tangible than form or sight. It had essence and structure. It supported Meg more firmly than the arms of Aunt Beast. It seemed to travel with her, to sweep her aloft in the power of song, so that she was moving in glory among the stars, and for a moment she, too, felt that the words Darkness and Light had no meaning, and only this melody was real.

Meg did not know when she fell asleep within the body of the music. When she wakened Aunt Beast was asleep, too, the softness of her furry, faceless head drooping. Night had gone and a dull gray light filled the room. But she realized now that here on this planet there was no need for color, that the grays and browns merging into each other were not what the beasts knew, and that what she, herself, saw was only the smallest fraction of what the planet was really like. It was she who was limited by her senses, not the blind beasts, for they must have senses of which she could not even dream.

She stirred slightly, and Aunt Beast bent over her immediately, "What a lovely sleep, my darling. Do you feel all right?"

"I feel wonderful," Meg said. "Aunt Beast, what is this planet called?"

"Oh, dear," Aunt Beast sighed. "I find it not easy at all to put things the way your mind shapes them. You call where you came from Camazotz?"

"Well, it's where we came from, but it's not our planet."

"You can call us Ixchel, I guess," Aunt Beast told her. "We share the same sun as lost Camazotz, but that, give thanks, is all we share."

"Are you fighting the Black Thing?" Meg asked.

"Oh, yes," Aunt Beast replied. "In doing that we can never relax. We are the called according to His purpose, and whom He calls, them He also justifies. Of course we have help, and without help it would be much more difficult."

"Who helps you?" Meg asked.

"Oh, dear, it is so difficult to explain things to you, small one. And I know now that it is not just because you are a child. The other two are as hard to reach into as you are. What can I tell you that will mean anything to you? Good helps us, the stars help us, perhaps what you would call *light* helps us, love helps us. Oh, my child, I cannot explain! This is something you just have to know or not know."

"But—"

"We look not at the things which are what you would call seen, but at the things which are not seen. For the things which are seen are temporal. But the things which are not seen are eternal."

DINNER TABLE AFFIRMATION

FEBRUARY 19

Eating has always been important to me, because the focal point of the day is the dinner table, a foretaste of the heavenly banquet. The dinner hour is a sacramental time for me, a time of gratitude for whoever is gathered around the table, for the food, for our being part of the great story of Creation. We share the day's events, tell stories, look up words in dictionaries, linger long after the meal is over while the candles burn down.

The family dinner table is no longer something to be taken for granted. In some families it doesn't even exist. People eat catch-as-catch-can, with various conflicting schedules, grabbing a bite, watching TV, running off, missing the wonderful time of communication. It is a great loss. Often during my marriage Hugh and I had to work hard to keep the tradition, eating at odd hours just so that we could get everybody together, but the effort is worth it, it is *worth* it. I know one family who eats breakfast together; it is their chief gathering time. For me the shared evening meal is the time for gathering together, the time when meaning is made clear—the value and validity of our lives. There have been times of trouble when the dinner table has been the only affirmation available.

RE-MEMBERING

FEBRUARY 20

My great-great-grandmother, great-grandmother, grandmother, mother are alive for me because they are part of my story. My children and grandchildren and I tell stories about Hugh, my husband. We laugh and we remember—*re-member*. I tell stories about my friend, the theologian Canon Tallis, who was far more than my spiritual director, with whom I had one of those wonders, a spiritual friendship. I do not believe that these stories are their immortality—that is something quite different. But remembering their stories is the best way I know to have them remain part of my mortal life. And I need them to be part of me, while at the same time I am quite willing for them all to be doing whatever it is that God has in mind for them to do. Can those who are part of that great cloud of witnesses which has gone before us be in two places at once? I believe that they can, just as Jesus could, after the Resurrection.

OUR INNER CHILD RECOGNIZES TRUTH

If we limit ourselves to the possible and provable, as I saw these people doing, we render ourselves incapable of change and growth, and that is something that should never end. If we limit ourselves to the age that we are, and forget all the ages that we have been, we diminish our truth.

FEBRUARY 21

Perhaps it is the child within us who is able to recognize the truth of story—the mysterious, the numinous, the unexplainable—and the grown-up within us who accepts these qualities with joy but understands that we also have responsibilities, that a promise is to be kept, homework is to be done, that we owe other people courtesy and consideration, and that we need to help care for our planet because it's the only one we've got.

I never want to lose the story-loving child within me, or the adolescent, or the young woman, or the middle-aged one, because all together they help me to be fully alive on this journey, and show me that I must be willing to go where it takes me, even through the valley of the shadow.

EUCHARIST

When I receive Communion I am partaking in the most sacred myth and ritual of the Christian church (and let us remember that myth is about *truth*). When we receive the bread and the wine we receive the truth of Jesus' promise, the truth of his love. We don't need to get hung up on words like *transubstantiation,* which tend to take the Eucharist out of the truth of myth and into the wimpiness of fact. What happens when we receive the bread and wine is a mystery, and when we try to explain it in any kind of way we destroy our own ability to partake in the truth of this marvelous and eternally mysterious ritual.

When we receive the bread and the wine we are indeed taking into ourselves Christ's love, that love that will be finally expressed in the Second Coming.

HAPPINESS IS NOT GUARANTEED

Joseph and his brothers did not dwell together in unity. And yet as the story unfolds we see that they *were* family, in the deepest sense of the word. Happiness is not a criterion for the truest kind of family loving, any more than instant gratification is a criterion for joy. There seems to be an illusion in some of Christendom today that Christians are always happy. No matter what tragedies happen, Christians are supposed to be happy if they truly have faith. It's only an illusion and can cause enormous trouble. Jesus was not always happy. He was, indeed, the *suffering servant* Isaiah talks about. Happiness, blind, unquestioning happiness, is not the sign of the Christian. Even the Holy Family was not, in the superficial sense of the word, happy. Simeon warned Mary that a sword of anguish would penetrate her own heart. And, indeed, it did.

A GOD WHO LETS US EXPAND

While she is walking her dog, Camilla Dickinson, the teen-aged protagonist of Camilla, *talks with Frank Rowan, the brother of her best friend, Luisa.*

FEBRUARY 24

L isten, Camilla Dickinson, do you believe in God?"
Frank looks very much like Luisa. His hair is a darker shade of red, but he has the same blue eyes and long arms with the naked wristbones always showing below his sweater and making him look younger than he is. And I saw now that he talked like Luisa, too, because that was the kind of question Luisa was apt to ask anybody new who interested her. She asks that sort of question partly because it shocks people and partly because she doesn't believe in God and she really wants to know what other people think. I think perhaps she feels that if she finds enough people who really believe in God, maybe she'll believe in Him again too.

It's the only thing we've ever really fought about—I mean a real fight, not just a spat. Luisa has to have a spat at least once a day. But about this all she'll ever say is "You're just a dope to believe in God, Camilla," with such scorn that I seem to shrivel and curl all up inside though I am determined to go on being a dope if that makes me a dope.

So now I said "Yes!" to Frank almost as though he had raised a whip over my head.

"That's very refreshing," Frank said, "very refreshing indeed. Do you know, oddly enough, so do I."

"Oh," I said.

"Maybe it's just a reaction because of Mona and Luisa. But I doubt very much if my God is the same kind of God you believe in, Camilla Dickinson."

"I don't believe in an old man in a nightgown and long white whiskers, if that's what you mean," I said rather sharply.

"Tell me about your God," Frank demanded. "What kind of a God *do* you believe in?"

We walked around the park and I didn't say anything because I was trying to think the kind of God I believe in into words. God wasn't anything I ever thought about at all before I met Luisa. He was just something that was always there, the way Mother and Father were before Jacques. And when Luisa talked to me about God it didn't make me want to think about Him; it just made me stubborn. But Frank made me want to think.

We paused for a moment to watch two old men wearing wool caps and big woolen scarves sitting on a bench with a chessboard between them. They sat as still as statues, almost as though the chill November air had frozen them. We waited until finally one of them reached out a hand in a gray woolen glove and made a move and then Frank walked me over to a bench and pushed me down on it and we sat there and a brown leaf dropped from the tree behind us and drifted down onto the sidewalk.

"Well," I said at last, "I don't think it's God's fault when people do anything wrong. And I don't think He plans it when people are good. But I think He makes it possible for people to be ever so much bigger and better than they are. That is, if they want to be. What I mean is, people have to do it themselves. God isn't going to do it for them."

LETTING GOD OUT OF THE BOX

Frank and Camilla are riding the ferry.

Frank dropped his arm from my waist and said abruptly, "You know, Cam, about God."

FEBRUARY 25

"What?" I asked, startled.

"You know what we need is a new God." I didn't say anything, so after a moment he went on. "I mean, what we need is a God people like me, or David, or you, or our parents, could really believe in. I mean, look at all the advances we've made scientifically since—oh, well, since Christ was born if you want to put a date on it. Transportation—look how that's changed. And communication. Telegraph and telephones and television. They're all new and a few thousand years ago we couldn't even have conceived of them but now we can't conceive of doing without them. But you take God. God hasn't changed any since Jesus took him out of a white nightgown and long whiskers. You know what I mean. Along about when Christ was born, just a few years A.D., it was time someone should conceive a new God and then have the power to give his new understanding to the world. So what we need again now is a new God. The God most people are worshiping in churches and temples hasn't grown since Christ's time. He's deteriorated. Look what the Middle Ages did to the Church. All this arguing about how many angels could stand on the point of a needle. All the velvet and gold on the outside and decadence on the inside. And then the Victorians. They tried to put God back in a long white nightgown and whiskers again. That kind of God isn't any good for today. You can't blame Mona for not believing in that kind of God. We need a God who's big enough for the atomic age."

DOORWAY TO THE STARS

Camilla is the narrator.

FEBRUARY 26 I walked slowly down the street and all of a sudden piano music came pouring out of an upper window of one of the houses. It wasn't somebody practicing a music lesson; it wasn't somebody playing carelessly at the piano just for fun, the way Mother sometimes does; it was somebody playing the piano the way a real astronomer would go to a new telescope that might show him an undiscovered star, or the way a scientist on the verge of a tremendous discovery would enter his laboratory; it was somebody playing the piano the way Picasso must have painted his harlequins or Francis Thompson have written "The Hound of Heaven." I stopped and listened and listened. I did not know what the music was, but it made me think of the names of stars, of the winter stars, Aquarius, Capricornus, Pisces, Mesartim, Cetus, Piscium.

THE POWER OF MUSIC

In A Severed Wasp, *Katherine Vigneras, a retired concert pianist, and Mimi Oppenheimer, an orthopedic surgeon and Katherine's tenant, attend an organ concert at the Cathedral of St. John the Divine. Llew Owen is the organist. He has recently lost his wife and baby during childbirth.*

FEBRUARY 27

A small stir of anticipation moved like a breeze through the audience, and the concert began. At first the notes of the great organ were muted, no more than a whisper. Then, slowly, a series of rich chords rose, swelled, burst into brilliant life. Katherine leaned her head back against the carved wood of the stall. Mimi's chatter was gone now, Mimi was gone, there was nothing but music.

The Cathedral was gone. Memory, memories were gone. The power of the music caught her up into pure being. Into is-ness. Reality. It was this transcendence into which music drew her which had been her salvation during the most intolerable periods of her life.

The concert may have lasted an hour, but music, which is inextricably intertwined with time, is also paradoxically a release from time, and when enthusiastic applause greeted the final notes, Katherine was scarcely aware of time having passed.

"He *is* superb, isn't he?" Mimi was still beating her hands together.

"Glorious. Of course, he played some of my favorite things." Katherine reached for her cane and the lacy shawl she had brought in case the weather should once again change suddenly.

Mimi put a restraining hand on her arm. "Let's wait until the place clears out. It's hell, isn't it, but Llew's playing has deepened enormously since he lost his wife and baby."

"Hell," Katherine agreed. "But that's the way it works. Look at Beethoven. The worse his deafness, the greater his music. And the best was composed when he was totally walled into a silent world. Did you notice that your Llew played one of Justin's pieces? Justin might never have started composing had his hands not been broken in Auschwitz."

BEING HONEST ABOUT
THE FEAR OF DEATH

FEBRUARY 28 Red, a seventeen-year-old boy who lived in our building in New York, often dropped into our apartment shortly before dinner. He was an only child, and our normal noisiness appealed to him. And he liked to wander into Hugh's and my room, where I had my desk, and talk. One evening he came in as I was, as usual, banging away on the typewriter. "Madeleine, are you afraid of death?"

I turned around. "Of course, Red."

"Thank God. Nobody's ever admitted it to me before."

I've had people tell me they aren't afraid of death. I don't think I believe them any more than I believe writers who tell me they don't care what anybody thinks of their work. My agnostic faith does not, at its worst, include pie in the sky. If it runs along the same lines as does William James's, it cannot evade acceptance of responsibility, judgment, and change. Whatever death involves, it will be different, a venture into the unknown, and we are all afraid of the dark. At least I am—a fear made bearable by faith and joy.

THE CERTAINTY OF BLESSING

Cursing is a boomerang. If I will evil towards someone else, that evil becomes visible in me. It is an extreme way of being forensic, toward myself, as well as toward whoever outrages me. To avoid contaminating myself and everybody around me, I must work through the anger and the hurt feelings and the demands for absolute justice to a desire for healing. Healing for myself, and my anger, first, because until I am at least in the process of healing, I cannot heal; and then healing for those who have hurt or betrayed me, and those I have hurt and betrayed. . . .

Perhaps most difficult of all is learning to bless ourselves, just as we are. Before we can ask God to bless us, we must be able to accept ourselves as blessed—not perfect, not virtuous, not sinless—just blessed.

If we have to be perfect before we can know ourselves blessed, we will never ask for the transfiguring power of God's love, because of course we are unworthy. But we don't have to be worthy, we just have to acknowledge our need, to cry out, "Help me!" God will help us, even if it's in an unexpected and shocking way, by swooping down on us to wrestle with us. And in the midst of the wrestling we, too, will be able to cry out, "Bless me!"

I am certain that God will bless me, but I don't need to know how. When we think we know exactly how the one who made us is going to take care of us, we're apt to ignore the angel messengers sent us along the way.

MARCH

THE CENTER IS GOD

In this fantasy, A Wind in the Door, *Meg Murry and a cherubim named Proginoskes are in the microscopic world inside one of her brother Charles Wallace's cells. Charles is seriously ill. To save him, Meg and the cherubim must Name (affirm and call into being) a farandola (an infinitesimally small imaginary creature) inside of a mitochondrion.*

What are we to do?" Mr. Jenkins asked.

"The second test," the cherubim urged. "We must pass the second test."

"And that is?"

"To Name Sporos. As Meg had to Name you."

"But Sporos is already Named!"

"Not until he has Deepened."

"I don't understand."

"When Sporos Deepens," Proginoskes told Mr. Jenkins, "it means that he comes of age. It means that he grows up. The temptation for farandola or for man or for star is to stay an immature pleasure-seeker. When we seek our own pleasure as the ultimate good we place ourselves as the center of the universe. A fara or a man or a star has his place in the universe, but nothing created is the center."

THE POWER OF ONE

Sporos is a microscopic farandola inside one of Charles Wallace's cells. Sporos must root or Deepen if the boy is to be saved.

B ut what does Sporos have to do with Charles Wallace?"
"The balance of life within Yadah is precarious. If Sporos
and the others of his generation do not Deepen, the balance
will be altered. If the farandolae refuse to Deepen, the song
will be stilled, and Charles Wallace will die. The Echthroi will
have won."

"But a child—" Mr. Jenkins asked. "One small child—why
is he so important?"

"It is the pattern throughout Creation. One child, one man,
can swing the balance of the universe. In your own Earth history what would have happened if Charlemagne had fallen at
Roncesvalles? One minor skirmish?"

ROOTED—FREE

*Senex, one of the already Deepened farandolae, and Meg try
to persuade Sporos to Deepen. Sporos is under the influence* · MARCH 3
of the Echthroi, who are evil entities.

U gliness seeped past Meg and to Sporos. "Why do you *want*
to Deepen?"

Sporos's twingling was slightly dissonant. "Farandolae are
born to Deepen."

"Fool. Once you Deepen and put down roots you won't be
able to romp around as you do now."

"But—"

"You'll be stuck in one place forever with those fuddy-
duddy farae, and you won't be able to run or move, ever
again."

"But—"

The strength and calm of Senex cut through the ugliness. "It is only when we are fully rooted that we are really able to move."

Indecision quivered throughout Sporos.

Senex continued, "It is true, small offspring. Now that I am rooted I am no longer limited by motion. Now I may move anywhere in the universe. I sing with the stars. I dance with the galaxies. I share in the joy—and in the grief. We farae must have our part in the rhythm of the mitochondria, or we cannot be. If we cannot be, then we are not."

"You mean, you die?" Meg asked.

"Is that what you call it? Perhaps. I am not sure. But the song of Yadah is no longer full and rich. It is flaccid, its harmonies meager. By our arrogance we make Yadah suffer."

NAMED, NOT NUMBERED

I do not know my social security number. I have no intention of ever knowing my social security number. I can look it up if absolutely necessary. But if we don't take care, if we don't watch out, society may limit us to numbers. I wonder if I could pray if I lost my name? I am not at all sure that I could.

If we are numbered, not named, we are less than human. One of the most terrible things done to slaves throughout the centuries, from Babylon to Rome to the United States, was to take away their names. Isn't one of the worst things we can do to any prisoner to take away his name or her name and call them by numbers? If you take away someone's name, you can treat that person as a thing with a clear conscience. You can horsewhip a thing far more easily than a person with a name, a name known to you. No wonder the people who were put in Nazi concentration camps had numbers branded on their arms. When Adam named the animals he made them real. My dog is named Timothy and my cat is named Titus. Farmers do not let their children name the animals who are going to be slaughtered or put in the pot. It is not easy to eat a ham you have known as Wilbur or a chicken called Flossy.

When we respond to our names, or call someone else by name, it is already the beginning of a community expressing the image of God. To call someone by name is an act of prayer. We may abuse our names, and our prayer, but without names we are not human. And Adam and Eve, no matter what else they were, were human.

THE DEMANDS OF TRUTH

Truth is frightening. Pontius Pilate knew that, and washed his hands of truth when he washed his hands of Jesus.

Truth is demanding. It won't let us sit comfortably. It knocks out our cozy smugness and casual condemnation. It makes us move. It? *It?* For truth we can read Jesus. Jesus *is* truth. If we accept that Jesus is truth, we accept an enormous demand: Jesus is wholly God, and Jesus is wholly human. Dare we believe that? If we believe in Jesus we must. And immediately that takes truth out of the limited realm of literalism.

MARCH 5

UNQUENCHABLE LOVE

One of the results of the Fall is that we have forgotten who we are, and so have forgotten how to be. Learning to be hurts. We can sing songs of happiness without knowing pain. But we can sing the joy of our creation and honor our Creator only from within the fire.

MARCH 6

We walked through fire and water, David the psalmist cried, and affirmed that even in the fire, even in the deep waters, God is there. And Solomon sings in his great love song, *Many waters cannot quench love, rivers cannot wash it away.* Nor can the fire destroy it.

That love which cannot be destroyed has been the central core of stories since stories were first told or chanted around the campfires at night. Sometimes that love is shown by what we human creatures do to hurt it. We learn about love by being shown the abuses of love in *Anna Karenina,* or *The Brothers Karamazov,* or *King Lear.* Often when I am tired at night my bedtime reading is a murder mystery. Most of the writers to whom I turn are committed Christians, because it takes a firm grounding in the love of God for a writer to go into the darkest depths of the human heart. Often in these mysteries that love which will make us more human shines through the ugliness of greed and murder. Love does not triumph easily or without pain, but story gives us the courage to endure the pain.

BREAD FOR THE WORLD

MARCH 7

Give us this day our daily bread. Not mine, but ours—everybody's. Our responsibility to the starving world is implicit in that sentence. As long as any part of the body is hungry, the entire body knows starvation. But again, we do not need to think of our obligations in terms of success; we would fail to do anything at all if we knew we had to succeed. We simply do what we can; we offer our little loaves and fishes and leave the rest to the Lord.

The story of the loaves and fishes is something explained away in a reasonable sort of manner. It was something like a potluck supper, I have been told. The people who had been listening to Jesus were so moved by his words that when it came time to eat, those who had brought picnics with them shared their food around.

The reasonable explanations don't really make much sense. Jesus took the stuff of nature, bread and fish, and working from what already existed, multiplied it. He refused to turn stones into bread, which he could have done. But stones are not bread; they are stones. Instead, when he fed the multitudes, he took the loaves, he took the fish, and there was enough for everybody. In John's Gospel it is pointed out that a lad came up and *offered* what he had, and this act of offering was essential for the miracle.

Another important part of the miracle is Jesus' concern for the fragments, because he is always concerned about the broken things, the broken people. Only when we realize that we are indeed broken, that we are not independent, that we cannot do it ourselves, can we turn to God and take that which he has given us, no matter what it is, and create with it.

TRANSFIGURATION

Suddenly they saw him the way he was,
the way he really was all the time,
although they had never seen it before,
the glory which blinds the everyday eye
and so becomes invisible. This is how
he was, radiant, brilliant, carrying joy

MARCH 8

63

like a flaming sun in his hands.
This is the way he was—is—from the beginning,
and we cannot bear it. So he manned himself,
came manifest to us; and there on the mountain
they saw him, really saw him, saw his light.
We all know that if we really see him we die.
But isn't that what is required of us?
Then, perhaps, we will see each other, too.

THE SPLENDOR OF THE LIGHT

MARCH 9   The myths of man have always made it clear that it is impossible for us to look at the flame of reality directly and survive. Semele insisted on seeing her lover in his own form, as god, and was struck dead. In the Old Testament it is explicitly stated, many times, that man cannot look on the living God and live. How, then, do "myths" become part of experience?

In my church we observe, with considerable discipline, the season known as Lent. After its austerities, the brilliance of Easter will shine with greater joy. In the Jewish religion candles are lit, one each night for seven nights, for Hanukkah. The Hindus celebrate Dewali, the festival of lights, in which every house is ablaze with lights to rejoice in the victory of good over evil. In every culture there is a symbolic festival of light conquering darkness.

MOVING BEYOND WAR

MARCH 10   But Scripture makes it clear that we are never to stay in one place, one way of thinking, but to move on, out into the wilderness, as El Shaddai moved Abraham, Isaac, and Jacob.

As promised, they had many descendants and, alas, a large population seems to encourage war.

But on a planet where population has grown beyond bounds, this warring way of life does not work any more. Wars in the name of religion not only give religion a bad name, they are a warning that it is time for us to move out of and beyond the old tribalism. Not easy, for it would seem that some form of tribalism is inherent in human nature. Science fiction writers often cast their characters in the old tribal mode, even when the tribe is the people of this planet, and the neighbours, "them," are from other planets. In Star Trek, the tribe includes a Martian, so "us" is the solar system, and "them" (usually the bad guys) are from the other solar systems. Sometimes it is this galaxy that is the tribe, versus other galaxies.

But everything we are learning about the nature of Being is making it apparent that "us" versus "them" is a violation of Creation. Tribalism must be transformed into community. We are learning from astrophysics and particle physics and cellular biology that all of Creation exists only in interdependence and unity.

A DOSE OF WONDER

We daily have to make choices between good and evil, and it is not always easy, or even possible, to tell the difference between the two. Whenever we make a choice of action, the first thing to ask ourselves is whether it is creative or destructive. Will it heal, or will it wound? Are we doing something to make ourselves look big and brave, or because it is truly needed? Do we know the answers to these questions? Not always, but we will never know unless we ask them. And

MARCH 11

we will never dare to ask them if we close ourselves off from wonder.

When I need a dose of wonder I wait for a clear night and go look for the stars. In the city I see only a few, but only a few are needed. In the country the great river of the Milky Way streams across the sky, and I know that our planet is a small part of that river of stars, and my pain of separation is healed.

Dis-aster makes me think of dis-grace. Often the wonder of the stars is enough to return me to God's loving grace.

PORTION, NOT PINNACLE, OF CREATION

MARCH 12

We are at a demanding threshold of understanding right now, as we move from deterministic, forensic thinking, to more indeterministic, vulnerable thinking. We are unique, incomparable creatures, but was creating us God's chief achievement or ultimate aim? We can no longer separate ourselves from the rest of creation, nor think of ourselves as more important in God's eyes than stars or butterflies or baboons. We are part of a whole which is so intricately balanced that the smallest action (watch that butterfly) can have cosmic consequences.

We need to step out of the limelight as being the pinnacle of God's work. I suspect that those first human creatures who walked upright on their hind legs and so freed their hands to make and use tools, most likely thought of themselves as the pinnacle of creation. Look at us! We are man who uses tools! God has done it at last!

Perhaps we have just as far to go on the long journey toward being truly human.

WHAT DO WE SEEK?

H ow do we reawaken a sense of the sacred?
First of all, we must look for it. Jacob fled Esau, and MARCH 13 was given a vision of God. He was realistic about people, including himself, but he did not look for evil. So he was given the greatest good. ·

What are we looking for? For God and love and hope? Or for wrongness and evil and sin?

If the totally interdependent, interconnected world of physics is true, then this oneness affects the way we look at everything—books, people, symbols. It radically affects the way we look at the cross. Jesus on the cross was at-one with God, and with the infinite mind, in which Creation is held. The anguish on the cross has to do with this at-one-ment in a way which a forensic definition of atonement cannot even begin to comprehend.

TRUTH PUSHES US BEYOND FACTS

I f truth and reason appear to be in conflict, then both must
be re-examined, and scientists are as reluctant to do this MARCH 14 tough work as are theologians. When the theory of plate tectonics and continental drift was first put forward (and how reasonable it seems now), the scientists got as upset as the theologians did when planet earth was displaced as the center of the universe. And as for those seven days of creation, nothing whatsoever is said in Genesis about God creating in human time. Isn't it rather arrogant of us to think that God had to use

our ordinary, daily, wristwatch time? Scripture does make it clear that God's time and our time are not the same. The old hymn "a thousand ages in thy sight are but a moment past" reprises this. So why get so upset about the idea that God might have created in divine time, not human? What kind of a fact is this that people get so upset about? Facts are static, even comfortable, even when they are wrong! Truth pushes us to look at these facts in a new way, and that is not comfortable, so it usually meets with resistance.

STORIES, MIDWIVES OF OUR WHOLENESS

MARCH 15

Stories, no matter how simple, can be vehicles of truth; can be, in fact, icons. It's no coincidence that Jesus taught almost entirely by telling stories, simple stories dealing with the stuff of life familiar to the Jews of his day. Stories are able to help us to become more whole, to become Named. And Naming is one of the impulses behind all art; to give a name to the cosmos we see despite all the chaos.

God asked Adam to name all the animals, which was asking Adam to help in the creation of their wholeness. When we name each other, we are sharing in the joy and privilege of incarnation, and all great works of art are icons of Naming.

When we look at a painting, or hear a symphony, or read a book, and feel more Named, then, for us, that work is a work of Christian art. But to look at a work of art and then to make a judgment as to whether or not it is art, and whether or not it is Christian, is presumptuous. It is something we cannot know in any conclusive way. We can know only if it speaks within our own hearts, and leads us to living more deeply with Christ in God.

HALLOWING

To relinquish our conscious, cognitive selves is an act of hallowing. It should be true of any activity, not just writing stories. It should be true of the doctor, and too often it isn't. Those who must make instant life and death decisions are put in the position of being God, and being God is woefully addictive. The great physicians are those who know that it is not their mortal hands which heal, but God's hand using the human one. It is God's name that should be hallowed, not ours. When we put ourselves before God then inevitably we come to grief—one of the most common griefs of all.

MARCH 16

RELINQUISHMENT

Thy will be done on earth, as it is in heaven. Heaven is not a place name. Heaven is wherever God's will is being done. When, occasionally, it is done on earth, then there is heaven. It is the most difficult thing in the world for most of us to give up directing our own story and turn to the Author. This has to be done over and over again every day. Time and again I know exactly how a certain situation should be handled, and in no uncertain terms I tell God how to handle it. Then I stop, stock-still, and (sometimes with reluctance) end by saying, "However, God, do it your way. Not my way, your way. Please."

MARCH 17

AGING INTO TRUE ADULTHOOD

So my hope, each day as I grow older, is that this will never be simply chronological aging—which is a nuisance and frequently a bore—the old "bod" at over half a century has

MARCH 18

had hard use; it won't take what it did a few years ago—but that I will also grow into maturity, where the experience which can be acquired only through chronology will teach me how to be more aware, open, unafraid to be vulnerable, involved, committed, to accept disagreement without feeling threatened (repeat and underline this one), to understand that I cannot take myself seriously until I stop taking myself seriously—to be, in fact, a true adult.

To be.

FELLOWSHIP AROUND THE DINNER TABLE

MARCH 19

The focus of our days is the dinner table, whether, as often happens in the winter nowadays, it is just Hugh and me or I am cooking for a dozen or more. When the children were in school I didn't care what time we ate dinner as long as we ate it together. If Hugh were going to be late, then we would all be late. If he had to be at the theatre early, we would eat early. This was the time the community (except for the very small babies) gathered together, when I saw most clearly illustrated the beautiful principle of unity in diversity: we were one, but we were certainly diverse, a living example of the fact that like and equal are not the same thing.

THE BLESSING OF SILENCE

MARCH 20

Why are we so afraid of silence? Teenagers cannot study without their records; they walk along the street with their transistors. Grownups are as bad if not worse; we turn on the TV or the radio the minute we come into the house or start the car. The pollution of noise in our cities is as destructive as the pollution of air. We show our fear of silence in our conversation: I wonder if the orally minded Elizabethans used "um" and "er" the way we do? And increasingly prevalent is what my husband calls an articulated pause: "You know." We interject "you know" meaninglessly into every sentence, in order that the flow of our speech should not be interrupted by such a terrifying thing as silence.

If I look to myself I find, as usual, contradiction. Ever since I've had a record player I've written to music—not all music, mostly Bach and Mozart and Scarlatti and people like that—but music: sound.

Yet when I went on my first retreat I slipped into silence as though into the cool waters of the sea. I felt totally, completely, easily at home in silence.

With the people I love most I can sit in silence indefinitely.

We need both for our full development; the joy of the sense of sound; and the equally great joy of its absence.

POETRY AND STORY, THE LANGUAGES OF FAITH

It's no coincidence that just at this point in our insight into our mysteriousness as human beings struggling towards MARCH 21 compassion, we are also moving into an awakened interest in the language of myth and fairy tale. The language of logical argument, of proofs, is the language of the limited self we know and can manipulate. But the language of parable and poetry, of storytelling, moves from the imprisoned language of the provable into the freed language of what I must, for lack of another word, continue to call faith. For me this involves trust not in "the gods" but in God. But if the word God has understandably become offensive to many, then the language of poetry and story involves faith in the unknown potential in the human being, faith in courage and honor and nobility, faith in love, our love of each other, and our dependence on each other. And it involves for me a constantly renewed awareness of the fact that if I am a human being who writes, and who sends my stories out into the world for people to read, then I must have the courage to make a commitment to the unknown and unknowable (in the sense of intellectual proof), the world of love and particularity which gives light to the darkness.

WITHIN THIS STRANGE
AND QUICKENED DUST

MARCH 22

O God, within this strange and quickened dust
The beating heart controls the coursing blood
In discipline that holds in check the flood
But cannot stem corrosion and dark rust.
In flesh's solitude I count it blest
That only you, my Lord, can see my heart
With passion's darkness tearing it apart
With storms of self, and tempests of unrest.
But your love breaks through blackness, bursts with
  light;
We separate ourselves, but you rebind

In Dayspring all our fragments; body, mind,
And spirit join, unite against the night.
Healed by your love, corruption and decay
Are turned, and whole, we greet the light of day.

AWESOME AUTHENTICITY

If Jesus was a threat to Herod two thousand years ago, he is still a threat today, because he demands that we see ourselves as we really are, that we drop our smug, self-protective devices, that we become willing to live the abundant life he calls us to live. It's too strong, so we react by trying to turn him into a wimp come to protect us from an angry Father God who wants us punished for our sins: not forgiven, but punished. And our response of fear hasn't worked, and we're left even more frightened and even more grasping and even more judgmental.

MARCH 23

LOVE, THE SURVIVAL KIT

In my hospital bed I was homesick. Here it was August, but I found myself thinking of Holy Week. Lonely week. The most painful part of the story. Jesus, at the end of his earthly mission, facing failure, abandonment, death.

MARCH 24

What kept him going? What keeps us going when we're in the middle of the worst of it? The knowledge that we are loved by our Creator. Everybody else left Jesus. The disciples, those he had counted on to be with him to the end, all left him in the Garden. No one understood who he was, what he was about, what he had come for. How many times in our lives have we faced that utter and absolute abandonment? He knew that his mission had been high, and it was in ruins about his feet.

He stood in front of Pontius Pilate and he held to his mission and his position because of love, God's love, which did not fail, not even when he questioned it on the cross.

What has happened during the centuries to that God of sustaining, enduring, total love? How can we survive without it?

I cannot.

INTELLECT AND INTUITION, TEAM PLAYERS

MARCH 25   We are meant to be whole creatures, we human beings, but mostly we are no more than fragments of what we ought to be. One of the great evils of twentieth-century civilization is the rift which has come between our conscious and our intuitive minds, a rift which has been slowly widening for thousands of years, so that now it seems as unbridgeable as the chasm which separated Dives, suffering the torments of hell, from Lazarus, resting on Abraham's bosom.

And this gap, separating intellect from intuition, mind from heart, is so frightening to some people that they won't admit that it exists. I heard an otherwise intelligent man announce belligerently that there was no gap whatsoever between his conscious and below-conscious mind; his conscious mind was in complete control of his unconscious mind, thank you very much.

HAVE WE LEARNED ANYTHING?

If Jesus came today, would we be any braver, any more open, any more willing to give ourselves to his love, than were those who cried out, "Crucify him! Crucify him!"? Would we be any more willing today to allow him to love all kinds of people, even those we don't much care about? MARCH 26

That, of course, was part of the problem—Jesus' friends. They were not the right people. He went to the wrong dinner parties (his first miracle took place at a big party). He loved children, and let them climb all over him with their sticky little hands and dirty little feet. He even told us that we had to be like little children ourselves if we wanted to understand God, and yet the world (and too often the church) taught then, and still teaches, that we have to outgrow our childhood love of story, of imagination, of creativity, of fun, and so we blunder into the grown-up world of literalism.

ATONEMENT REDEFINED

A young friend said to me during Holy Week, "I cannot cope with the atonement." MARCH 27

Neither can I, if the atonement is thought of forensically. In forensic terms, the atonement means that Jesus had to die for us in order to atone for all our awful sins, so that God could forgive us. In forensic terms, it means that God cannot forgive us unless Jesus is crucified and by this sacrifice atones for all our wrongdoing.

But that is not what the word means! I went to an etymological dictionary and looked it up. It means exactly what it says, at-one-ment. I double-checked it in a second dictionary. There is nothing about crime and punishment in the makeup of that word. It simply means to be at one with God. Jesus on the cross was so at-one with God that death died there on Golgotha, and was followed by the glorious celebration of the Resurrection.

SETTING PRIORITIES

MARCH 28

One of my icons for Good Friday is Bach's "St. Matthew Passion," music which speaks deeply into the soul and affirms that God's love cannot be understood; it can only be affirmed.

I believe that if I was asked to, I could die for my children. I know that God died for me, and that because of this death, God gives us life.

I listen to Bach's music and it expresses for me that incredible love which our Maker shows us, a love which is willing to die for our sakes, in order that we may know life. If I need a visible icon, then I will take a seed, knowing that the seed is useless until it is put into the ground, dies as a seed, and is resurrected as a flower, or tree, or blade of grass—whatever God means it to be.

Can my Good Friday icons become idols? Everything can. One Good Friday I had a call from a friend who was in deep trouble and needed help. If I went to my friend, I would not be able to listen to the "St. Matthew Passion"; I would not be able to go to church and offer my presence during the three-hour service.

Wouldn't both the music and the church have become idols if I had paid more attention to them than to my friend? We never know for absolute certain whether or not we have made the right choice. I pray that I did.

THE INCOMPREHENSIBLE GIFT OF IDENTIFICATION

The enfleshing of the Word which spoke the galaxies made the death of that Word inevitable. All flesh is mortal, and MARCH 29
the flesh assumed by the Word was no exception in mortal terms. So the birth of the Creator in human flesh and human time was an event as shattering and terrible as the eschaton. If I accept this birth I must accept God's love, and this is pain as well as joy because God's love, as I am coming to understand it, is not like man's love.

What one of us can understand a love so great that we would willingly limit our unlimitedness, put the flesh of mortality over our immortality, accept all the pain and grief of humanity, submit to betrayal by that humanity, be killed by it, and die a total failure (in human terms) on a common cross between two thieves?

JESUS, AT-ONE

For Jesus, at-one-ment was not being at-one only with the glory of the stars, or the first daffodil in the spring, or a MARCH 30
baby's laugh. He was also at-one with all the pain and suffering that ever was, is, or will be. On the cross Jesus was at-one with the young boy with cancer, the young mother hemorrhaging, the raped girl. And perhaps the most terrible anguish

came from being at-one with the people of Sodom and Gomorrah, the death chambers at Belsen, the horrors of radiation in the destruction of Hiroshima and Nagasaki. It came from being at-one with the megalomania of the terrorist, the coldness of heart of "good" people, or even the callous arrogance of the two men in criminal court.

We can withdraw, even in our prayers, from the intensity of suffering. Jesus, on the cross, experienced it all. When I touch the small cross I wear, that, then, is the meaning of the symbol.

THE ASTONISHING RESURRECTION

MARCH 31

When Christ was born as a human baby, he ensured that he would die, because death is something that comes to every human being. But because Jesus Christ was wholly God as well as wholly human, he rose from the grave, to the astonishment not only of the Roman overlords and the powerful Jews in the Sanhedrin, but to the astonishment of all those who had been with him during his earthly life. The Resurrection, too, is beyond the realm of fact (Do you believe in the literal fact of the Resurrection? No! I believe in the Resurrection!) and bursts into the realm of love, of truth, for in Jesus, truth and love are one and the same.

APRIL

CRUCIFIXION AS BEGINNING

But God, the Good Book tells us, is no respecter of persons, and the happy ending isn't promised to an exclusive club, as many groups, such as the Jehovah's Witnesses believe. It isn't—face it—only for Baptists, or Presbyterians, or Episcopalians. What God began, God will not abandon. *[H]e who began a good work in you will carry it on to completion. . . .* God loves *every one*, sings the psalmist. What God has named will live forever, Alleluia!

The happy ending has never been easy to believe in. After the Crucifixion the defeated little band of disciples had no hope, no expectation of Resurrection. Everything they believed in had died on the cross with Jesus. The world was right, and they had been wrong. Even when the women told the disciples that Jesus had left the stone-sealed tomb, the disciples found it nearly impossible to believe that it was not all over. The truth was, it was just beginning.

FROM ST. LUKE'S HOSPITAL (2)

If I can learn a little how to die,
To die while body, mind, and spirit still
Move in their triune dance of unity,
To die while living, dying I'll fulfill
The purpose of the finite in infinity.
If God will help me learn to die today,
Today in time I'll touch eternity,
And dying, thus will live within God's Way.
If I can free myself from self's iron bands,

Freed from myself not by myself, but through
Christ's presence in this simple room, in hands
Outstretched in holy friendship, then, born new
In death, truth will outlive the deathly lie,
And in love's light I will be taught to die.

RIGHT RESURRECTION

*Zachary Gray, a spoiled rich kid who pursued teenaged
Vicky Austin during the Austins' ten-week camping trip in*
The Moon by Night, *has come back into the Austin family's
life (in* A Ring of Endless Light*). Vicky's parents do not care
for Zachary. Zachary has just asked Vicky and her family if
they know anything about cryonics.*

APRIL 3

Zachary was explaining, "We belong to a group in California called the Immortalists. We believe that it isn't necessary for people to die as early as they do, and when we understand more about controlling DNA and RNA it will be possible for people to live for several hundred years without aging—and that time is not so far in the future as you might think."

We were all silent, listening to him. Mother glanced at Daddy, and then took the silver pitcher and headed for the kitchen for more iced tea.

Zachary went on, "Cryonics is the science of freezing a body immediately after death, deep-freezing, so that later on—in five years, or five hundred—when scientists know more about the immortality factor, it will be possible for these people of the future to revive the deep-frozen bodies, to resurrect them."

Grandfather spoke with a small smile, "I think I prefer another kind of resurrection."

Zachary's lips moved in a scornful smile. "Of course, the problem at the moment is cost. Not many people can afford it. We feel lucky that we can."

"You did—you did that to your mother?" Rob sounded horrified. I was, too, come to that. I'd known, vaguely, that this kind of thing was being done in California, but not by or to anybody I knew. I looked at Grandfather.

He gave me his special grandfather-granddaughter smile. "Resurrection has always been costly, though not in terms of money. It took only thirty pieces of silver."

"Oh, that," Zachary said, courteously enough. "We think this is more realistic, sir. While only the rich can afford it now, ultimately it should be available to everybody."

Into my mind's eye flashed an image of the afternoon before, when we were standing by a dark hole in the ground, waiting for Commander Rodney's body to be lowered into it. Somehow that struck me as being more realistic than being deep-frozen. Being deep-frozen went along with plastic grass and plastic earth and trying to pretend that death hadn't really happened.

"Of course," Zachary said, "nowadays a lot of people get cremated, basically because of lack of space in cemeteries."

Rob was looking at him in fascinated horror. "You mean your scientists couldn't do anything with ashes?" He was sitting next to Grandfather and he reached out to hold his hand.

Now Rob was bathed in Grandfather's luminous smile. "I'm not depending on super scientists, Rob. When one tries to avoid death, it's impossible to affirm life."

82

GENUINE IMMORTALITY

Grandfather and Vicky discuss Zachary Gray's suicide attempt, which had precipitated the death of Commander Rodney. Rodney had jumped into the water to save Zachary and had suffered a heart attack. Grandfather asks:

How well do you know him, Vicky?"

"I don't think anyone knows Zachary well. Not even Zachary. You never know what he's going to say or do. And, Grandfather—just to make it more complicated, he wasn't just some dumb kid who didn't know how to handle a sailboat. The boat's capsizing wasn't an accident. He wanted to drown. He wanted to die."

"Do you know why?"

"He has a heart condition, and I think it's made him sort of flirt with death. But he keeps talking about being a lawyer, so he can take care of himself and not let other people get the better of him."

The ceiling fan whirred softly. "Do you think he really wanted to die?"

I thought about this for quite a while before answering. "It's funny—even when he courts death, I don't think he really believes in it. But maybe I'm wrong, because I just don't understand anybody wanting to die, at least not somebody young, with everything going for him the way Zachary has. But you heard him this morning, all that cryonics junk and Immortalists."

"I heard."

"But that kind of stuff isn't what immortality is about, is it?"

"Not to me." The smile lines about his eyes deepened. "To live forever in this body would take away much of the joy of living, even if one didn't age but stayed young and vigorous."

I didn't understand, but I had a hunch he was right. "Why?"

"If we knew each morning that there was going to be another morning, and on and on and on, we'd tend not to notice the sunrise, or hear the birds, or the waves rolling into shore. We'd tend not to treasure our time with the people we love. Simply the awareness that our mortal lives had a beginning and will have an end enhances the quality of our living. Perhaps it's even more intense when we know that the termination of the body is near, but it shouldn't be."

I wanted to reach over to him and hold him and say "It is, oh, it is," but I couldn't.

Again his eyes smiled at me. "I like the old adage that we should live each day as though we were going to live forever, and as though we were going to die tomorrow." He ruffled my hair again. "This cryonics business strikes me as fear of death rather than joy in life."

ETERNITY IS TOTAL IS-NESS

APRIL 5   We are all going to die, and I suppose whether it is sooner or later makes little difference in eternity, for eternity is total is-ness, immediacy, now-ness. Living in eternity is, in fact, the way we are supposed to live all the time, right now, in the immediate moment, not hanging onto the past, not projecting into the future. The past is the rock that is under our feet, that enables us to push off from it and move into the future. But we don't go bury ourselves in the past, nor should we worry too much about the future. "Sufficient unto the day..." my grandmother was fond of quoting. God in Jesus came to be in time with us and to redeem human time for us—human time, wristwatch time *(chronos)*, and God's time *(kairos)*. But even *chronos* is variable. How long is a toothache? How long is a wonderful time? When I fly from New York to San Francisco to see my eldest daughter and her family, I have to set my watch back three hours and I always have jet lag. Even chronological time is full of surprises.

AT COMMUNION

Whether I kneel or stand or sit in prayer
I am not caught in time nor held in space,
But, thrust beyond this posture, I am where
Time and eternity are face to face;
Infinity and space meet in this place
Where crossbar and upright hold the One
In agony and in all Love's embrace.
The power in helplessness which was begun
When all the brilliance of the flaming sun
Contained itself in the small confines of a child
Now comes to me in this strange action done
In mystery. Break time, break space, O wild
and lovely power. Break me: thus am I dead,
Am resurrected now in wine and bread.

APRIL 6

STEPS TOWARD NEW LIFE

APRIL 7 So now, as we take the next steps into the wilderness into which God is sending us now; as the human creature has moved from being the primitive hunter to the land-worker to the city-dweller to the traveller in the skies, we must move on to a way of life where we are so much God's one people that warfare is no longer even a possibility. It is that, or dis-aster, and we must not let Satan, the great separator, win.

The phrase, "the butterfly effect," comes from the language of physics. It is equally the language of poetry, and of theology. For the Christian, the butterfly has long been a symbol of resurrection.

The butterfly emerges from the cocoon, its wings, wet with rebirth, slowly opening, and then this creature of fragile loveliness flies across the blue vault of sky.

Butterflies and angels, seraphim and cherubim, call us earthbound creatures to lift up our mortal dust and sing with them, to God's delight.

Holy. Holy. Holy!

A CALL TO REPENTANCE

APRIL 8 If God is in and part of all creation, then any part can be a messenger, an angel. Sometimes our very questions are angelic. Questions allow us to grow and develop and change in our understanding of ourselves and of God, so that nothing that happens, and nothing that science discovers, is frightening, or disturbs our faith in God.

Some scientists in their arrogance have done terrible things.

But the great scientists are humble, and have imaginations as vivid as any poet's—"The butterfly effect," for instance. What a marvellous concept, and what a marvellous way of expressing it, and by a scientist, not an artist!

The quark, one of the smallest, if not *the* smallest, of our subatomic particles, is named from James Joyce's *Finnegans Wake*. The world of subatomic particles is so extraordinary that even to contemplate it implies an open imagination.

We have discovered the world of subatomic physics because we have split the atom. This has revealed many things which are horrible indeed. A considerable number of scientists have repented of the use made of their discoveries. True repentance opens our eyes to the God who heals and redeems.

As a nation we have yet to come to terms with our fire bombs which destroyed German cities and their civilian population during World War Two. We have yet to come to terms with having dropped not one, but two atom bombs, leaving the horror of death and radiation, maiming men, and women, and children who had nothing to do with battle lines. Part of our fascination with the atom bomb may be caused by our refusal, as a nation, to repent. We have yet to come to terms with Vietnam, and Lebanon, and El Salvador, because repentance is no longer part of our national vocabulary.

PRAYER POWER

What would those who were responsible for the making of the automobile have done if some kind of prescience APRIL 9 had shown them that the death toll from automobile accidents is already greater than the death toll of all of the world's wars put together? What would the scientists working on the splitting of the atom have done if they could have foreseen Hiroshima and Nagasaki? Many of the scientists who worked on early fusion and fission were appalled at the gigantic Pandora's box they had opened. A considerable number of those who had approached the work as humanistic atheists turned from their atheism to become deeply committed theists. A good many, not all, but a good many, looked at what they had unleashed and got down on their knees.

And the power of prayer is greater than the Pentagon. It is greater than the greed and corruption which can still conceive of a nuclear holocaust as survivable. It is greater than the bomb. It can help bring wisdom to our knowledge, wisdom which is all that will keep us from destroying ourselves with our knowledge.

In an accidental and godless universe, where the human race on this particular planet in this particular galaxy appeared by happenstance, there would be very little hope. But in a purposeful universe created by a caring, loving God, there is great hope that ultimately el's purposes will be worked out in history.

ALL THINGS ARE LINKED

APRIL 10

Troubling a Star *is the story of Vicky Austin's trip to Antarctica. She is going to visit her friend Adam Eddington, who is working at a research station there. During the voyage, the ship stops near the Falkland Islands. Passengers go ashore in Kodiaks (small boats). Siri, one of the passengers, has come ashore with Vicky.*

Siri spread her parka on the rough beach and sat on it, then took her harp, which had been slung over her shoulder with a wide canvas strap, out of its canvas carrier. She began to sweep her fingers over the strings. Then she hummed a little, softly, and finally began to sing. I'd half slept through the words when she sang in our hotel room in San Sebastián, but now I was paying attention.

> All things by immortal power,
> Near or far,
> Hiddenly
> To each other linked are,
> That thou canst not stir a flower
> Without troubling of a star.

Her fingers on the strings reprised the melody. Then she sang the last two lines again.

> Thou canst not stir a flower
> Without troubling of a star.

As I was drawn closer to Siri and her harp, so were the penguins, and three of them waddled right up to her.

ACTIONS HAVE CONSEQUENCES

It is Adam Eddington's Aunt Serena who is responsible for Vicky Austin's trip to Antarctica. Vicky travels with an old friend of the Eddington family, Adam Cook. Cook, as he is called, travels to Antarctica every year to visit his brother. Cook is supposed to keep an eye on Vicky. Vicky asks:

APRIL 11

89

D o you think it's true? Every action has inevitable consequences?"

"I'm not sure about inevitable. Actions do have consequences, and not all of them are bad. Some of them are mirac-
ulously good."

I looked at him questioningly. We went out onto the fo'c'sle
and stood at the rail.

He said, "I believe in a pattern for the universe, a pattern
that affirms meaning, and perhaps especially when things
seem meaningless. Everything we do has a part in the weaving
of the pattern, even our wrong decisions. But I believe that the
beauty of the pattern will not be irrevocably distorted. That is
a hope we learn to live with."

I looked out at the water, thinking.

He glanced at me briefly, then back out to sea. "When the
pattern is torn, there is a healing power that can mend. Let me
make a metaphor. Sometimes our angels come and give us a
nudge and we go in a direction we might have missed otherwise, and so we are helped to make a right step, or to avoid
doing something which might have terrible consequences.
Sometimes we are not able to or choose not to heed the nudge.
We are creatures who have been given the terrible gift of free
will, and that means we are responsible for our actions and
have to suffer the consequences. Without our angels, I believe
we would be in a worse state than we are."

I thought of Aunt Serena and Owain both asking angels to
watch over me.

I looked at Cook and he smiled. "I believe in angels. I can't
give you any proof or any further explanations, because an-

gelic guidance is not to be understood by our finite minds. But
believe in it."

"Okay. Thank you. I get it. Sort of."

"Sort of is good enough."

CONTINUING EDUCATION

Carrying my babies was a marvelous mystery, lives growing
unseen except by the slow swelling of my belly. Death is
an even greater mystery. I don't want to be afraid to ask the
big questions that have no answers. The God I cry out to in
anguish or joy can neither be proved nor disproved. The hope
I have that death is not the end of all our questions can neither
be proved nor disproved. I have a great deal left to learn, and
I believe that God's love will give me continuing opportunities
for learning. And in this learning we will become truer to
God's image in us.

APRIL 12

COMMUNION WITH GOD
OVERCOMES OUR FEARS

When we are in communion with the Creator we are less
afraid, less afraid that the wrong people will come to
the party, less afraid that we ourselves aren't good enough,
less afraid of pain and alienation and death. Jesus, who comes
across in the Gospels as extraordinarily strong, begged in the
garden, with drops of sweat like blood running down his face,
that he might be spared the terrible cup ahead of him, the betrayal and abandonment by his friends, death on the cross.

APRIL 13

Because Jesus cried out in anguish, we may, too. But our fear is less frequent and infinitely less if we are close to the Creator. Jesus, having cried out, then let his fear go, and moved on.

HIEROPHANY

APRIL 14

Sometimes the loveliness of God's presence comes in the midst of pain.

I wasn't quite over a bad case of shingles when I went south to conduct a retreat. I felt miserable. The shingles blisters, which had managed to get even into my ear, had burst my eardrum. The weather was not cooperating. Instead of being warm and sunny (I had hoped to be able to sit on the beach and bask in the sun and heal) it was cold, rainy, and raw.

When the rain finally stopped, I went for a silent walk on the beach with two caring friends. The ocean was smothered in fog, but occasionally the curtain lifted enough to reveal a fishing boat, and a glimpse of muted silver on sea. One of my companions found some lovely driftwood. The other picked up some tiny donax shells and put them in my palm. And there, in the silence, in the fog, in my pain, was a sensation of being surrounded by the almighty wings of God, right there, at that time, in that place, God with us.

ANCIENT WITNESS TO THE WONDER

APRIL 15

And it came to me as I stood on the desert sand, looking at the Great Pyramid, that what any civilization says about God tells us more about that civilization than it does about God. Nothing we say about the Creator can begin to be adequate. It is always small and fumbling and human and an-thropomorphic—no matter how mighty our monuments.

What those ancient Egyptians were saying to me in their frescoes and carvings was that life would have meant nothing to them at all without their faith in God, even if their gods frequently came to them in both animal and human form.

ENJOYING GOD'S HANDIWORK

You really seem to enjoy your faith," the young woman said. Yes, I hope I do. So what is it about my faith that I APRIL 16 enjoy? I enjoy it because I believe it to be true, not necessarily factual, but true. If it's factual I don't need faith for it. I enjoy my faith because I believe that God created this wondrous universe out of love, and that God had fun in the act of Creation—hydrogen clouds and galaxies and solar systems and planets capable of sustaining life, and fish and birds and beasts and us human creatures. And then God rested, and I, too, enjoy my day of rest and (occasionally and wonderfully) several days of rest when I go on retreat.

I enjoy my faith because it is full of story, marvelous story, and sometimes terrible story.

COURAGE TO QUESTION

My faith in God, who is eternally loving and constant even as my understanding grows and changes, makes APRIL 17 life not only worth living, but gives me the courage to dare to disturb the universe when that is what el calls me to do. Sometimes simply being open, refusing to settle for finite answers, disturbs the universe. Questions are disturbing, especially those which may threaten our traditions, our institutions, our security. But questions never threaten the living God, who is constantly calling us, and who affirms for us that love is stronger than hate, blessing stronger than cursing.

THE LADY OF THE LAKE

APRIL 18

Dragons in the Waters is a book of intrigue set primarily on a ship bound for Venezuela. The protagonist, Simon Renier, is thirteen. Trouble erupts, and Simon is in danger. His aunt, Leonis Phair, is summoned to Venezuela to rescue him. At one point in the story, she visits a tribe of peaceful Indians, the Quiztanos, who were visited generations ago by Simon's distant relative Quentin Phair. Ouldi is a young Indian guide, The Umara is a very old Indian who is greatly honored by the tribe, and Umar Xanai is the tribal leader.

Ouldi said, "Grandfather says that you will be more comfortable here than at the new so-modern hotel. Always at night a breeze comes over the lake and the forest lends us the coolness of its shadows and the mountain gives us the strength of its peace. And"—he gestured toward the statue—"she gives us her blessing."

"Your Lady of the Lake," Miss Leonis said.

Ouldi translated, "Not of the lake only. She speaks to us not merely of the waters, but of the wind and the rain and the mountain and the stars and the power behind them all."

Miss Leonis looked out over the peaceful scene. "I, too, trust the same power."

The Umara, who seemed to have fallen asleep, spoke.

Ouldi listened carefully. "She says that this Power is the Power which has all Memory. Even her Memory is as nothing compared to the Memory of the Power behind the stars."

Miss Leonis said, "To be part of the memory of this power is for life to have meaning, no matter what happens." She had based her life on this faith. She could not begin to doubt it now.

HELPING THE SUN TO RISE

Miss Leonis wakes early, dresses, and joins Umar Xanai at the edge of the lake. Her walk has made her slightly out of breath. Simon is her great-grandson.

APRIL 19

Umar Xanai was there before her, alone, sitting in Charles's favorite position.

The old woman sat down silently, slightly to one side and behind him. Around her she could sense the sleeping village. Someone was moving on the porch of one of the Caring Places. Soon Dragonlake would be awake. All around her she heard bird song. A fish flashed out of the lake and disappeared beneath the dark waters. Above her the stars dimmed and the sky lightened.

When the sun sent its first rays above the mountain, Umar Xanai rose and stretched his arms upward. He began to chant. Miss Leonis could not understand the velvet Quiztano words, but it seemed clear to her that the old chieftain was encouraging the sun in its rising, urging it, enticing it, giving the sun every psychic aid in his power to lift itself up out of the darkness and into the light. When the great golden disc raised itself clear of the mountain the chanting became a triumphal, joyful song.

At the close of the paean of praise the old man turned to the old woman and bent down to greet her with the three formal kisses.

She asked, "You are here every morning?"

He nodded, smiling. "It is part of my duties as chief of the Quiztanos."

"To help the sun rise?"

"That is my work."

"It will not rise without you?"

"Oh, yes, it would rise. But as we are dependent on the sun for our crops, for our lives, it is our courtesy to give the sun all the help in our power—and our power is considerable."

"I do not doubt that."

"We believe," the old man said quietly, "that everything is dependent on everything else, that the Power behind the stars has not made anything to be separate from anything else. The sun does not rise in the sky in loneliness; we are with him. The moon would be lost in isolation if we did not greet her with song. The stars dance together, and we dance with them."

Miss Leonis smiled with joy. "I, too, believe that. I am grateful that you help the sun each morning. And when the moon wanes and the sky is dark—you are with the dying moon, are you not?"

"When the tide ebbs and the moon is dark, we are there."

"My tide is ebbing."

"We know, Señora Phair."

"It will be an inconvenience to you. I am sorry."

"Señora Phair, it is part of our Gift. We will be with you."

"I am not afraid."

"But you are afraid for the Phair."

"I am afraid for Simon."

"Do not fear, Señora Phair. You have come to redeem the past."

"That is not in my power," she said sadly.

He looked at her calmly. "You will be given the power."

UNITED BY THE POWER
BEHIND THE STARS

Simon sat between Umar Xanai and Ouldi. On the old chieftain's other side was Aunt Leonis, with Mr. Theo by her. She looked as frail as old glass, and yet her expression was full of peace.

APRIL 20

She looked at him and smiled, calmly and reassuringly.

Not everybody was seated, but Umar Xanai picked up a piece of fruit as a signal that the feast was to begin. Then he rose and spoke:

> Power behind the stars
> making life from death
> joy from sorrow
> day from night
> who heals the heart
> and frees the lake
> of dragons and all ill
> come feast with us

that we may share your feast
with all we touch.

Then he bowed his head silently.

When he looked up, Miss Leonis spoke:

"Thou didst divide the sea through thy power; thou break-est the heads of the dragons in the waters. Thou broughtest out fountains and waters out of the hard rocks; the day is thine, and the night is thine; thou hast prepared the light and the sun. Oh, let not the simple go away ashamed, but let the poor and needy give praise unto thy Name." She did not bow her head, but looked briefly up at the sky, then out over the lake, and closed her eyes.

"Lady, Señora Phair," Umar Xanai said, "we are as one."

CONSUMERS DO NOT CONSERVE THE EARTH

After quoting theologian Martin Buber, who said that the world is a reality created to be hallowed, Madeleine writes:

APRIL 21 Probably the worst thing that has happened to our under-standing of reality has been our acceptance of ourselves as consumers. Our greed is consuming the planet, so that we may quite easily kill this beautiful earth by daily pollution without ever having nuclear warfare. Sex without love con-sumes, making another person an *object,* not a *subject.* Can we change our vocabulary and our thinking? To do so may well be a matter of life and death. Consumers do not under-stand that we must live not by greed and self-indulgence but by observing and contemplating the wonder of God's universe as it is continually being revealed to us.

A BLESSING FOR THE EARTH

In this fantasy, An Acceptable Time, *Polly O'Keefe has traveled through a time door three thousand years in the past. There is friction between two tribes, the People Across the Lake and the People of the Wind. There has been a drought. Karralys, holy man from the People of the Wind, prays. The snake referred to is an old black snake named Louise the Larger, not the snake in the garden of Eden.*

APRIL 22

Karralys stood at the water's edge and raised his arms to the sky. "Bless the sky that holds the light and life of the sun and the promise of rain," he chanted, and one by one the other council members joined him, echoing his song.

"Bless the moon with her calm and her dreams. Bless the waters of the lake, and the earth that is strong under our feet. Bless those who have come to us from a far-off time. Bless the one who summoned the snake, and bless the snake who came to our aid. Bless the east where the sun rises and the west where it goes to rest. Bless the north from where the snows come, and the south that brings the spring. Bless the wind who gives us our name. O Blesser of all blessings, we thank you."

He turned from the lake and smiled at the people gathered around skins spread out on the ground. A deer was being roasted on a spit, and a group of young warriors danced around it, chanting.

"What're they singing about?" Zachary asked Polly.

"I think they're thanking it for giving them—us—its life."

"It didn't have much choice," Zachary pointed out.

Perhaps it didn't, but Polly felt a graciousness in the dance and in the singing.

GOOD MORNING SONG
TO OUR MOTHER

APRIL 23

In An Acceptable Time, *Polly O'Keefe meets Anaral, a girl from the three-thousand-year-ago past, while she is out walking on her grandparents' property.*

Who are you?" Polly asked.

"Anaral." The girl pointed to herself as she said her name. She had on the same soft leather tunic and leggings she had worn the night before, and at her throat was the silver band with the pale stone in the center. The forefinger of her right hand was held out a little stiffly, and on it was a Band-Aid, somehow utterly incongruous.

"What were you singing? It was beautiful. You have an absolutely gorgeous voice." With each word, Polly was urging the girl not to run away again.

A faint touch of peach colored Anaral's cheeks, and she bowed her head.

"What is it? Can you tell me the words?"

The color deepened slightly. Anaral for the first time looked directly at Polly. "The good-morning song to our Mother, who gives us the earth on which we live" — she paused, as though seeking for words—"teaches us to listen to the wind, to care for all that she gives us, food to grow"—another, thinking pause—"the animals to nurture, and ourselves. We ask her to help us to know ourselves, that we may know each other, and to forgive"—she rubbed her forehead—"to forgive ourselves when we do wrong, so that we may forgive others. To help us walk the path of love, and to protect us from all that would hurt us." As Anaral spoke, putting her words slowly into English, her voice automatically moved into singing.

"Thank you," Polly said. "We sing a lot in my family. They'd love that. I'd like to learn it."

ENJOYING GOD

In the Portuguese convent, Joaquina is an overly pious nun, and Mother Escolastica is one of the senior nuns. Mariana is APRIL 24 *playing with some of the convent children. At the time of this story, the middle of the seventeenth century, Portugal was still struggling to win her freedom from Spain.*

The refectory rang with unaccustomed laughter.

Sister Joaquina, unable to share the pleasure, was saying, "I'm not sure it's a good idea."

Beatriz directed her clear gaze at Joaquina. "What? Being free of Spain?"

"Counting buttons."

—What? Mother Escolastica, sitting across from the younger nuns, focused her dark old eyes, still bright as beads on Joaquina's pasty face. Did the young nun, like Sister Maria da Assunção, suffer from dyspepsia? Her diet should be checked.

Why should a casual remark from silly little Michaela on the brightness of the buttons on the French soldiers' jackets be made into an issue?

Joaquina, overly fond of mortifications, took the driest, hardest crust from the bread tray. "It keeps our minds from the contemplation of inward visions."

Mariana burst into such a peal of laughter that all heads in the refectory turned in her direction.

Joaquina flushed. "What's so funny?"

"Forgive me," Mariana said quickly as she reached for an orange and began to peel it. "I wasn't laughing at you. You're quite right. I should spend more time, as you do, worrying about saving my soul, but I can't seem to do it, because surely *I* cannot save my soul. Only God can do that. And when I see—" she looked out the long, open windows to the garden, "—the way the evening sun is touching the flowers right now—or when I look at this orange, look at the brilliance of its color and smell the sharpness of its scent—isn't that as much a vision of God as anything we see inwardly?"

"I don't know," Joaquina said flatly. She looked across the table at Mother Escolastica. "I don't mean to criticize, Mother, but there's something wrong with it."

"With what, child?"

"The way Sister Mariana looks out the window at the flowers, and the way she enjoys that orange."

"Well?"

"She enjoys it too much."

Mariana's mouth was full of juicy pulp. "Aren't we supposed to?"

ANNUNCIATION

To the impossible: Yes!
Enter and penetrate
O Spirit. Come and bless
This hour: the star is late.
Only the absurdity of love
Can break the bonds of hate.

APRIL 25

After Annunciation

This is the irrational season
When love blooms bright and wild.
Had Mary been filled with reason
There'd have been no room for the child.

BEWARE! HIGH VOLTAGE

In literal terms the Annunciation can only confound us. But the whole story of Jesus is confounding to the literal-minded. It might be a good idea if, like the White Queen, we practised believing six impossible things every morning before breakfast, for we *are* called on to believe what to many people is impossible. Instead of rejoicing in this glorious "impossible" which gives meaning and dignity to our lives, we try to domesticate God, to make his mighty actions comprehensible to our finite minds. It is not that the power to understand is not available to us; it is; he has promised it. But it is a power far greater than the power stations for our greatest cities, and we find it easier not to get too close to it, because we know that this power can kill as well as illuminate. Those who try to use it for

APRIL 26

their own advantage come to disaster, like Simon Magus in the Acts of the Apostles. But then, Simon Magus thought that he was qualified, that power was his due. And this has been the downfall of dictators throughout history, and this century seems to have had an inordinate number of them.

ROCK BOTTOM

APRIL 27

It's a good thing to have all the props pulled out from under us occasionally. It gives us some sense of what is rock under our feet, and what is sand. It stops us from taking anything for granted.

WISE ONES, ANCIENT AND MODERN

APRIL 28

When I am looking for theologians to stimulate my creativity, theologians who are contemporary enough to speak to these last years of our troubled century, I turn to the Byzantine and Cappadocian Fathers of the early years of the Christian era, because their world was more like ours than the world of such great theologians as Niebuhr and Tillich and Bultmann, who were writing in the framework of a world which was basically pre–World War II, and definitely pre-the-splitting-of-the-atom. In the first few centuries A.D., Rome was breaking up; civilization was changing as radically as is our own; people were no longer able to live in the luxury they had become accustomed to, as the great aqueducts and water-heating systems broke down and the roads were no longer kept up. Such people as St. Chrysostom, Basil the Great, Gregory of Nyssa and his brilliant sister, Macrina, were facing the same kind of change and challenge that we are, and from them I get great courage.

And when I try to find contemporary, twentieth-century mystics, to help me in my own search for meditation and contemplation, I turn to the cellular biologists and astrophysicists, for they are dealing with the nature of being itself, and their questions are theological ones: What is the nature of time? of creation? of life? What is human creativity? What is our share in God's work?

IGNORE INTUITION AT OUR PERIL

One of the many sad results of the Industrial Revolution was that we came to depend more than ever on the intellect, and to ignore the intuition with its symbolic thinking. The creator, and the mystic, have tended more towards Platonism than Aristotelianism, and to be willing to accept Plato's "divine madness," with its four aspects of prophecy, healing, artistic creativity, and love.

APRIL 29

These divine madnesses have been nearly lost in this century, and so we've lived almost entirely in the pragmatic, Cartesian world. I wonder if Descartes knew what he was doing when he wrote his famous *I think, therefore I am,* and subsequently, if not consequently, we began even more than before to equate ourselves with our conscious minds. *Cogito, ergo sum* nudges us on to depend solely on intellectual control, and if we insist on intellectual control we have to let go our archaic understanding and our high creativity, because keeping them means going along with all kinds of things we *can't* control.

REALITY EMBRACES REASON
AND INTUITION

APRIL 30 And yet, ultimately, our underwater, intuitive selves are never really incompatible with the above water, intellectual part of our wholeness. Part of Jesus' freedom came from the radical view of time which allowed him to speak with Moses and Elijah simultaneously, thus bursting through the limitations of time accepted by the intellect. Yet what he did is not at all inconsistent with what contemporary astrophysicists are discovering about the nature of time. Secularists have long tended to laugh away the story of "Sun, stand thou still upon Gibeon," but according to some new research, it now seems as though something actually did happen to the physical world at that time; the earth may have shifted slightly on its axis, and time would have been affected, and the sun for a moment may indeed have stood still.

MAY

UNIVERSE-DISTURBERS

MAY 1 If we disturb the universe, no matter how lovingly, we're likely to get hurt. Nobody ever promised that universe-disturbers would have an easy time of it. Universe-disturbers make waves, rock boats, upset establishments. Gandhi upset the great British Empire. Despite his non-violence, he was unable to stop the shedding of blood, and he ended with a bullet through his heart. Anwar Sadat tried to work for peace in one of the most unpeaceful centuries in history, knowing that he might die for what he was doing, and he did.

Does it encourage our present-day universe-disturbers to know that Abraham, Isaac, and Jacob before them were universe-disturbers? Their vision of God, while undeniably masculine, was also the vision of a God who cared, who appeared to his human friends and talked with them. The patriarchs lived in a primitive, under-populated world, and yet their vision of God as Creator of all, of God who cared, of God who was part of the story, was very new.

Jesus was a great universe-disturber, so upsetting to the establishment of his day that they put him on a cross, hoping to finish him off. Those of us who try to follow his Way have a choice, either to go with him as universe-disturbers (butterflies), or to play it safe. Playing it safe ultimately leads to personal diminishment and death. If we play it safe, we resist change. Well. We all resist change, beginning as small children with our unvarying bedtime routine, continuing all through our lives. The static condition may seem like security. But if we cannot move with change, willingly or reluctantly, we are closer to death and further from life.

TURNING THE TABLES
ON A BLOOD TABOO

So Jesus healed this unclean woman, and by her touch he became ritually unclean himself. He was on his way to the MAY 2 house of Jairus, whose daughter was mortally ill. But Jesus did not stop to follow the law, to purify himself. Ritually unclean, so that anybody who touched him was also unclean, he went to Jairus's house, and raised the little girl from the dead. Thereby he broke another taboo, going against the proscription against touching a dead body. He touched her, and she was alive, and he suggested that she be given food. Shocking behaviour. Everybody he touched, after being touched by the woman with the issue of blood, was unclean. But he brought a dead child back to life, making himself doubly unclean, and the child, also. Ritually unclean, but alive! Jesus acted on the law of love, not legalism. As far as we know, he never did anything about getting himself ritually cleansed. Because love, not law, is the great cleanser. In obeying this higher law he shocked everybody, including his closest friends, in his extraordinary and unacceptable ways of acting out love. Of being Love.

THE MEDIUM
IS THE MESSAGE

Christ can speak to me through the white china Buddha who sits on my desk at Crosswicks and smiles at me tolerantly when I fly into a torrent of outrage or self-pity. That forbearing smile helps restore my sense of proportion, and rids me of that self-will which keeps me caught up in myself so that I am isolating myself from Christ. Of course I am no more likely to become a Buddhist than my parents were likely to turn to Islam when they framed those lovely verses from the Koran.

There is no limit to the ways in which Christ can speak to us, though for the Christian he speaks first and most clearly through Jesus of Nazareth. Indeed, my icons would be idols if they did not lead me to follow more closely in Jesus' steps.

THE CROSS
AS ANCIENT SYMBOL

MAY 4

For the human being the cross is an ancient symbol, used thousands of years before Jesus of Nazareth was crucified. The Bushmen of South Africa painted small red crosses in their caves, and it is thought that these small, apricot-skinned people originally came to South Africa from Egypt. They listened for guidance from God in the tapping of the stars. Sometimes on a cold, clear night I think I can hear their tapping, too. The Bushmen were not separated from the stars, or the coinherence of all of creation. Other peoples have tried to exterminate these tiny, untamed people. Surely their loss is felt in great waves throughout the galaxies, an agonizing butterfly effect.

Jesus of Nazareth could not be tamed, either, and so he, too, had to be wiped out, hung on a cross in the dust and the heat and the flies. Those who cannot be tamed are disturbers of the universe, and without them we would be infinitely poorer. But because they are a threat to the control of local governments they must be put down, ruthlessly.

JESUS—GOD'S SHOW AND TELL

*At a writers' workshop at Mundelein College that Madeleine
was teaching, the class sat in a circle and shared meaningful*   MAY 5
stories.

A teacher of small children told us of a child who said to
her, "Jesus is God's show and tell."

How simple and how wonderful! Jesus is God's show and
tell. That's the best theology of incarnation I've ever heard.
Jesus said, if you do not understand me as a little child, you
will not be able to enter the kingdom of heaven.

That child's insight works more powerfully for me than
dogma. When I am informed that Jesus of Nazareth was exactly like us except sinless, I block. If he was sinless he wasn't
exactly like us. That makes no sense. Jesus was like us because
he was born like any human child, grew up like the rest of us,
asked questions in the temple when he was twelve, lost his temper in righteous indignation at the money lenders in the temple, grieved when at the end his disciples abandoned him. I
want Jesus to be like us because he is God's show and tell, and
too much dogma obscures rather than reveals the likeness.

If Jesus is God's show and tell, the wonder, the marvel is
that Jesus and the Father are one. Not I, says Jesus over and
over, but the Father in me, the Father who is such love that he
is willing to be in the story with us.

THE ETERNAL CHRIST I

A true symbol is an open window, never leading to a
closed, deterministic world, but to an open, indeterminis-   MAY 6
tic one. Symbols are mind, heart, and soul stretchers.

Recently I was shown a colour photograph of an icon—from Armenia, I think—which absolutely delights me. It is a picture of King David, sitting and holding his harp with one hand. With the other he holds a child who is sitting on his knee, and the caption under the picture reads: *King David with Christ on his lap.*

What a glorious reminder that Christ always was! Jesus of Nazareth lived for a brief life span, but Christ always was, is, and will be, and the picture of King David with Christ on his lap is my treasure for this year, a treasure largely in my mind's eye, because I do not have a copy of the picture of this icon.

So, like King David, we may hold Christ on our laps, and we will be taught to live lovingly with paradox and contradiction, with yes and with no, light and dark, in and out, up and down.

EVERY KNEE SHALL BOW

MAY 7 On the cross Jesus was at one with God and the holy angels and rainbows and butterflies. And he was also, to his anguish, at one with Satan and all the fallen angels, with those who would viciously destroy what God has made with love and joy, with those whose pride is even greater than that of the terrorist. Because Jesus took into himself on the cross every evil and every sin and every brokenness to come upon this planet, there is the fragile but living hope that one day even Satan may once again join the sons of God when they gather round their Maker, and that he will beg to be allowed once again to carry the light. For, as Saint Paul wrote to the people of Philippi, "Every knee shall bow in heaven and on

arth and under the earth, and every tongue confess that Jesus
Christ is Lord, to the glory of the Father."

THE ASCENSION, ANOTHER MYSTERY

However the Ascension happened, what we do know is
that Jesus did not want his friends to hold on to him.   MAY 8
They were thrilled with the Resurrection body, once they recognized it to be the Lord, and they wanted to keep him with
them forever. But he told them, in no uncertain terms, that it
was better for them for him to leave them. He would send
them the Holy Spirit; that was the promise. He would go, and
then the Comforter would come.

How did they understand? When would they understand?
Probably never completely, as we at our best do not understand completely. We need to move beyond the dominance of
the intellect and understand with the spirit if we are to contemplate the reality of the Ascension. But we must also take great
care that the understanding of the heart does not deteriorate
into sentimentality and become idolatrous. With God's help it
need not.

JOY'S FOUNDATION

It is faith that what happens to me matters to God as well as
to me that gives me joy, that promises me that I am eternally   MAY 9
the subject of God's compassion, and that assures me that the
compassion was manifested most brilliantly when God came
to us in a stable in Bethlehem. God gave us the wonderful
story of Jesus, and that story dignifies my story, your story, all

our stories. As we read it in the Gospels we see that Jesus was
not only a great storyteller, he also came in for much frightened and irrational criticism. He was accused of having fun
with his friends. His enjoyment of his faith, too, was suspect.
This joy came from his constant awareness of his Source. And
it is that awareness of our Source that takes away our fears
and not only allows us, but prods us, even commands us to
enjoy our faith.

PERFECT LOVE CASTS OUT FEAR

MAY 10 Story helps us dare to take seriously Jesus' promise that every
hair of our head is counted—one of the Maker's joyous ex-
aggerations. Or is it exaggeration? Are there angels whose job
is to do such counting? What has happened to Christianity that
there is so little joy? (Not mere happiness. Joy. Someone told
me that the difference between happiness and joy is sorrow.)
Why do we forget the promise of the rock under our feet? Why
is there so much fear, so much antagonism, so much judgmentalism? Why do some people read story looking for something
to criticize rather than applaud? It is a human tendency to
draw together when a common enemy can be found. If there is
no real enemy, or if the real enemy is too fearful to be faced,
then one has to be made up. That frightens me more than the
real enemy.

THE GIFT OF GOD'S PRESENCE

MAY 11 Heaven is nothing we can seek through our own virtue; it
cannot be earned; it is a gift of the God of love. When we
are self-emptied enough to make room for this love, it is not a

result of our own moral rectitude or willpower. But it is sometimes given to us, this lovely emptiness, and then the Holy Spirit
can fill it, with prayer, or music, or a poem, or a story. Or, sometimes, it goes beyond all these to the greatest gift of all, being
filled with that which is beyond all symbols, with God's Presence.

And then we *are*, far more than when we are filled with self-
probing, self-centeredness, or self-righteousness.

WINDOWS TO THE SOUL

*The Small Rain is Madeleine's first novel. Young Katherine
Forrester, the protagonist, is a talented pianist. In this scene,
near the end of the novel, Katherine is sick. Her fiancé, Pete,
leaves her with their friend Felix Bodeway while he and
Katherine's roommate go out for a drink. Felix and Katherine begin to talk. Felix says,*

MAY 12

Well, shall we talk or shall we just sit?"
"Whatever you say."
"Shall I tell you about myself?"
"All right."
He sat hunched up on a low, yellow, wooden bench, holding
the tip of his nose between two curved fingers in a way that he
had. His blond hair was a little too shaggy, and a lock fell across
his forehead and over one eye. "I'm a window cleaner," he said.
"A window cleaner and a musician?"
"No 'and.' Music is my window cleaning. If I weren't so
sick of it, I'd quote the Bible. You know that bit. Through a
glass darkly. That's how people see. It's as though nobody was
out in the world. You know what I mean? We're all shut up in

rooms. Everybody. And nobody can ever get in to anybody else's room. That's because we've got bodies. And the only way we can have contact with people is through the windows in our rooms. You get what I mean? And some people have more windows than others. And everybody's windows get dirty. So there have to be window cleaners. I'm one. At least maybe I will be one someday. That's what I want to be."

"Oh."

"The trouble is that my own windows need cleaning."

"Do they?"

"Sometimes I read things and I can see out better. Usually it's music (you must play for me). Or a great actress. Or a painting. Usually I just get drunk, so I can forget I'm locked up all by myself in a room and it's foggy outside . . . You know, Miss Forrester—Katherine—I don't talk this way to most people. . . . It's just easy, somehow, to say things to you."

GROWING PAINS

MAY 13

In this scene from The Small Rain, *Sarah Courtmont, Katherine Forrester's roommate, is making her stage debut in Tchekov's play* The Three Sisters. *Katherine's actress mother, Manya, attends the performance. When it is over, she goes backstage to speak to Sarah. Manya criticizes her performance, especially in the third act. Dejected, Sarah says, "I'm sorry." Manya responds:*

Why are you sorry? There's nothing to be sorry about. I'd rather have you be terrible than mediocre. And in the moments when you were good you were excellent. But you're

116

simply not ready to play a part like Masha. You aren't anything as a human being yet. You're still wishy-washy. Your most definite quality at the moment is your self-centeredness. You have the welfare of Miss Sarah Courtmont, and Miss Sarah Courtmont alone, in mind, and if other people have to be sacrificed, you'll sacrifice them. That's all right in moderation. But watch out for it. It may make for quick success, but it'll be bad for you as an actress in the long run, if you don't check it. You have great potentialities of power and strength, but as yet they are only potentialities that come out in spite of yourself. Guard them. Use them. Don't kill them. Because you can kill them, you know. There are some things that can't die, but there is nothing that can't be murdered. . . ."

BEING TIME

When I am constantly running there is no time for being. When there is no time for being there is no time for listening. MAY 14 I will never understand the silent dying of the green pie-apple tree if I do not slow down and listen to what the Spirit is telling me, telling me of the death of trees, the death of planets, of people, and what all these deaths mean in the light of love of the Creator who brought them all into being; who brought me into being; and you.

This questioning of the meaning of being, and dying, and being, is behind the telling of stories around tribal fires at night; behind the drawing of animals on the walls of caves; the singing of melodies of love in spring, and of the death of green in autumn. It is part of the deepest longing of the human psyche, a recurrent ache in the hearts of all of God's creatures.

LISTENING—PRAYING—BEING

MAY 15 When we are at Crosswicks I usually take time to go to the brook, taking heavy clippers with me to try to keep the bittersweet from strangling the trees, to cut new paths to the rocks overlooking the water or leading to a particularly beautiful grove of birch or pine. Sitting, or, better, lying on one of my favorite sun-warmed rocks, I try to take time to let go, to listen, in much the same way that I listen when I am writing. This is praying time, and the act of listening in prayer is the same act as listening in writing. And again, comparisons need not come into it; the prayer of the saint is not necessarily "better" than the prayer of the peasant.

And then there is time in which to be, simply to be, that time in which God quietly tells us who we are and who he wants us to be. It is then that God can take our emptiness and fill it up with what he wants, and drain away the business with which we inevitably get involved in the dailiness of human living.

AMNESIA

MAY 16 In one of his dialogues, Plato talks of all learning as remembering. The chief job of the teacher is to help us to remember all that we have forgotten. This fits in well with Jung's concept of racial memory, his belief that when we are enabled to dip into the intuitive, subconscious self, we remember more than we know. One of the great sorrows which came to human beings when Adam and Eve left the Garden was the loss of memory, memory of all that God's children are meant to be.

REMEMBERING RIGHTLY

God is always calling on us to do the impossible. It helps
me to remember that anything Jesus did during his life
here on earth is something we should be able to do, too.

When spring-fed Dog Pond warms up enough for swimming, which usually isn't until June, I often go there in the late
afternoon. Sometimes I will sit on a sun-warmed rock to dry,
and think of Peter walking across the water to meet Jesus. As
long as he didn't remember that we human beings have forgotten how to walk on water, he was able to do it.

If Jesus of Nazareth was God become truly man for us, as I
believe he was, then we should be able to walk on water, to
heal the sick, even to accept the Father's answer to our prayers
when it is not the answer that we hope for, when it is *No.*
Jesus begged in anguish that he be spared the bitter cup, and
then humbly added, "but not as I will, Father; as you will."

In art, either as creators or participators, we are helped to
remember some of the glorious things we have forgotten, and
some of the terrible things we are asked to endure, we who are
children of God by adoption and grace.

KNOWING CHRISTIANS BY THEIR LOVE

How often we children have been unwilling, unwilling to
listen to each other, unwilling to hear words we do not
expect. But on that first Pentecost the Holy Spirit truly called
the people together in understanding and forgiveness and
utter, wondrous joy. The early Christians, then, were known
by how they loved one another. Wouldn't it be wonderful if

people could say that of us again? Not an exclusive love, shutting out the rest of the world, but a love so powerful, so brilliant, so aflame that it lights the entire planet—nay, the entire universe!

I had such an experience once, in Ayia Napa, Cyprus, when I was with a group of Christians from all over the world and from all denominations. We celebrated Holy Communion together in an upper room, and we sang "We're one in the Spirit, we're one in the Lord," and I knew it to be true. That gathering was an icon of love for me, an icon of Pentecost, an icon of what Christians ought to be, known by our love.

The icon becomes idol when any one part of the body wants the rest of the body to be just like it. In that upper room we ranged from Seventh-day Adventist all the way through to Roman Catholic, and we rejoiced in our individual ways of proclaiming our faith; at the same time we honored the ways of the others whose expression of faith was different from ours. The icon did not become idol because no one person or group professed to have the only truth or the only way to affirm that truth. How odd it would be if the body were all hands or knees or teeth!

TEMPER MY INTEMPERANCE

Temper my intemperance, O Lord,
O hallowed, O adored,
my heart's creator, mighty, wild,
temper thy untempered child.
Blaze my eye and blast my ear,
let me never fear to fear,

nor forget what I have heard,
even your voice, my Lord.
Even your Word.

BELIEF AND DOUBT

A winter ago I had an after-school seminar for high-school students and in one of the early sessions Una, a brilliant fifteen-year-old, a born writer who came to Harlem from Panama five years ago, and only then discovered the conflict between races, asked me out of the blue: "Mrs. Franklin, do you really and truly believe in God with no doubts at all?"

MAY 20

"Oh, Una, I really and truly believe in God with all kinds of doubts."

But I base my life on this belief.

THE PARTICULARITY OF GOD'S LOVE

Una kept pushing me, wanting to know (I think wanting to be reassured) if I really believed in God. One day she brought it up at the beginning of the class, and the others seemed to want to talk too, so I plunged in: "There are three ways you can live life—three again—remember that the great writers almost always do things in threes. You can live life as though it's all a cosmic accident; we're nothing but an irritating skin disease on the face of the earth. Maybe you can live your life as though everything's a bad joke. I can't."

MAY 21

They couldn't, either, though for some of the kids who sat around the table that day not much had happened to make them think that life is anything else.

"Or you can go out at night and look at the stars and think, yes, they were created by a prime mover, and so were you, but he's aloof perfection, impassible, indifferent to his creation. He doesn't care, or, if he cares, he only cares about the ultimate end of his creation, and so what happens to any part of it on the way is really a matter of indifference. You don't matter to him, I don't matter to him, except possibly as a means to an end. I can't live that way, either."

Again there was general agreement.

"Then there's a third way: to live as though you believe that the power behind the universe is a power of love, a personal power of love, a love so great that all of us really *do* matter to him. He loves us so much that every single one of our lives has meaning; he really does know about the fall of every sparrow, and the hairs of our head are really counted. That's the only way I can live."

PRAYER—AN ACT OF LOVE

MAY 22 *In* A Ring of Endless Light, *Adam Eddington calls Vicky Austin to tell her that his supervisor at the marine biology laboratory, Jeb Nutteley, was seriously injured when a motorcycle hit him as he walked to his car. Vicky's father is a doctor. John and Suzy are Vicky's siblings.*

When he hung up, I asked, "Is Jeb going to be all right?"

"We won't know for a while. The sooner he regains consciousness, the more hopeful the prognosis."

I didn't like the sound of his voice. A shadow seemed to move across the kitchen windows. I kept on wiping the knives although they'd been dry for a long time. "Well, but—" I said at last. "You don't think he's going to die?"

"A skull fracture's pretty critical, but as long as the CAT scan was okay he's got a good chance if he doesn't stay unconscious too long."

John added in a low voice, "Better he die than—" His voice trailed off.

"Be a vegetable?" I asked.

John simply nodded.

Mother turned off the water, which had been running all this time. Even though the Island is surrounded by water, Grandfather's drinking supply comes from a well and we're careful not to waste it.

"Wonder who'll be the next to go?" the woman had asked at Commander Rodney's funeral. Maybe it wouldn't be our grandfather after all. Maybe it would be Jeb Nutteley, struck down as wantonly as his wife and child. I had an irrational desire to run across the Island to the dolphin pens. But if Ynid needed to be told, she would surely know from Adam.

"I'm going to help Father get ready for bed," Daddy said.

Suzy demanded, "So, are you going to ask him to pray for Jeb?"

"Why not?" Daddy responded mildly.

"You mean, it may not do any good but it probably won't do any harm?"

Daddy's voice was still mild. "I think it well may do good."

Suzy snorted and turned away from Daddy, so that she was facing Mother.

Mother put her hand against Suzy's cheek. "I believe in prayer. You know that."

"But you don't even know Jeb! You've never even met him!"

"What's got into you?" John demanded sharply.

Suzy still sounded angry. "Prayer didn't keep Jeb from being hit by a motorcycle. It didn't stop Grandfather from having leukemia."

"Prayer was never meant to be magic," Mother said.

"Then why bother with it?" Suzy scowled.

"Because it's an act of love," Mother said.

DON'T GIVE IN TO DARKNESS

MAY 23

While Vicky is at the hospital visiting her ill grandfather, a distraught woman hands Vicky her child, Binnie, to hold while she goes to the nurses' desk. The child dies in Vicky's arms. The day after this incident, Grandfather is home. Vicky is terribly upset and enters Grandfather's room. He asks her what is wrong. Caro is Grandfather's wife who died several years ago.

How could I tell him? "Don't you know?"

"I know what happened last night, yes."

"To Binnie?"

"Yes. That's a hard one, Vicky, and you're young to learn it, but it's part of life."

"Not life. Death."

He looked at me steadily. "It is time, Vicky, for me to give you my last instructions." . . .

"Oh, Grandfather . . . "

He smiled. "*Other men's crosses are not my crosses* . . . remember? Perhaps holding Binnie while she died was a cross prepared for you at the foundation of the world. But telling me when to let go is not. I cannot ask that even of your father, because even a doctor does not necessarily know."

"But—"

He held up his hand for me to stop, and again the loveliness of his smile washed over me. "Caro." But he was not confusing Caro with me. "I am at that place where the wall between here and hereafter is so tenuous that it is no longer a barrier. Caro will tell me when it is the right time. She will let me know. Vicky, are you hearing me?"

"No," I said flatly. . . .

"You may not think you are hearing me, but you will not forget. When I am on the other side you will remember, and you will be able to let me go."

"No—" My whisper was so faint it was almost inaudible.

Grandfather's voice was quiet but strong. "Empty yourself, Vicky. You're all replete with very thee."

No, no. Not with me. With darkness.

Grandfather reprimanded. "You have to give the darkness permission. It cannot take over otherwise."

But I hadn't given it permission. It had come, as suddenly and unexpectedly as death had come and taken the child in my arms.

"Vicky, do not add to the darkness."

I stood at the hospital bed, still alien in Grandfather's study, and looked at him, thin and translucent as an El Greco— . . .

I heard him and I did not hear him.

"Vicky, this is my charge to you. You are to be a light-bearer. You are to choose the light."

"I can't . . ." I whispered.

"You already have. I know that from your poems. But it is a choice which you must renew now."

I couldn't speak.

He reached out and drew me to him, kissing me gently on the forehead. "I will say it for you. You will bear the light." He kissed me again. "Now go." He lowered the bed and closed his eyes.

DOLPHIN HEALING SERVICE

MAY 24

Vicky Austin is plunged into darkness by the illness of her grandfather and the death of the child in her arms at the hospital. Adam Eddington comes to Grandfather's house and takes her to the beach. When they arrive, Adam orders Vicky to take off her shorts and shirt so she can swim. He pushes her into the ocean and swims with her. Then the dolphins come. Basil, Norberta, and Njord are the dolphins that have swum with Adam and Vicky before. These dolphins have been befriended by Adam as part of his summer project at the marine biology laboratory.

Surrounded
by flashing silvery bodies
tossed up into the air
caught
held between the sleekness of two dolphins
holding me but not hurting
holding and swimming
and then leaping with me up into the air
Basil and Norberta leaping into joy
with me between them

and before us and behind us and beside us
the others of the pod flashing and leaping
and I was being passed from pair to pair
And I knew they were trying to bring me out of the darkness and into the light, but the darkness remained because the
light was too heavy to bear
Then I sensed a withdrawing
the pod moving away from me
not out to sea, but away, swimming backward and looking
at me, so that I was in the center of a circle
but I was not alone
Norberta was with me
Suddenly she rose so that her flipper was raised, and then
she brought it down, wham, on my backside
Ouch!
I submerged, down into the strange green darkness of sea,
shot through with ribbons of gold
gulping sea water
choking
rising, sputtering, up into the air
into the blazing blue of sky
and Njord was there, nudging me, and laughing as I choked
and spat out salt water, coughing and heaving
And the light no longer bore down on me
but was light
and Njord nudged and poked and made laugh noises
and I grabbed his fin and he soared into the air.
And I played with Njord.

The pod began to sing, the same alien alleluias I had heard
first from Basil, then from Norberta and Njord, and the sound

wove into the sunlight and into the sparkles of the tiny wavelets and into the darkest depths of the sea.

One last alleluia and they were gone, leaving Basil and Norberta to watch Njord and me play.

And then they were gone, too, flashing out to sea, their great resilient pewter bodies spraying off dazzles of light, pure and endless light.

I watched them until they disappeared into the horizon.

Then I turned and swam into shore.

Adam was at the beach ahead of me, standing on his head.

I body-surfed in, stood up, shaking water, and splashed in to meet him.

He flipped over onto his feet and I looked at him wonderingly. "I called you—"

"And I came," he said.

I moved toward him and we were both caught and lifted in the light, and I felt his arms around me and he held me close.

A SYMBOL FOR COMMUNITY AND UNITY

MAY 25

When Hugh and I worshiped in the small Congregational Church in our village it was not a liturgical church and we didn't pay any attention to Trinity Sunday. We paid attention to Christmas and Easter, but that was all. We didn't observe Lent, or Epiphany, or Advent, or any of the other great seasons of the church year. Now that our Congregational church has joined the United Church of Christ, this has changed, and we mark the seasons and this, to me, gives an added richness to our observance.

But now Trinity Sunday in even the most liturgical of churches is paid little heed. The Trinity is a wholeness which has become too difficult for us to understand. It's never been easy, but at least we used to declare our belief in the Trinity as intrinsic to Christianity. Now we have the great feast of Pentecost, and Trinity Sunday comes and goes and after that we're into the long series of Sundays after Pentecost, replacing what I used to think of as the long green Sundays after Trinity.

The Trinity proclaims a unity that in this fragmented world we desperately need. We are mortals who are male and female, and we need to know each other, love each other. The world gets daily more perilous. Our cities spawn crime. Terrorists are around every corner. Random acts of violence increase. . . .

The Trinity was never meant to be comprehensible in the way that a mathematical formula is comprehensible. The writers of the Apostles' and the Nicene creeds affirmed that. Another thing we must remember about the Trinity is that it was always there, an icon of all three Persons, whole, undivided. The hardest Person of the Trinity to comprehend is Christ, because we must let go all our rational preconceptions and move into the mystery of love.

REENTRY

When our children were born, two things happened simultaneously. We cleaned up our language; we had been MAY 26 careless about four-letter words—I'd been rather proud of those I'd picked up from stage hands; we no longer used them indiscriminately. And we discovered that we did not want our children to grow up in a world which was centered on man to the exclusion of God. We did know that bedtime prayers were not enough and that it made no sense whatsoever to send the children to Sunday School unless we went to church ourselves. The inconsistency of parents who use the church as a free baby-sitting service on Sunday mornings, while they stay home and read the Sunday papers, did not have to be pointed out to us. I found myself earnestly explaining to the young minister that I did not believe in God, "but I've discovered that I can't live as though I didn't believe in him. As long as I don't need to say any more than that I try to live as though I believe in God, I would very much like to come to church—if you'll let me."

So I became the choir director.

INTEGRITY

MAY 27

The most "whole" people I know are those in whom the gap between the "ontological" self and the daily self is the smallest. The Latin *integer* means untouched; intact. In mathematics, an integer is a whole number. The people I know who are intact don't have to worry about their integrity; they are incapable of doing anything which would break it.

It's a sad commentary on our world that "integrity" has slowly been coming to mean self-centeredness. Most people who worry about their integrity are thinking about it in terms of themselves. It's a great excuse for not doing something you really don't want to do, or are afraid to do: "I can't do that and keep my integrity." Integrity, like humility, is a quality which vanishes the moment we are conscious of it ourselves. We see it only in others.

The gap between our "real" and "actual" selves is, to some degree, in all of us; no one is completely whole. It's part of what makes us human beings instead of gods. It's part of our heritage from our mythical forebears, from Adam and Eve. When we refuse to face this gap in ourselves, we widen it.

SEARCH FOR COMMUNITY

I knew the beauty of community in the birthing of my babies. We human beings are not meant to give birth to our MAY 28 offspring alone, any more than the dolphin, who delivers her babies with the help of midwife dolphins, in community. The need of the mother for support at this incredible moment has too often been forgotten by science, and it is good that once again the father can be present at the birth of his seed and share in this marvelous communal act.

I wish I knew it more often in church, and that I were a less reluctant Christian. The Church is too grownup for me, too reasonable, too limited. One reason nearly half my books are for children is the glorious fact that the minds of children are still open to the living word; in the child, nightside and sunside are not yet separated; fantasy contains truths which cannot be stated in terms of proof. I find that I agree with many college-age kids who are rejecting the adult world—not those with bad cases of Peter Pantheism, but with those who understand that the most grownup of us is not very grownup at all, that the most mature of us is pretty immature; that we still have a vast amount to learn.

THE ETERNAL CHRIST II

MAY 29

In An Acceptable Time, *Zachary Gray, a young man who has courted both Vicky Austin and Polly O'Keefe, shows up at Polly's grandparents' home. Eventually he becomes involved in a fantastic adventure that takes Polly, Zachary, and a family friend, Bishop Colubra, back to 1000 B.C. Zachary has become a prisoner of the People Across the Lake, one of the two tribes the time travelers meet in the past. Bishop Colubra prays.*

When they got to the standing stones there was someone lying on the altar. With a low cry, Anaral hurried forward, then drew back. "It is Bishop talking with the Presence."

While Polly watched, the bishop slowly pushed himself into a sitting position and smiled at her and Anaral. Then he returned his stare to some far distance. *"But, Lord, I make my prayer to you in an acceptable time,"* he whispered. "The words of the psalmist. How did he know that the time was acceptable? How do we know? An acceptable time, now, for God's now is equally three thousand years in the future and three thousand years in the past."

"We are sorry," Anaral apologized. "We did not mean to disturb your prayers."

The bishop held out his hands, palms up. "I have tried to listen, to understand."

"Who are you trying to listen to?" Polly asked.

"Christ," the bishop said simply.

"But, Bishop, this is a thousand years before—"

The bishop smiled gently. "There's an ancient Christmas hymn I particularly love. Do you know it? *Of the Father's love begotten—*"

"*E'er the worlds began to be.*" Polly said the second line.

"*He is alpha and omega, He the source, the ending—*" the bishop continued. "The Second Person of the Trinity always was, always is, always will be, and I can listen to Christ now, three thousand years ago, as well as in my own time, though in my own time I have the added blessing of knowing that Christ, the alpha and omega, the source, visited this little planet. We are that much loved. But nowhere, at any time or in any place, are we deprived of the source. Oh, dear, I'm preaching again."

"That's okay," Polly said. "It helps."

WHY ARE YOU A CHRISTIAN?

Faith and religion are not the same thing. Although my faith may falter, it has to do with the constancy of God's love. MAY 30 Religion, which is the expression of faith, may find different expressions appropriate in different times and places and to different people, and the variety of these expressions can enlarge our perceptions and deepen our faith.

John Wesley Watts, who lived in West Virginia in the nineteenth century, wrote his own epitaph as he lay dying, and subsequently it was engraved on his tomb: *John Wesley Watts: A Firm Believer in Jesus Christ, Jeffersonian Democracy, and the Methodist Episcopal Church.*

I respect his conviction, but it is conviction, not faith. I come closer to defining and describing faith when I remember the great preacher Phillips Brooks, who was asked by an earnest questioner why he was a Christian. He thought seriously for a moment, then replied, "I think I am a Christian because of my aunt, who lives in Teaneck, New Jersey."

Or, as my friend Canon Tallis puts it, "A Christian is someone who knows one."

If I have faith, it is because I have met faith, I have seen it in action. And this faith is never a vague, pie-in-the-sky kind of thing. Heaven is not good because life is bad; the quality of our lives while we live them is preparation for heaven.

TRUE HEROES,
OUR POINTS OF REFERENCE

MAY 31

But I can't do it myself. I need a hero. Sometimes I have chosen pretty shoddy ones, as I have chosen faulty mirrors in which to see myself. But a hero I must have. A hero shows me what fallible man, despite and even *with* his faults, can do: I cannot do it myself; and yet I can do anything: not as much of a paradox as it might seem.

In looking towards a hero, we are less restricted and curtailed in our own lives. A hero provides us with a point of reference.

Charlotte Napier, in *The Love Letters,* tries to explain this to João Ferreira: "Supposing you were sitting in a train standing still in a great railroad station. And supposing the train on the track next to yours began to move. It would seem to you that it was your train that was moving, and in the opposite direction. The only way you could tell about yourself, which way you were going, or even if you were going anywhere at all, would be to find a point of reference, something standing still, perhaps a person on the next platform; and in relation to this person you could judge your own direction and motion. The person standing still on the platform wouldn't be telling you where you were going or what was happening, but without him you wouldn't know. You don't need to yell out the train window and ask directions. All you need to do is see your point of reference."

JUNE

THE INDESCRIBABLE DEITY

Athanasius and his friends, hammering out the *Quicunque Vult* in order to defend the Trinitarian God they adored, struggled to move beyond the literal level of daily words and yet make the point, and sometimes blundered into absurdity (as Dorothy Sayers noted): the Father incomprehensible, the Son incomprehensible, the Spirit incomprehensible—the whole thing incomprehensible. Of course it is. That's partly the point of Athanasius's powerful wielding of words as though he were trying to catch hold of the whirlwind. The Trinity is trapped in neither time nor space. *Before Abraham was, I am,* cries the second person. *I will be what I will be,* shouts the first. And through the brilliant flame of the Spirit I know that the Christ on whose name I call was creating galaxies and snowflakes long before there were living beings naming the animals in the Garden.

Perhaps the morning stars still sing together, only we have forgotten the language, as we have forgotten so much else, limiting Christianity to a mere two thousand years. We've known it by that name for even less, but that is our shortsightedness. When God came to us as one of us he was misunderstood and betrayed and part of that misunderstanding and betrayal is our dimming his brilliance because it's too much for our feeble eyes; our limiting his power because we're afraid of the unsheathed lightning; our binding him with ropes of chronology instead of trying to understand his freedom in *kairos*. Not that we've done any of this to the Lord himself, only to our image of the One we worship, and that's bad enough.

THE DANGER OF VANITY IN GOODNESS

In this excerpt from A Ring of Endless Light, *Zachary Gray has told Vicky Austin that he is going to hang around because he needs her. This is confusing to her. She discusses this with her grandfather.*

JUNE 2

That's a pretty heavy burden, Vicki."

"Do you think I'm strong enough to carry it?"

"I think we're given strength for what we have to carry. What I question is whether or not this burden is meant for you."

"He needs me, Grandfather."

"You, Vicki Austin, specifically?"

"Well—yes. I think so." I did not like the way Grandfather's eyes were stern as they looked at me.

He said, "There's a sermon of John Donne's I have often had cause to remember during my lifetime. He says, *Other men's crosses are not my crosses.* We all have our own cross to carry, and one is all most of us are able to bear. How much do you owe him, Vicky?"

I replied slowly. "I don't think of it in terms of owing, like paying a debt. The thing is—he needs me."

Grandfather looked away from me and out to sea, and when he spoke, it was as though he spoke to himself. "The obligations of normal human kindness—*chesed,* as the Hebrew has it—that we all owe. But there's a kind of vanity in thinking you can nurse the world. There's a kind of vanity in goodness."

139

I could hardly believe my ears. "But aren't we supposed to be good?"

"I'm not sure." Grandfather's voice was heavy. "I do know that we're not good, and there's a lot of truth to the saying that the road to hell is paved with good intentions."

I said, slowly, "I can't make Zachary leave the Island if he wants to stay."

THE CLOSELY WOVEN PATTERN

JUNE 3   *Leo Rodney, whose father recently died of a heart attack while saving Zachary Gray, is talking with Vicky Austin about his plans to attend Columbia University in this selection from* A Ring of Endless Light. *They discuss the fact that Adam Eddington's parents both teach at Columbia. Grandfather, Adam Eddington, and Vicky's brother John are also in on the conversation.*

Grandfather says there's no such thing as coincidence," I said, and looked at him.

Grandfather's lips quirked into a small smile. "The pattern is closely woven."

Adam, who had been silent all through the discussion . . . spoke up. "You really think there's a pattern, sir?"

"It seems evident to me."

"What does that do to free will?" John asked.

"Not a thing. Any one of us can cause changes in the pattern by our responses of love or acceptance or resentment." He held a thin hand out toward Leo. "You're finding that out, ren't you? And your mother. Her response is always on the side of life. She's going back to nursing, isn't she?"

THE SOLID GROUND OF MYTH

Jung says that we are a sick society because we have lost a valid myth to live by, and in my small back room I was absorbing a mythic view of the universe, a universe created by a power of love far too great to be understood or explained by tenets or dogmas. That power of love was offered me by those writers and artists whose imaginations took me beyond literalism. Long before Joseph Campbell and others popularized a mythic view of the universe, that was my view; and probably the most important influence in deepening my mythic understanding was George MacDonald. He comforted me, but not with cozy platitudes. The mythic world he offered me promised no easy solutions. Rather, it gave me solid ground under my feet, a place where I could stand in a world which was confusing and dangerous and unfriendly. I read the books in my small bookcase. I read the books on my parents' shelves. And the world widened.

JUNE 4

WHAT IS REALITY?

When I look at the stars to help me find perspective, I am seeking an alternate reality, one which is deeper and more real than the world of immediate consciousness.

JUNE 5

Different people have different perceptions of reality, and our own perceptions change as we move from infancy to childhood to adolescence to adulthood. As Americans, as people whose background is from the Judeo-Christian tradition, the terms of our reality are very different from that of a fundamentalist Muslim whose presuppositions involve bloodbaths and the ritual killing of anyone who disagrees. But to someone within the framework of this reality, his is right, and ours is wrong. Can we be sure we are right? What about the Spanish Inquisition, the burning of anyone accused of being a witch, even if the accusation was false?

We have strayed far from the reality of those peoples of the world who live close to the land, who listen to the language of the birds, the singing of the trees, the message of the clouds in the sky. Our loss.

We are far from the reality of many of the people we encounter every day. I am light years away from the perception of reality of people who find that story is a lie, who believe that to act in a play is a sin, because it is to "make believe," and who have fallen for one of the devil's cleverest deceptions, that myth is not a vehicle of truth, but a falsehood.

REDEFINING MYTH AS TRUTH

JUNE 6 It doesn't bother me when people talk condescendingly about the Christian myth, because it is in myth that sunside and nightside collaborate and give us our glimpses of truth. But when I use the word *myth* I bump headlong into semantic problems, because myth, to many people, is a lie. Despite the fact that during the last decade myth has been rediscovered as a vehicle of truth, there are still those who cannot help thinking of it as something which is false. We give children the

Greek and Roman myths, the Norse or Celtic myths, and expect them to be outgrown, as though they are only for children and not to be taken seriously by realistic adults. If I speak of the Christian myth it is assumed not only that I am certainly not a fundamentalist, but that I am an intellectual who does not need God and can speak with proper condescension of the rather silly stories which should be outgrown at puberty. But I am far closer to the fundamentalist than the atheist when I speak of myth as truth.

The rediscovery of myth hasn't helped, because what does his Satanic Majesty do when the sons of Adam stumble upon something which would further the coming of the Kingdom and destroy the Prince of this World? He infiltrates, and so myth becomes part of the jargon, and jargon has no power.

Nonetheless, myth is the closest approximation to truth available to the finite human being. And the truth of myth is not limited by time or place. A myth tells of that which was true, is true, and will be true. If we will allow it, myth will integrate intellect and intuition, night and day; our warring opposites are reconciled, male and female, spirit and flesh, desire and will, pain and joy, life and death.

THE TRUTH OF MYTH

A study of the myths of various religions and cultures shows us not how different we human beings are, but how alike we are in our longing for God, for the Creator who gives meaning and dignity to our lives.

JUNE 7

I am not sure how much of the great story of Abraham, Isaac, and Jacob is literally true, how much is history, how much the overlapping of several stories. Did *both* Abraham and Isaac pretend to Abimelech that their wives were their sisters, or have the two stories mingled over the ages? Does it really matter? The mythic truths we receive from these stories enlarge our perception of the human being, and that unique being's encounters with God. When the angel of God comes to wrestle with us we must pray to be able to grapple with the unexpected truth that may be revealed to us. Because Jacob, later in the story, had the courage to ask for God's blessing, we may too.

If we take the Bible over-literally we may miss the truth of the poetry, the stories, the myths. Literalism can all too easily become judgmentalism, and Jesus warned us not to judge, that we might not be judged.

How difficult it is! When I worry about those who castigate me for not agreeing with them, am I in my turn falling into judgmentalism? It's hard not to. But not all the way, I hope. I don't want to wipe out those who disagree with me, consigning them to hell for all eternity. We are still God's children, together. At One. Even if I am angry, upset, confused, I must still see Christ and Christ's love in those whose opinions are very different from mine, or I won't find it in those whose view fits more comfortably with mine.

THE LOVE OF THE FATHER

JUNE 8 — We are so familiar with the Parable of the Prodigal Son that we forget part of the message, and that is the response of the elder brother. As I read and reread Scripture it seems evident that God is far more loving than we are, and far more forgiving. We do not want God to forgive our enemies, but Scripture teaches us that all God wants is for us to repent, to say, "I'm sorry, Father. Forgive me," as the Prodigal Son does when he *comes to himself* and recognizes the extent of his folly and wrongdoing. And the father rejoices in his return.

Then there's the elder brother. We don't like to recognize ourselves in the elder brother who goes off and sulks because the father, so delighted at the return of the younger brother, prepares a great feast. Punishment? A party! Because the younger brother has learned the lesson he has, in a sense, already punished himself. But, like the elder brother, we're apt to think the father much too lenient.

REDISCOVERING THE NEED FOR MYTH

In these strange and difficult years since man has learned to split, though not to fathom the dark and dangerous heart of the atom, the attitude towards the language of myth has altered radically. It is the scientists themselves who have shaken our faith in their omnipotence, by their open admission that they have rediscovered how little they know, how few answers they really have. JUNE 9

Before they discovered nuclear fission and fusion, before they discovered the terrible fallibility this power revealed to them, many scientists were atheists; we don't need God if everything is explainable—in which case we would not need the language of the imagination and there would be no poets or storytellers. But on that day in 1945 in the desert in New Mexico when a group of men exploded the first atomic bomb, on that day when a light brighter than a thousand suns touched the sands of Alamogordo and those who had made it happen watched the mushroom cloud that has hovered over us ever since, this attitude changed. It is the scientists themselves who today are telling us that they cannot tell us everything—even as we walk on the surface of the moon, even as we probe into the strange and further field of genetics. The deepest scientific truths cannot be expressed directly. We hear this from men like Pollard, who has remained a distinguished scientist and has also become a priest. Fred Hoyle is a famous astrophysicist; but when he has an idea that goes beyond present knowledge (something very different from wisdom) or that might upset some tired old pragmatic scientist, he turns to writing fantasy, where he can communicate ideas that are too big, too violent, too brilliant to be rendered directly.

LIVING MYSTERIES

JUNE 10

Often we forget that [God] has a special gift for each one of us, because we tend to weigh and measure such gifts with the coin of the world's market place. The widow's mite was worth more than all the rich men's gold because it represented the focus of her life. Her poverty was rich because all she had belonged to the living Lord. Some unheard-of Elizabethan woman who led a life of selfless love may well be brought before the throne of God ahead of Shakespeare, for such a person may be a greater force for good than someone on whom God's blessings seem to have been dropped more generously. As Emmanuel, Cardinal Suhard says, "To be a witness does not consist in engaging in propaganda, nor even in stirring people up, but in being a living mystery. It means to live in such a way that one's life would not make sense if God did not exist."

The widow's mite and Bach's *St. Matthew's Passion* are both "living mysteries," both witness to lives which affirm the loving presence of God.

LAUGHTER, A WEAPON AGAINST THE DARK

We can surely no longer pretend that our children are growing up into a peaceful, secure, and civilized world. JUNE 11 We've come to the point where it's irresponsible to try to protect them from the irrational world they will have to live in when they grow up. The children themselves haven't yet isolated themselves by selfishness and indifference; they do not fall easily into the error of despair; they are considerably braver than most grownups. Our responsibility to them is not to pretend that if we don't look, evil will go away, but to give them weapons against it.

One of the greatest weapons of all is laughter, a gift for fun, a sense of play which is sadly missing from the grownup world. When one of our children got isolated by a fit of sulks, my husband would say very seriously, "Look at me. Now, don't laugh. Whatever you do, don't laugh." Nobody could manage to stay long-faced for very long, and communication was reestablished. When Hugh and I are out of sorts with each other, it is always laughter that breaks through the anger and withdrawal.

Paradox again: to take ourselves seriously enough to take ourselves lightly. If every hair of my head is counted, then in the very scheme of the cosmos I matter; I am created by a power who cares about the sparrow, and the rabbit in the snare, and the people on the crowded streets; who calls the stars by name. And you. And me.

OUR NEED FOR MYSTERY

A Russian priest, Father Anthony, told me, "To say to anyone 'I love you' is tantamount to saying 'You shall live forever.'"

I am slowly beginning to learn something about immortality.

Our children are hungry for words like Father Anthony's. They have a passionate need for the dimension of transcendence, mysticism, way-outness. We're not offering it to them legitimately. The tendency of the churches to be relevant and more-secular-than-thou does not answer our need for the transcendent. As George Tyrrell wrote about a hundred years ago, "If [man's] craving for the mysterious, the wonderful, the supernatural, be not fed on true religion, it will feed itself on the garbage of any superstition that is offered to it."

BACK INTO JOY

Madeleine is with Dana and Margie, two of their "summer children." They had attended a carnival with Hugh and had brought home enormous trumpets.

Sunday evening was clear and luminous so we went to the star-watching rock and welcomed the arrival of each star with a blast of trumpet. We lay there, in an odd assortment of coats; I had on an embroidered coat a friend had bought in

Dubrovnik; the two girls had on ancient fur coats; and we were covered with blankets. We needed them, even though the rock itself still held the warmth of the sun, our own star, and radiated a gentle heat to us as we lay there and watched the sky, blowing the trumpets and sharing a can of insect repellent and listening to the crickets and the katydids and trying to identify the other night singers, and then outsinging them with all the nursery rhymes and songs and hymns we could think of which had stars and alleluias in them.

And I was totally back in joy. I didn't realize I had been out of it, caught in small problems and disappointments and frustrations, until it came surging back. It was as radiant as the rock, and I lay there, listening to the girls trumpeting, and occasionally being handed one of the trumpets so that I could make a loud blast myself, and I half expected to hear a herd of elephants come thundering across the far pastures in answer to our call.

And joy is always a promise.

HUMAN BEINGS MAKE MISTAKES

Emma Wheaton, the protagonist of Certain Women, *and her younger brother, Louis, talk with her grandfather, a southerner who is a country preacher.*

JUNE 14

Grandpa Bowman often used theatrical terms. "You see, my dear children, that the people God has chosen to use throughout history, and still today, are never the good and moral and qualified people. They're faulty and flawed and complicated enough to be fascinating and infuriating."

"Like you." Emma sat with Louis on her grandfather's porch.

"Saul or Samuel?" Grandpa Bowman asked.

"Samuel, of course."

The old man laughed. "I came to the Lord late, after I was fully grown and working on my own. I was walking in the woods when the Lord came to me in a vision."

"Grandpa," Emma asked without guile, "have any of your visions come true?" She froze, as he turned on her, shouting.

"Many of them. Many, many. Your mother turned away from my visions and refused to fulfill them."

"Okay, Grandpa, okay. I didn't mean to upset you."

"Only the Lord can upset me," he bellowed.

"Hey, Grandpa," Louis said eagerly, "have you ever had any visions about me?"

"You, child? No. I have had no visions about you. Are you disappointed?"

"It would depend on what the visions were."

"You're a good boy. Your mother has brought you up well."

"You do like my mom?"

"She's a pet lamb, like you."

"Grandpa, would it have been better if my papa hadn't married all those other wives?"

Grandpa Bowman huffed softly. "I'm not comfortable with better or worse. It is simply a fact, Louis, that he did. He is a human being."

"And human beings make mistakes?"

"Inevitably."

"Grandpa, do you think God ever makes mistakes?"

Grandpa Bowman turned to Emma. "How would you answer that question?"

Emma thought, frowning. "Well. We often think God makes mistakes because we'd rather blame God than blame ourselves."

"Heah, heah! So go on."

Emma paused and scratched a mosquito bite. "Well. Human beings make mistakes because we have free will."

"And?"

"It was pretty risky of God to give us free will."

"Very risky," Grandpa Bowman said.

"Do you think it was a mistake?"

"I am not God," Grandpa Bowman said. "But I am happy that I am a human being who can make mistakes, and not an insect, who cannot."

Louis asked, "Have you made mistakes, Grandpa?"

"A great many."

PARENTS AREN'T PERFECT

Nik, Emma Wheaton's estranged husband, has come to the Portia, *the fifty-foot boat on which Emma's aged father, actor David Wheaton, dying of cancer, is spending his last days. Nik is a playwright. He has discovered that David is reading an old, incomplete play he had written about the biblical character King David.*

JUNE 15

E m, why—why is your father—"

"Why is he rereading your play?"

"Yes. He can't be reading it just as a play. It's tied in with too much pain—"

"It's pain that has to be exorcised. I think that talking about the play has helped."

"And you?"

Emma clasped her hands together tightly. "We've talked, whenever he's wanted to. He's said some amazing things."

Nik looked at her questioningly.

"He said that it was only after David lusted after Bathsheba, caused Uriah's death, only after he had failed utterly with Tamar and Amnon and Absalom, only after he was fleeing his enemies, fleeing his holy city of Jerusalem, that he truly became a king."

Nik looked down at his hands clenched on the yellowed pages of his play. "Maybe we have to sin, to know ourselves human, faulty, and flawed, before there is any possibility of greatness. I think your father's right. David did become great only after he'd lost everything."

"Is it always the hard way?" Emma asked.

"Isn't it?" Nik unclenched his fists. "David's grief over Absalom—it was grief over his own failure as a father."

"Oh, Nik—yes—Papa, too. He believes that he failed all of us."

Nik's voice was calm. "Parents always fail their children. If we'd had children, we'd have failed ours. That's simply how it is, and the kids have to get along as best they can. My parents were who they were. Dave is Dave."

ACCEPTANCE

JUNE 16 *After a concert in the Cathedral of St. John the Divine, Katherine Vigneras, the protagonist of* A Severed Wasp, *is*

152

introduced to the organist Llewellyn Owen by the dean of the cathedral.

N ow," Dr. Davidson said firmly, "Llew, we've run the gamut but we're here at last. Madame Vigneras, our organist, Llewellyn Owen."

Llewellyn Owen leapt to his feet to take her hand.

"That was a splendid performance, Mr. Owen," Katherine said. "I especially enjoyed my husband's Toccata and Fugue. Far too many people play it at a gallop, and you hit exactly the right controlled and serious tempo."

A quick flush suffused his pale skin. "Thank you. That means more to me than I can say, coming from you. I'm particularly fond of that piece—there's so much—so much acceptance in it."

She nodded. "Justin was not a very accepting person, but he worked through a good deal while he was composing that."

The young organist's eyes were bleak. "Is it worth it?"

"Oh, yes, Mr. Owen. It is worth it. I promise you that."

"In spite of—death and war and terror—"

"In spite of everything." He looked at her with so much pain that she repeated, "I promise."

CATHARSIS

Llew Owen talks with Katherine about the death of his wife and child. Bishop Undercroft had wanted him at the cathedral at the same time his wife was delivering a baby and dying. He has still not forgiven either the bishop or himself for not being at the hospital when the baby was born.

JUNE 17

The baby wasn't right, and Dee—started to bleed—and they couldn't control it—and I wasn't with her. I was here, at the Cathedral—" He was choking on dry sobs.

Katherine did not move to touch him, but sat quietly at the piano, waiting.

"It was his fault." The words were muffled. "I could at least have been with her. I'll never forgive him."

"Or yourself?"

"Both of us. I wasn't there, and she died."

"I wasn't with Justin when he died. I knew he was ill, and I still went on with my work. I was in Poland. I know something of what you've been going through. As for Bishop Undercroft, I gather he was brought up in the British tradition, where the chief purpose of education is to train you to do what you have to do, when you have to do it, whether you want to or not. It isn't a bad tradition, you know." —Without it, how could I have gone on playing, giving that first concert after Michou's death? "It wasn't Bishop Undercroft's fault that things went wrong."

Llew was half kneeling, half sitting on the stone floor, and he put his head in her lap. She touched his fine, thick hair. "The doctors said it was something that no one could have predicted."

"Then let it go. Stop blaming. You have to get on with things. You *are* getting on. I have heard you play."

"I'm alive only when I'm at the organ. Everywhere else I'm lost. I want to kill someone, to—"

"That's all right at first," Katherine said, "but you can't let it go on too long. If you do, it will destroy your music, and you are not permitted to do that."

"Who won't permit me?"

"I, for one."

He laughed then, a strangled sound. "At least you didn't say God."

She continued to stroke the lustrous black hair. His head was heavy on her lap, and suddenly she realized that he had fallen asleep, there on the hard stone floor of St. Ansgar's chapel.

Bishop Chan emerged slowly from the pew. "Thank you, Madame. You've done more for Llew than the rest of us together."

"But I haven't—"

"You're Katherine Vigneras. He can hear a musician where he cannot hear a priest."

"He's asleep—"

"I'll wake him in a moment. He was holding vigil for Merv most of last night. You've been a catalytic agent among us, Madame. We get very lost in our own world, here on the Close, very ingrown." The bishop leaned down and touched Llew on the shoulder. "Son." Llew shuddered and opened his eyes. "We must leave Madame Vigneras to the piano."

The young organist sprang to his feet, looked around wildly. "What did I do? I dumped it all on you—"

Katherine spread out both her hands and made a gesture as though throwing. "There. I've dumped it on these stones where it can't hurt anyone. Let it go. Serve your music."

He nodded. "I'm tired of being told to serve God. Serving my music is something I understand."

"Isn't it the same thing?" Bishop Chan crossed to him. "Come."

GLIMPSES OF GOD KEEP US GOING

A priest assigned to the cathedral has been murdered. A special worship service is being held. Bishop Chan has read the scripture from Job. Felix, a retired bishop of the cathedral and friend of Katherine, preaches the sermon. Katherine is present and listening.

She was too busy looking at him, thinking that he did indeed look like a bishop, to hear his first words. She picked up as he was saying, "Job is one of the dark books of the Bible, and although it is shot through with light, it has never been one of my favorite books. I turn more often to Jonah, which says much of the same things—that God's love for his Creation is boundless, and that all he wants from us is that we love him in return.

"But today's reading from Job has one of the greatest cries of affirmation in the entire Bible. Out of the depths of his pain, loss, anger, Job cries out, *I know that my Redeemer lives!* and he adds the equally extraordinary words, that he himself will see him, face to face. Not now, not in the midst of this mortal journey, because we couldn't bear it now. Moses asked to see God, and God put him in the cleft of a rock and protected him with his hand, and Moses saw God's hindquarters as he passed by.

"God's hindquarters. That's all we get, in this earthly part of our journey. But it's the glimpses that keep us going.

"The New Testament reading, too, is a promise, a promise that what God creates, he will not abandon, that ultimately we will be as we were meant to be."

For a moment Katherine had a glimpse of Juliana, successful at cross-breeding chickens, and yet unable to complete fifth-grade work.

". . . and then we, too, will see God face to face, as Adam and Eve did when God walked and talked with them in the cool of the evening—before the choices made then and throughout the centuries brought us to the world of pain and confusion in which . . ."

Choices again. Katherine looked at Felix, but she was no longer listening, even though she was feeling grateful that she liked what he was saying, that his delivery was authoritative and vibrant. When he preached, the years seemed to drop from him.

OUR SUFFERING MATTERS TO GOD

Katherine has tuned Felix out and done some remembering. Now she turns her attention back to Felix and his sermon.

She shook her head and moved carefully from the past to the present, away from the cathedral in Munich, to the larger one in New York. JUNE 19

She turned her attention to Felix, heard him saying, "The psalmist sings that he has never seen the good man forsaken, nor his children begging for bread. But good men and their children go hungry every day. And we come to the ancient question: If God is good, why do the wicked flourish, and the innocent suffer? They do; the wicked flourish, and children die of malnutrition or drugs; there is continuing war and disease and untimely death, and we cry out, Why!?

"And God answers by coming to live with us, to limit himself willingly in the flesh of a human child—how can that be? The power that created the stars in their courses contained in an infant? An infant come to live with us, grow for us, die for us, and on the third day rise again from the dead for us.

"And what did this incredible sacrifice accomplish? Nothing. On the surface, nothing at all. More than half the world is starving. The planet is torn apart by wars, half of them in the name of religion. We have surely done more harm throughout Christendom in the name of Christ than we have done good. Rape and murder and crimes of violence increase. . . . So what is it all about? How can it possibly matter?

"I don't know how it matters; I only know that it does, that when we suffer, God suffers, and he will never abandon the smallest fragment of his creation. He suffered with us during his sojourn as Jesus of Nazareth. And from the moment of Creation on, he suffers when any part of his creation suffers. Daily I add to his suffering and only occasionally to his gladness. But he will not give up on me, not now, not after my mortal death. He will not give up on any of us, until we have become what he meant us to be.

"I know this. I do not know how it will be done, but I know that it will be. I know that my Redeemer lives, and that I shall see him face to face." He stood for a moment, regarding the congregation with a gentle and loving gaze. Then he said, "Amen," and returned to his seat.

MUSIC MAGIC

JUNE 20
Zachary Gray takes Vicky Austin to a piano concert played by Katherine Vigneras. Basil is a dolphin. Adam Eddington, one of the special young men in Vicky's life in A Ring of Endless Light, *is working with at the marine biology laboratory during this summer. Vicky narrates.*

At that moment there was a burst of applause and a woman climbed the steps to the platform, bowed to the audience, and sat down at the piano. She was small and slight, with dark hair piled high on her head, showing a beautiful neck.

When she raised her hands over the keyboard I had a sense of total authority, and also a sense of terrific love, as though the piano were not an inanimate object but a dearly beloved person. And when she started to play, it was as though she and the piano were playing together.

Music has always been part of my life, taken for granted like the air I breathe. At home, Mother has the record player going most of the time; she says she'd never do any house-work without the help of music: for cleaning she puts on something loud, like a Brahms or Beethoven symphony, which can be heard over the vacuum cleaner. For cooking, which she enjoys, it's more likely to be Bach or Scarlatti or Mozart, or chamber music of some kind. So, sitting there in the gathering twilight, I was lifted up on the music, soaring with almost the same freedom and joy as Basil leaping into the sky.

The notes of the Bach hit against the air as clear as stars on a cold night. The audience shifted and stirred and then, caught in the music, stilled and listened. The wind blew softly and the heat of the day fled away. The lanterns moved in the breeze and the shadows rippled to the music like dancers. The long, lingering mid-July day slowly faded to streaks of rose and mauve, forecasting another clear, hot day. And then the color was gone and the stars began to come out, seeming to tangle with the Japanese lanterns. It was magic. I put my head down on Zachary's shoulder and closed my eyes and let the music wash over me like the ocean.

STAR SENSE

Vicky Austin is riding with Zachary Gray after the concert.
Vicky narrates.

Not only had I never been up in a plane, I'd never ridden in an open car before today. After the heat of the day it was so cool that I had to put Mother's shawl up over my head, and Zachary spread a rug over my knees.

"It's too pretty to put the hood up."

It was. The sky was purply black, with the galaxies clustered above us and a lopsided moon just rising. If music means a lot to me, so do stars, and I missed them desperately in the city, where the street lights and neon signs take away from the stars so that only the most brilliant ones are visible. If I'm confused, or upset, or angry, if I can go out and look at the stars I'll almost always get back a sense of proportion. It's not that they make me feel insignificant; it's the very opposite; they make me feel that everything matters, be it ever so small, and that there's meaning to life even when it seems most meaningless.

MODERN MYSTICS

Vicky Austin is the narrator.

After breakfast I read to Grandfather. A lot of what I read was over my head, because, somewhat unexpectedly, he asked me to read the works of scientists, mostly cellular biologists or astrophysicists.

"Grandfather, I didn't know you were interested in science."

"I'm interested in everything," he said gently, "but I want the scientists right now because they are the modern mystics, much more than the theologians." So we read about mitochondria, and we read about black holes, those weird phenomena which follow the death of a giant star. I found myself nearly as fascinated as Grandfather obviously was. When a giant star dies, there's what one article called a "catastrophic gravitational collapse." The extraordinary thing is that the star collapses so totally that it actually collapses itself out of existence and becomes what mathematicians call a "singularity." How can you take an enormous mass and shrink it down to nothing? But this nothing isn't really nothing. Its gravity is so great that nothing can escape it, and if you went through a black hole you might find yourself in a completely different time, or even a different universe. And this isn't science fiction. I began to see what Grandfather meant about the scientists being mystics.

GOING TO THE BROOK TO BE

Madeleine goes to her favorite brook, about a ten-minute walk from Crosswicks.

The path becomes full of tussocks and hummocks; my legs are etched by the thorns of blackberry brambles and wild JUNE 23 roses. Earlier this summer the laurel burst from snow into fire, and a few weeks later we found a field of sweet wild strawberries. And then there are blueberry bushes, not very many, but a few, taller than I am and, to me, infinitely beautiful. . . .

I go to the brook because I get out of being, out of the essential. So I'm not like the bush, then. I put all my prickliness, selfishness, in-turnedness, onto my *is*ness; we all tend to, and when we burn, this part of us is consumed. When I go past the tallest blueberry bush, where my twine is tied to one of the branches, I think that the part of us that has to be burned away is something like the deadwood on the bush; it has to go, to be burned in the terrible fire of reality, until there is nothing left but our ontological selves; what we are meant to be.

I go to the brook and my tensions and frustrations are lost as I spend a happy hour sitting right in the water and trying to clear it of the clogging debris left by a fallen tree.

LOSING OURSELVES TO FIND OURSELVES

JUNE 24 When we are *self*-conscious, we cannot be wholly aware; we must throw ourselves out first. This throwing ourselves away is the act of creativity. So, when we wholly concentrate, like a child in play, or an artist at work, then we share in the act of creating. We not only escape time, we also escape our self-conscious selves.

The Greeks had a word for ultimate self-consciousness which I find illuminating: *hubris:* pride: pride in the sense of putting oneself in the center of the universe. The strange and terrible thing is that this kind of total self-consciousness invariably ends in self-annihilation. The great tragedians have always understood this, from Sophocles to Shakespeare. We witness it in history in such people as Tiberius, Eva Perón, Hitler.

THE WONDER OF
UNSELF-CONSCIOUSNESS

Creativity is an act of discovering. The very small child, the baby, is still unself-conscious enough to take joy in discovering himself: he discovers his fingers; he gives them his complete, unself-conscious concentration. . . . JUNE 25

The kind of unself-consciousness I'm thinking about becomes clearer to me when I turn to a different discipline: for instance, that of playing a Bach fugue at the piano, precisely because I will never be a good enough pianist to play a Bach fugue as it should be played. But when I am actually sitting at the piano, all there is for me is the music. I am wholly in it, unless I fumble so badly that I perforce become self-conscious. Mostly, no matter how inadequate my playing, the music is all that matters: I am outside time, outside self, in play, in joy. When we can play with the unself-conscious concentration of a child, this is: art: prayer: love.

THE EVER-CHANGING SELF

We *can* give a child a self-image. But is this a good idea? Hitler did a devastating job at that kind of thing. So does Chairman Mao. To settle for this because we can't give a child a self is manipulation, coercion, and ultimately the coward's way out. JUNE 26

I haven't defined a self, nor do I want to. A self is not something static, tied up in a pretty parcel and handed to the child, finished and complete. A self is always becoming.

Being does mean becoming, but we run so fast that it is only when we seem to stop—as sitting on the rock at the brook—that we are aware of our own *is*ness, of being. But certainly this is not static, for this awareness of being is always a way of moving from the selfish self—the self-image—and towards the real.

Who am I, then? Who are you?

IT IS I

JUNE 27 I first became aware of myself as self, as Pascal's reed ("Man is only a reed, the feeblest reed in nature; but he is a thinking reed"), when I was seven or eight years old. We lived in an apartment on East 82nd Street in New York. My bedroom window looked out on the court, and I could see into the apartments across the way. One evening when I was looking out I saw a woman undressing by her open window. She took off her dress, stretched, stood there in her slip, not moving, not doing anything, just standing there, being.

And that was my moment of awareness (of ontology?): that woman across the court who did not know me, and whom I did not know, was a person. She had thoughts of her own. She *was*. Our lives would never touch. I would never know her name. And yet it was she who revealed to me my first glimpse of personhood.

When I woke up in the morning the wonder of that revelation was still with me. There was a woman across the court, and she had dreams and inner conversations which were just as real as mine and which did not include me. But she was there, she was real, and so, therefore, was everybody else in the world. And so, therefore, was I.

I got out of bed and stood in front of the mirror and for the first time looked at myself consciously. I, too, was real, standing there thin and gawky in a white nightgown. I did more than exist. I *was*.

That afternoon when I went to the park I looked at everybody I passed on the street, full of the wonder of their realness.

MOMENTS OF COMPLETENESS

My moments of being most complete, most integrated, have come either in complete solitude or when I am being part of a body made up of many people going in the same direction. A vivid example is a great symphony orchestra, where each instrument is completely necessary for the whole; a violin cannot take the place of a trombone, nor cymbals of the harp; and there are even times when the lowly triangle is the focus of the music.

JUNE 28

(I love Chaliapin's definition of heaven: "There will be five thousand sopranos, five thousand altos, ten tenors—I don't much like tenors—a thousand baritones, and I will sing bass.")

Where have I known this unity?

In the Holy Mysteries. Yes.

And years ago when I was in the theatre and was privileged to be a small part of bringing a play to life, I remember one evening during the rehearsal lying up on the grid and looking down from this great height to the stage and yet being a complete part of all that was being said and done.

THE SEPARATION IS THE SIN

JUNE 29 As I read and reread the great stories in the Bible it seems more and more clear that sin is separation from God, and one way to separate ourselves from God is to over-define God. If Jesus was like us, but sinless, it wasn't that he never did anything the moral majority of his day considered wrong. Indeed, he did many things that they considered sin, such as breaking the law by healing people on the Sabbath. But he was never separate from the Source, while we, of our essence, separate ourselves over and over.

The first great story in the Bible, after the wonderful paean of praise to Creation, is a story of separation from God, the story of Adam and Eve in the Garden. It doesn't really matter who was the first to eat of the fruit of the tree of the knowledge of good and evil. What is important is that in going against God's wishes, they separated themselves from their Maker. Both of them.

Like many of the tales in Scripture, the story of the expulsion of the human beings from the Garden is an ambiguous one. It is a story not of punishment, but of separation, the two human beings' separation from God, and separation from their own natures.

ALPHA AND OMEGA

JUNE 30 The true universe disturber has no arrogance. The arrogance and vanity of the terrorist is chilling. It takes humility and faith in God's loving concern to cross battle lines, be they geographical or ideological.

I was given a small Mexican cross, a copy of an ancient one, many thousands of years old, and it, like the cross of the African Bushmen, gives me a feeling of continuity and hope. The second person of the Trinity was with us "before the worlds began to be. He is alpha and omega, he the source, the ending," as the ancient hymn says. All of God has always been part of creation, part of the story, taking us in the everlasting arms as the shepherd clasps the lost lambs.

JULY

WE NEED A BIGGER PICTURE

JULY 1

In The Moon by Night, *Zachary Gray has taken Vicky Austin to see the play* The Diary of Anne Frank. *It has upset her, particularly the question about how there can be a good God if bad things happen to good people. She is talking with Uncle Douglas, who is an artist, while he is sketching her. She tries to express how unfair it seems.*

Uncle Douglas just nodded slowly, as though to himself, and went on sketching me. Finally he said, "It's a bit of a shock, isn't it, when you realize that things aren't fair in life? It comes particularly hard to you, Vicky, because your parents are eminently fair. It comes hard because of your grandfather. But it was your grandfather who once recited a little poem to me. Want to hear it?"

"Sure," I said without much enthusiasm. I expected something religious and *comforting,* and the whole point was that the *comforting* things were what *scared* me most, because Zachary was right, they didn't make sense.

"The rain is raining all around,"

Uncle Douglas quoted,

"It rains on both the just and the unjust fellow.
But more, it seems on the just than on the unjust,
For the unjust hath the just's umbrella.

All I'm trying to get at, Vicky, is that life isn't fair, and your grandfather, who is one of the greatest human beings I've ever known, is quite aware of it. He doesn't have anything to do with pie in the sky." (Pie in the sky again. It almost sounded as though Uncle Douglas could read people's minds.) "Your grandfather knows that the wicked flourish and the innocent suffer. But it doesn't destroy him, Vicky. He still believes, with a wonderful and certain calm, that God is our kind and loving father."

A THEODICY

Vicky and Uncle Douglas continue talking. Douglas is sketching Vicky. Evidently Uncle Douglas has less than conventional views about God. He prepares to share them with Vicky to help her understand the suffering and evil in the world.

JULY 2

U ncle Douglas sighed. For a while he worked on his sketch of me. Then he sighed and said, "One of the biggest facts you have to face, Vicky, is that if there *is* a God he's infinite, and we're finite, and therefore we can't ever understand him. . . . So in my heathen way, Vicky, when I wasn't much older than you, I decided that God, a kind and loving God, could never be proved. In fact there are, as you've been seeing lately, a lot of arguments *against* him. But there isn't any point to life without him. Without him we're just a skin disease on the face of the earth, and I feel too strongly about the human spirit to be able to settle for that. So what I did for a long time was to live life *as though* I believed in God. And eventually I found out that the *as though* had turned into a reality. I think the thing that did it for me was a jigsaw puzzle."

"A *jig*saw puzzle?"

"A jigsaw puzzle. Hold still. . . . You know those puzzles with hundreds of tiny pieces? You take one of those pieces all by itself and it doesn't make sense, does it? You look at one piece and it doesn't seem to be part of a picture. But you put all the pieces together and you see the meaning of it all. Well, what I, in my heathenish way, Vicky, feel about life, and unfairness, is that we find it hard to realize that there *is* a completed puzzle. We jump to conclusions and decide that the one little piece we have in our hand is all there is and that it doesn't make sense. We find it almost impossible to *think* about infinity, much less comprehend it. But life only makes sense if you see it in infinite terms. If the one piece of the puzzle that is this life were all, then everything would be horrible and unfair and I wouldn't want much to do with God, either. But there are all the other pieces, too, the pieces that make up the whole picture."

LIFE IS NOT FAIR

JULY 3   The stories of the great scriptural characters are not stories about fairness. Life is not fair. Indeed, the idea of fairness and unfairness didn't come into being until after the Fall. In Eden there was no need to think about such things, because life was the joy of at-one-ment with the Creator. It is after the fracture of this union, this separation (the first apartheid), that we begin to get caught up in shoulds and oughts, and fair and unfair. Children tend to stamp their feet and cry out, "It's not fair!" and very likely it isn't. When we think in terms of fairness and unfairness, we begin to want to "pay back" whoever has been unfair, we begin to want to get even, to punish. That is the beginning of forensic thinking.

Unfortunately, as many of us move on in chronology, we tend to stay stuck in the "It's not fair!" frame of mind, which, for the adult, is crippling. It takes great courage to live in a world where fairness simply doesn't play a part, and hasn't, since Adam and Eve ate of the fruit of the tree of the knowledge of good and evil. And one of Satan's most successful ploys is his insistence that things ought to be fair. The good should be rewarded; the bad should be punished. If we think forensically and earn enough merit badges everything will work out just as we would like. But that is not how grace works.

NOT CHOOSING IS NOT AN OPTION

Freedom is a terrible gift, and the theory behind all dictatorships is that "the people" do not want freedom. They want JULY 4 bread and circuses. They want workman's compensation and fringe benefits and TV. Give up your free will, give up your freedom to make choices, listen to the expert, and you will have three cars in your garage, steak on the table, and you will no longer have to suffer the agony of choice.

Choice is an essential ingredient of fiction and drama. A protagonist must not simply be acted upon, he must act, by making a choice, a decision to do this rather than that. A series of mistaken choices throughout the centuries has brought us to a restricted way of life in which we have less freedom than we are meant to have, and so we have a sense of powerlessness and frustration which comes from our inability to change the many terrible things happening on our planet.

FREEDOM'S TERRIBLE COST

Why would God give the gift of freedom to creatures who are not ready for it, who have kept making wrong JULY 5 choices for thousands and thousands of years—ever since Eve listened to the snake? Freedom is a mistake, we might well agree with the Grand Inquisitor, as we drive through the slums of any of our great cities, where buildings are gutted by tenants who are so frustrated by lack of heat in winter, no hot water ever and sometimes no water at all, that they resort to burning the buildings in order to get relocated. Or buildings gutted by landlords who cannot afford to heat them at the present price of oil, or to keep the water hot (not *all* landlords are vicious and greedy), and in desperation burn the building for insurance money, and get out. If all our freedom has done is build up our financially bankrupt, corrupt, tottering cities, what good is it?

Neither philosophy nor theology help me much here. The painters and writers who see the abuse and misuse of freedom and cry out for justice for the helpless poor, the defenseless old, give me more hope; as long as anybody cares, all is not lost. As long as anybody cares, it may be possible for something to be done about it; there are still choices open to us; all doors are not closed. As long as anybody cares it is an icon of God's caring, and we know that the light is stronger than the dark.

WHAT IS REAL?

JULY 6　For a human being, truth is verisimilitude, a likeness to what is real, which is as close as we can get to reality. It has taken me many years to learn that reality is far more than meets the human eye, or ear, or mind, and that the greatest minds have never attained more than fragmentary flashes of what is really real.

Below me on a flat, mossy stone in the brook sits a small green frog. What is a frog? What is the reality of a frog? I was fascinated by a scientific article which showed pictures of a frog as seen by a human eye, by a bird's eye, by a snake's eye. Each saw a very different creature. Which frog was more real?

DEATH, A NEW BIRTHING

Somehow, despite the fact that I feel that my mother's slow dying and birth are opposites, I still turn to the analogy of birth. When I walk down the lane at night and pray for Mother's death, I must know what I am praying for, and I am praying not just for her release from the prison her body has been turned into, but for birth. Alan was with Josephine during Charlotte's birth, and was amazed not only by the violence with which the mother works to expel the baby but by the violence with which the baby struggles to be born. Charlotte—typically—did not need to be spanked into life; she emerged shouting. Only a few hours earlier she had been safely inside her mother's womb, swimming comfortably in the amniotic fluid. Everything was done for her; she was sustained and nourished in the dark warmth. And suddenly the calm waters started churning, and she was shoved through a dark tunnel into blinding light, air knifed into her unused lungs, and she greeted the trauma of birth with a bellow of rage.

JULY 7

It's a good analogy for me, birth, and certainly has nothing to do with pie in the sky by and by. Perhaps the great-grandmother is as much afraid of the violence of a new birth as she is of the act of dying.

Do I believe all this? Not with my intellect. But my intuition keeps insisting that there are more things in heaven and earth Horatio, than your philosophies can tell.

EXTINCTION IS NOT AN OPTION

JULY 8 *Madeleine's father died when she was seventeen. Shortly after her father's death, she had a conversation on the beach one night with a friend named Yandell. Yandell believed that her father was just nothing after his death, and he told her that. She records this conversation in* The Summer of the Great-Grandmother.

I was both angry and frightened. I stood up, and sand slid under my feet. "Yandell, I saw him when he was dead. I saw Father, and it just wasn't Father. It's like looking at a photograph; it looks like the person, but the person isn't there. Father wasn't there, not what's really Father. And if he wasn't there, he's got to be somewhere."

The caustic note had gone from Yandell's voice, and he spoke slowly and calmly. "But what's a soul without a body, without senses? Can you imagine existing, being yourself, if you couldn't see? Or hear? Or feel? And after all, we think with our brains. How could you be you without your cerebral cortex?"

I was so angry that I nearly burst into tears, but they wouldn't have been the right kind of tears. "It's idiotic," I said, "it's crazy. If you die and then you're just nothing, there isn't any point to anything. Why do we live at all if we die and stop being? Father wasn't ready to be stopped. Nobody's ready to be stopped. We don't have *time* to be ready to be stopped. It's all crazy."

"Don't think the idea of extinction appeals to me," Yandell drawled.

I had put on my glasses so that I could see the stars. Now I took them off and the sky became nothing but a dark curtain. I waved my glasses at him. "Look at my glasses. I can't even see that there are any stars in the sky without them, but it's not the glasses that are doing the seeing, it's me, Madeleine. I don't think Father's eyes are seeing now, but *he* is. And maybe his brain isn't thinking, but a brain's just something to think through, the way my glasses are something to see through."

"Calm down," Yandell said. "Let's go walk on the beach and go wading."

MEDITATION—LETTING GO OF SELF

Vicky Austin takes a dinner tray in to her grandfather.

He was propped up in the hospital bed, his Bible by him, but he wasn't reading. I thought he probably knew most of it by heart.

He jerked slightly as I knocked and came in.

JULY 9

"Here's your dinner, Grandfather. I'm sorry if I woke you."

"You didn't wake me. I was meditating."

Mrs. Rodney had brought over a hospital table, which I swung over the bed for the tray. "What were you meditating about?" I asked, unfolding his napkin for him.

"You don't meditate *about*." His nicest smile twinkled at me. "You just meditate. It is, you might say, practice in dying, but it's a practice to be begun as early in life as possible."

"Sort of losing yourself?" I asked.

"It's much more finding than losing."

I wanted to stay and talk, because his mind seemed completely clear, but I knew I had to get back to the dining table.

"Vicky," Grandfather said as I turned to go, "I'll come out to the porch for the reading."

THOUGHTS ABOUT ETERNITY

JULY 10

Vicky Austin is talking with her friend Adam Eddington on the beach, while her dog, Mr. Rochester, lies at her feet. Vicky is depressed by the deaths that have taken place. Ynid and Basil are dolphins. Adam speaks:

You're upset because Ynid lost her baby."

"Of course. Probably not as upset as you are, but sure of course I'm upset."

"You're more upset than just *of course*. Why?"

"It's just—it's just—there's death everywhere—Commander Rodney—and watching Grandfather, and now Ynid's baby for no reason—it's just everywhere."

"Always has been. It's part of the price of being born."

"It just seems that lately . . ." My voice trembled and I leaned forward and carefully scratched Rochester behind the ears.

"Is the price too high?" Adam asked.

I shrugged, in the way that Mother hates.

"Are you afraid?" he asked softly.

Yes. I didn't say it aloud. I didn't need to.

"Of what, Vicky?" He picked up another handful of sand and started trickling it through his fingers. "Dying?" His voice wasn't loud, but the word seemed to explode into the night.

Mr. Rochester shifted position and I continued absent-mindedly to scratch behind his ears ... "Not so much of dying, if—I'm afraid of annihilation. Of not being."

Adam let all the sand fall. "I guess we all are, if it comes to that."

"Is that what you think it comes to? That Commander Rodney was just snuffed out? And Ynid's baby? And that Grandfather will be? And all of us?"

There was a long silence ...

At last Adam spoke. "I'm not a churchgoer, Vicky. I hadn't darkened the doors of a church since I sang in choir at school till—till Commander Rodney's funeral. So maybe what I think is kind of heretical."

"What *do* you think?" I desperately wanted to know. Maybe because of Basil, I trusted Adam. The breeze lifted and blew across us, pushing my hair back from my forehead. I must have shivered, because Adam put one arm lightly across my shoulders.

"When are you most completely you, Vicky?"

It wasn't at all what I had expected him to say. I was looking for answers, not more questions.

"When?" he repeated.

Maybe because I was feeling extraordinarily tired I was thinking in scenes, rather than logical sequences, and across my mind's eye flashed a picture of the loft, with the old camp cots, and the windows overlooking the ocean, and the lighthouse at night with its friendly beam, and on the far wall the lines of the poem Grandfather had painted there, *If thou could'st empty all thyself of self* ...

I was *not* really myself when I was all replete with very me. So when was I?

"When you first took me to meet Basil," I said slowly, "and when I was petting him and scratching his chest . . . "

"Who were you thinking about?"

"Basil."

"Were you thinking about *you?*"

"No."

"But you were really being you?"

"Yes."

"So that's contradiction, isn't it? You weren't thinking about yourself at all. You were completely thrown *out* of yourself in concentration on Basil. And yet you were really being really you."

I leaned my head against Adam's shoulder. "Much more than when I'm all replete with very me."

His right hand drew my head more comfortably against his shoulder. "So, when we're thinking consciously about ourselves, we're less ourselves than when we're not being self-centered."

"I suppose . . ."

"Okay, here's another analogy. Where are you when you write poetry?"

"This summer I'm usually up in the loft."

"You know that's not what I mean. When you're actually writing a poem, when you're in the middle of it, where are you?"

"I'm not sure. I'm more in the poem than I am in me. I'm using my mind, really using it, and yet I'm not directing the poem or telling it where to go. It's telling me."

His strong fingers moved gently across my hair. "That's the

way it is with science, too. All the great scientists, like Newton, like Einstein, repeat the same thing—that the discoveries don't come when you're consciously looking for them. They come when for some reason you've let go conscious control. They come in a sudden flash, and you can receive that flash, or you can refuse to. But if you're willing to receive it, then for that instantaneous moment of time you're really you, but you're not conscious in the same way you have to be later on when you look at what you saw in the flash, and then have to work out the equations to prove it."

. . . I asked, "Has that happened to you, that knowing in a flash?"

"Not in the way it did to Einstein, with his theory of relativity. Or to Dr. O'Keefe, with his work on limb regeneration. But in little ways with Basil, yes. He's taught me more about himself than I could have learned with just my thinking self. And Basil—Basil has taught you, hasn't he?"

"Yes. Oh, yes.". . .

"And you saw Jeb with Ynid."

Yes, I had seen Dr. Nutteley with Ynid. In the midst of his pain, Jeb had been wholly real.

"What I think . . . is that if we're still around after we die, it will be more like those moments when we let go, than the way we are most of the time. It'll be—it'll be the self beyond the self we know."

At that moment there was a rip in the clouds and an island of star-sparkled sky appeared, its light so brilliant it seemed to reach down beyond the horizon and encircle the earth, a ring of pure and endless light.

WE DIE MANY DEATHS

I must never lose sight of those other deaths which precede the final, physical death, the deaths over which we have some freedom; the death of self-will, self-indulgence, self-deception, all those self-devices which, instead of making us more fully alive, make us less.

The times I have been most fully me are when I have been wholly involved in someone or something else; when I am listening, rather than talking; cooking a special, festive dinner; struggling with a fugue at the piano; putting a baby to bed; writing. A long-dead philosopher said that if we practice dying enough during our lives we will hardly notice the moment of transition when the actual time comes. But I am far from a saint, and I am seldom able to practice consciously this kind of dying; it is not a do-it-yourself activity. I know about it only after it has happened, and I am only now beginning to recognize it for what it is.

It has nothing to do with long-faced self-righteousness, with pomposity or piousity. It does not preclude play or laughter. It is light, not heavy; merry, not sad; and it is realistic and never sentimental.

Our lives are given a certain dignity by their very evanescence. If there were never to be an end to my quiet moments at the brook, if I could sit on the rock forever, I would not treasure these minutes so much. If our associations with the people we love were to have no termination, we would not value them as much as we do. Human love is an extraordinary gift, but like all flesh it is corruptible. Death or distance separates all lovers. My awareness of my husband is sharpened by impermanence.

Would we really value anything we could have forever and ever?

A METAPHOR FOR THE AFTERLIFE

Frank Rowan and Camilla Dickinson talk about death.

"You know, Cam, we live on a pretty stinking little planet in a second-rate constellation in a backwash of the universe." JULY 12
"Yes, I know," I said.

"And when you think of all the millions of stars your astronomers see and then all the millions of stars that must be out there somewhere beyond the reach of even the most gigantic telescope that could ever be invented, who are we to say that there aren't stars or planets somewhere else with life on them, and life much better than ours? Why should the Earth, which is, as I said—well, it isn't even second-rate, it's lower than that—why should the Earth be the only planet with life on it when you think of stars and constellations and everything going on forever and ever and ever? I mean, you take space, and space goes on and on and on. And does it end the way Einstein says it does? And if it does, what's beyond that? So what I figured out was this: nobody ever gets a chance to finish on this Earth. And even if there's a heaven nobody's good enough at the end of life on this Earth to be ready to go to heaven. In the first place, we haven't got the equipment. And I don't think it's fair of God to give us brains to ask questions if He isn't going to let us answer them some-times. So I figured that when we die, maybe we go to another planet, the next planet in the scale. Maybe we get better brains there that will make us able to learn and understand just a little more than anyone—even someone like Einstein—is able to understand on this Earth. And maybe we might get another sense. I mean, maybe before we got born on the Earth we were on another planet where no one could see. If every-body in the world was born blind, if there wasn't any such thing as sight, we wouldn't have the slightest idea what it was. We couldn't conceive of it even in our wildest dreams. So maybe on the next planet there's a new sense, just as impor-tant as sight, or even more important, but which we can't conceive of now any more than we could conceive of sight if we didn't know about it. And then when we'd finished on that planet we'd go on to another planet and develop even more, and so on and on and on, for hundreds and thousands or maybe even millions of planets, learning and growing all the time, until at last we'd finally know and understand everything—absolutely everything—and then maybe we'd be ready for heaven.

"I guess when you're ready for heaven you're able to stop caring about being an individual. And I don't think I could ever stop caring about being an individual unless I'd lived bil-lions and billions of years and really *did* know and understand everything. I mean, then maybe I'd be ready for God."

"I think that's wonderful!" I cried. "Oh, Frank, I think it's wonderful. I could believe in something like that. I should think anyone could."

WHERE THERE'S LIFE, THERE'S HOPE

*Camilla is upset about her mother's attempt at suicide and
also that her mother seems to be having an affair. She meets* JULY 13
Frank. He asks her if she wants to talk, and they sit down.

L isten, Camilla," Frank said, and then he said to me what
he had already said, "listen, Camilla, you're alive. As long
as you're alive that's the most important thing in the world.
People die, young people, who haven't ever had any chance,
and it's awful, and they're the ones you cry about because
they're dead and they haven't got any more life again, ever.
But you're alive and as long as you're alive everything's really
all right, in spite of everything else. No matter what happens,
as long as you're alive everything's all right."

DOLPHIN ALLELUIAS!

*Vicky Austin and Adam Eddington are swimming with Basil
the dolphin. Adam has discovered that Vicky can communi-* JULY 14
*cate mentally with the dolphins. Adam, who works at the
marine center, is studying their interaction.*

Then Basil came to me.
What shall we do? I asked him silently, and listened for
his response with my inner ear. I seized his dorsal fin and we
went flying through the air. Then he dove into the water . . .
and up, up into the air again. He was much gentler with me
than he was with Adam; it was, in fact, a completely different

game. He wasn't trying to dislodge me, but to see how high he could leap into the air with me holding on, how deep he could go without my having to let go and surface. Leap, dive, in a regular but increasing rhythm, so that each time we were longer out of the water, deeper under the wrinkled skin of the surface.

He seemed to know just when it would have been impossible for me to hold my underwater breath one moment longer, for he broke up into the air and gently flipped me off. Then he swam rapid and widening circles around Adam and me, then came back and nudged me, as though wanting something.

I began to scratch his chest, gently but firmly, and he wriggled with pleasure.

"Right," Adam said. "Playtime's over. Ask him something."

I pushed slightly away from Basil and he bathed me with his smile, and my hand almost automatically reached for his dorsal fin, and he did a dolphin cartwheel with me holding on.

Now a backward one with Adam. Aloud, I said, to Adam, "Take his dorsal fin."

And Basil flipped over, backward.

"Terrif," Adam said. "Try something else. Simple. In a few minutes you can try something more complicated."

Swim, dear darling Basil, and I mean every bit of dear and darling because you're very dear and darling to me. Swim out to the horizon and then turn around and come back to us.

Like a flash he was gone, and then as he was about to vanish from sight he was back.

"Right," Adam said. "Now maybe you could try something a little more subtle."

What I wanted to do was to ask Basil to give me all the answers to everything, as though he weren't a dolphin but some kind of cosmic computer. And I knew that that was not only not realistic, it wasn't fair. But I wondered . . .

I thought of Ynid and her grief at her dead baby, and I asked Basil, *Is Ynid's baby all right? (Is Commander Rodney all right? Is my grandfather all right? Am I? Is it all right?)*

Basil pulled himself up out of the water and a series of sounds came from him, singing sounds.

And what it reminded me of was Grandfather standing by Commander Rodney's open grave and saying those terrible words and then crying out, full of joy, *Alleluia, alleluia, alleluia!*

Then Basil was gone, flashing through sea and sky, to disappear at the horizon.

Adam beckoned to me, and turned to swim into shore. I followed.

NON-LINEAR TIME

Again, Vicky and Adam are in the water. Norberta, Basil's consort, and Njord, their baby, approach.

"Calm them down," Adam said. "Tell them you want to ask them some serious questions."

JULY 15

What should I ask? What would be serious to both the dolphins and to me—and to Adam?

Dearest Norberta and Njord. Do you live in the now, or do you project into the future, the way I do, far too often?

I felt a gentle puzzlement coming from Njord.

Maybe he's too young to understand about the future. When Rob was a baby, everything was *now* for him. Now embraced both yesterday and tomorrow.

Norberta?

Again I felt puzzlement, not puzzlement about her understanding, but my own. Norberta wasn't sure I'd be able to understand.

Try me.

I rolled over onto my back and floated and Norberta moved her great body toward me until we were touching, and I was pressed against the beautiful resiliency of dolphin skin. And a whole series of pictures came flashing across the back of my eyes, in the dream part of my head.

The ocean.

Rain.

A rainbow, glittering with rain.

Snow, falling in great white blossoms to disappear as it touched the sea.

And then the snow turned to stars, stars in the daytime, drenched in sunlight, becoming sunlight.

and the sunlight was the swirling movement of a galaxy

and the ocean caught the light and was part of the galaxy

and the stars of the galaxies lifted butterfly wings and flew together, dancing

And then Norberta, with Njord echoing her, began making strange sounds, singing sounds, like the alleluia sounds Basil had made, and they did something to my understanding of time, so that I saw that it was quite different from the one-way road which was all I knew.

Norberta was right. There was much she understood that was beyond anything I'd ever dreamed of.

She and Njord slapped the water with their flukes in fare-
well and vanished over the horizon.

I rolled over and began to tread water.

"What did you ask them?" Adam swam to me.

"About time. Adam, their time and ours is completely different."

"How?"

"Norberta tried to tell me, but it was in a language I didn't
know, and it translated itself into images, not words."

Treading water, he held out his hands to me. "Hold. And
try to tell me what she told you."

I held his hands tightly. Kept moving my legs slowly. Closed
my eyes. Imaged again what Norberta had imaged me.

I heard Adam sigh, and opened my eyes.

"Non-linear time," he said. "She was trying to tell you
about non-linear time."

"What's that?" I was still holding on to the beauty of
Norberta's images, so it didn't quite hit me that Adam and I
had communicated in the same way that I communicated with
the dolphins.

"Time is like a river for most of us, flowing in only one direction. Get John to explain it to you. Physics isn't my strong
point. But there's a possibility that time is less like a river than
a tree, a tree with large branches from which small branches
grow, and where they touch each other it might be possible to
get from one branch of time to another." He let go my hands.
"I'm not explaining it well."

"Do you mean, maybe for dolphins time is less—less restricted and limited than it is for us?"

"Isn't that what Norberta was trying to tell you?"

"Yes. Adam, did you see the butterflies?"

He nodded. "Like the one we saw at the cemetery."

"You saw it, too?"

"And so did your grandfather."

"And Grandfather would know what Njord and Norberta were singing."

"Dolphins don't sing." Adam's voice was flatly categorical. "Only humpbacked whales sing."

"Call it what you like," I said. "To me it was singing."

A GLIMPSE OF KAIROS

JULY 16

In the heart and spirit we are less restricted by time. We are given glimpses of *kairos* in our own living, moments that break free of time and simply are. It is fascinating that music is so bound up with time and yet some of the greatest moments of music are the silences between notes. We all have moments of *kairos*, though we seldom recognize them till afterwards. One such glimpse that I remember with particular delight came after a long and very difficult labour when my doctor and friend dropped a small wet creature between my breasts, saying, "Here's your son, Madeleine." And I heard the angels sing.

PERSPECTIVE I

JULY 17

Human pride and self-satisfaction got yet another blow when it was seen that our sun is only one of many in our great galaxy the Milky Way—so gorgeous to look at when I am at Crosswicks, our house in the Litchfield hills, and I walk the dogs at night and see it flowing across the sky. I look up and try to understand that our solar system is a tiny pinprick in that great river of stars, and a relatively unimportant one in the exurbs of our spiral galaxy. It is the way we now understand God's Creation, but it is still only partial understanding. The truth I hold to is that it is all God's, joyfully created, and that it is good.

PERSPECTIVE II

JULY 18

After it had been accepted that our planet was part of a solar system in the Milky Way, then came the even more humbling realization that the Milky Way itself is not unique, but is an ordinary spiral galaxy among hundreds of billions of galaxies all rushing away from each other to the distant reaches of space.

It was no doubt a good thing for the human ego to learn about the immensity of the universe. And in this century we have discovered not only the vastness of the macrocosm, but the equal vastness of the microcosm, the almost unimaginably small world of sub-atomic particles. It gives some idea of the smallness when we realize that sub-atomic particles are as much smaller than we are as the galaxies are larger than we are.

But this knowledge also had the effect of making the thinking, questioning human creature seem pretty unimportant. Who are we that God should be mindful of us? Worse than that, to some people it seemed that we are God's biggest mistake, with our unending wars, our terrorism, our greed which has caused us to be poor stewards of the land given us to nurture. How do we account for man's inhumanity to man? What has happened to God's image in us?

Even when we list our great saints and artists, Teresa, Julian of Norwich, Bach, Shakespeare, Rembrandt, nothing we do seems very important, set against the enormity of Creation.

THE SACRAMENT OF HUMAN TOUCH

Meanwhile we are in time, and the flesh is to be honored. At all ages. For me, this summer, this has been made clear in a threefold way: I have fed, bathed, played pat-a-cake with my grandbabies. In the night when I wake up, as I usually do, I always reach out with a foot, a hand, to touch my husband's body; I go back to sleep with my hand on his warm flesh. And my mother is almost ninety and preparing to move into a different country. I do not understand the mysteries of the flesh, but I know that we must not be afraid to reach out to each other, to hold hands, to touch.

JULY 19

PREPARATION FOR THE LORD'S TABLE

If the Lord's table is the prototype of the family table, then, if I think in terms of the family table, I know that I cannot sit down to bread and wine until I've said I'm sorry, until reparations have been made, relations restored. When one of our children had done something particularly unworthy, if it had come out into the open before dinner, if there had been an "I'm sorry," and there had been acceptance, and love, then would follow the happiest dinner possible, full of laughter and fun. If there was something still hidden; if one child, or as sometimes happens, one parent, was out of joint with the family and the world, that would destroy the atmosphere of the whole meal.

JULY 20

MEANING PROVIDES
A LIFEBOAT

What do I believe, this summer, about death and the human being? I'm not sure. But I know that it is in the language of the fugue, not the language of intellectual certainty. And I know that I could not survive this summer if I could not hope for meaning, meaning to my mother's life, to Hugh's and mine, to our children's, to all the larger family, to everybody, to all things, including the rock at the brook and the small frog. What that ultimate meaning may be I do not know, because I am finite, and the meaning I hope for is not. But God, if he is God, if he is worth believing in, is a loving God who will not abandon or forget the smallest atom of his creation. And that includes my mother. And everybody, everybody without exception.

THE MEANING MAKERS

I cannot believe in meaning by myself, alone, but it is often the small things which sustain me. Someone will say, after a particularly difficult, tiring day, "Madeleine, dinner tonight was just great." Or I will sit, in the twilight, in the old rocker with one of the babies and sing, and take strength from the small and perfect body drooping into sleep in my arms. At least once a week Alan, or Tallis, will celebrate Communion, and from this I receive the same kind of strength which, in a different way, comes to me in the C minor Fugue, and I am able to return to the routine of these difficult days with a lighter touch.

A GOD WHO COMES

Madeleine thinks of the irrationality of the damage a tornado has done.

I couldn't stop myself from asking, Why the old apple tree? Why the grand maples? Why did the twister skip the ancient willow, fading with age, or a sapling which wasn't doing well, and attack the strongest and healthiest trees? If the tornado wasn't consciously evil, it was still evil.

I wrestle with these questions which do not have logical answers, wrestle with mysteries, much as Jacob wrestled with the angel. How do we even attempt to understand the meaning of tempest and tragedy, love and hate, violence and peace?

I struggle, and as always when I struggle to find the truth of something, I turn to story for illumination. And, as I grapple with the angels of difficult questions, I think of Jacob who saw a ladder of angels, reaching from earth to heaven, with the angels of God ascending and descending, linking heaven and earth, the creation to the Creator, not separated from each other, but participating in each other. Delight. At-one-ment.

For God is beyond all our forensic thinking. God is Love.

GOD LOVES EVEN US

The glorious message of Scripture is that we do not have to be perfect for our Maker to love us. All through the great stories, heavenly love is lavished on visibly imperfect people. Scripture asks us to look at Jacob as he really is, to look at ourselves as we really are, and then realize that this is who God loves. God did not love Jacob because he was a cheat, but because he was Jacob. God loves us in our complex *isness*, and when we get stuck on the image of the totally virtuous and morally perfect person we will never be, we are unable to accept this unqualified love, or to love other people in their rich complexity.

If God can love Jacob—or any single one of us—as we really are, then it is possible for us to turn in love to those who hurt or confuse us. Those we know and those we do not know. And that makes me take a new look at love.

HOLY HUMILITY

Madeleine recounts a rabbinical story about humility and then comments on it.

There's an old story of a student who went to a famous old rabbi and said, "Master, in the old days there were people who could see God. Why is it that nobody sees God nowadays?" JULY 25

The old man answered, "My child, nowadays nobody can stoop so low."

Why are we afraid of stooping so low? Didn't the second person of the Trinity stoop lower than we can even conceive when he willingly relinquished all power and glory to come to earth as a human baby?

We find it difficult to understand that the magnificence and might of all Creation is also small and vulnerable. Isn't the

Creator supposed to be invulnerable? Isn't that what used to be taught in seminary? If God can be hurt, what kind of protection can this suffering servant give us?

But God, in choosing to become incarnate, with all our human limitations, also chose the possibility of being hurt. Possibility? Probability? Inevitability? Those who are fully alive are also usually those who have been deeply wounded, and the God who came to us in Jesus of Nazareth was fully alive, with an awareness and a joy and a perceptiveness most of us can only wonder at. Along with the joy was a willingness to assume all of our human sufferings, which should make us look differently at our own pain.

AWE FULL

JULY 26 Oh, I am in awe of the maker of galaxies and geese, stars and starfish, mercury and men (male and female). Sometimes it is rapturous awe; sometimes it is the numinous dread Jacob felt. Sometimes it is the humble awe of knowing that ultimately I belong to God, to the Maker whose thumb print is on each one of us. And that is blessing.

HEADING HOME

JULY 27 With my naked intellect I cannot believe in God, particularly a loving God. My intellect is convinced that any idea of the person's continuing and growing after death is absurd; logic goes no further than dust to dust. Images, in the literary sense of the word, take me much further. Without my glasses I can see nothing but a vague blur. When I put them on, I become functional. But who is doing the seeing? The lenses of the spectacles are not. I am. There is an essential, ontological me—that part of me which is not consumed in the burning—which is (to use imagery again) that which I was created to be, the imaginative Adam and Eve as they were in the pre-history days of the Garden. Some of our children talk about going back to the garden; we can't do that; but we can travel in the direction which will lead us to that place where we may find out who we really are.

LOVE IS A PERSON

Love can't be pinned down by a definition, and it certainly can't be proved, any more than anything else important in life can be proved. Love is people, is a person. A friend of ours, Hugh Bishop of Mirfield, says in one of his books: "Love is not an emotion. It is a policy." Those words have often helped me when all my feelings were unlovely. In a summer household as large as ours I often have to act on those words. I am slowly coming to understand with my heart as well as my head that love is not a feeling. It is a person.

JULY 28

CHRISTIANITY, OFF BASE?

It wasn't till this summer that it occurred to me that most of my favorite mystery writers are English, and use the language literately; their syntax is not an insult to the reader. Even more important, most of them write out of a belief in a universe created by a God of love.

JULY 29

Something odd and sad: I originally wrote that many of my favorite mystery writers were practicing Christians, and two people whose opinion I respect told me that the word "Christian" would turn people off. This certainly says something about the state of Christianity today. I wouldn't mind if to be a Christian were accepted as being the dangerous thing which it is; I wouldn't mind if, when a group of Christians meet for bread and wine, we might well be interrupted and jailed for subversive activities; I wouldn't mind if, once again, we were being thrown to the lions. I do mind, desperately, that the word "Christian" means for so many people smugness, and piosity, and holier-than-thouness. Who, today, can recognize a Christian because of "how those Christians love one another"?

PERFECTION IS A PRISON

JULY 30 Perfectionism is imprisoning. As long as I demand it, in myself or anybody else, I am not free, and all my life—fifty-two this summer—I've believed that freedom is important, that, despite all our misuse and abuse of it, freedom is what makes us a little lower than the angels, crowned with glory and honor, according to the psalmist; how like a god, according to Shakespeare; freedom to remember, to share, to dream, to accept irrationality and paradox is what makes us human animals.

THE AUTONOMY OF GOD

JULY 31 How do I make more than a fumbling attempt to explain that faith is not legislated, that it is not a small box which works twenty-four hours a day? If I "believe" for two minutes once every month or so, I'm doing well.

The only God worth believing in is neither my pal in the house next door nor an old gentleman shut up cozily in a coffin where he can't hurt me. I can try to be simple with him, but not vulgar. He is the *mysterium tremendens et fascinans;* he is free, and he understands the *ousia* of this frightened old child of his. No wonder I can't believe in him very often!

AUGUST

A LESSON ON MEDITATION

*Vicky Austin goes in to her grandfather's room. She notices
how frail he is as he lies in his hospital bed.*

AUGUST 1

Did I interrupt you?" I asked. "Were you meditating?"
He smiled at me, his welcoming smile, so I pulled up the
chair and sat down. "I was meditating. But I'm glad to see
you." His eyes twinkled. He looked relaxed and very much
himself.

"What *is* meditation, Grandfather? How do you do it?"

"It isn't exactly something you do."

"What, then?"

He was silent a long time, and I thought he wasn't going to
answer. I was beginning to get used to his removing himself as
completely as though he had left the room; suddenly he just
wasn't there. Sometimes he seemed to retreat deep within himself; sometimes he would mumble as though he didn't quite
know where he was, as though he was trapped in a bad dream.
But now he said to me, and I wasn't sure whether or not he
was answering me, or if he was changing the subject, "You
like to go down to the cove by yourself, don't you, Vicky? And
sit on the rock and look out to sea?"

"Yes, and usually at the wrong moment, when Mother or
Daddy needs me to do something else."

"But *you* need to go to the rock and look out to sea, don't
you?"

"Yes, and sometimes I think you're the only one who understands why."

"What do you do when you go to the rock?"

"I don't do anything. I sit."

"Do you think?"

"Sometimes. But those aren't the best times."

"What are the best times?"

"When I sit on the rock—and I feel—somehow—part of the rock and part of the sky and part of the sea."

"And you're very aware of the rock and the sky and the sea?"

"Sometimes."

"And sometimes?"

"Sometimes it seems to go beyond that."

"And then what is it like?"

I thought for a moment. "It's hard to explain because it's beyond words. It's as though I'm out on the other side of myself." I thought of what Adam and I had talked about the other night. I tried to tell Grandfather some of what we had said, and ended, "And it's being part of everything, part of the rock and the sky and the sea and the wind and the rain and the sun and the stars . . ."

"And you, Vicky? Are you still there?"

No. Yes. How do you explain no and yes at the same time?

"I'm there—but it's as though I'm out on the other side of myself—I'm not in the way."

"There's your answer," Grandfather said. "That's meditation."

I didn't say anything. I was thinking.

JUST BEING IN THE LIGHT

Vicky Austin is narrating. Norberta and Njord are dolphins she has met through her friend Adam Eddington.　　　　AUGUST 2

203

I went down to the beach and sat on my rock. The rain seemed to be slackening off with the drop in the wind. I watched the waves breathing quietly. Adam's call had left me churning, and I thought perhaps if I meditated I'd see more clearly.

Mother says my seesaw moods are part of my adolescence and they'll moderate as I grow older. The hospital had thrown me into a pit of darkness; then Norberta and Njord, responding to my need, had lifted me back up to the light. Maybe you have to know the darkness before you can appreciate the light.

Meditation, I thought, sitting there on the rock in Grandfather's cove, has something to do with that light.

I let my mind drift toward the dolphins, and as I stared out at the horizon there was the lovely leap I was half expecting, and I was sure it was one of my friends. My breathing quietened, slowed, moved to the gentle rhythm of the sea. The tenseness left my body until it seemed that the rock on which I sat was not embedded deep in the sand but was floating on quiet waters.

My mind stopped its running around like a squirrel on a wheel, and let go. I sat there and I didn't think. I was just *being*. And it felt good.

THE UNREASONABLE WONDER

AUGUST 3

In the hospital in San Diego I didn't get much comfort from facts. First of all, it's easy to believe in facts. We certainly don't need faith, not for facts. Faith is for the part of the story that superficially isn't believable. Virgin births? Miracles? Resurrections? Unrealistic. Childish.

Or is it maybe not so much childish as child-hearted? Children are better believers than grown-ups, and better theologians than many academicians. One child whose sister told her that there is no Santa Claus answered calmly, "That's your problem."

In a world where we're brainwashed by the media into thinking that life should be easy and painless and reasonable, it is not easy or painless or reasonable to be a Christian—that is, to be one who actually dares to believe that the power that created all the galaxies, all the stars in their courses, limited that power to the powerlessness of an ordinary human baby. That's not reasonable.

It is equally unreasonable to believe that this ordinary baby grew into a man who was totally human and simultaneously totally divine. Who was, as the Athanasian Creed affirms, totally incomprehensible.

TRUTH—NOT PROVABLE FACT

B ut who wants a comprehensible God in the aftermath of an incomprehensible accident?

AUGUST 4

I remembered a conference during which a man announced, "I am a devout literalist. If I cannot believe that the stories in Scripture are literally and factually true, then I have to accept that there can be more than one interpretation of a story."

"Yes," I said. "That's right."

"Then how can I know which is the right one?"

Aye, there's the rub. We can't. But one thing I'm learning is that I do not always have to be right. Or maybe we can look at two different interpretations of a story and understand that they are *both* right. If I have to take every story in the Bible as literal, and capable of only one interpretation, I will lose the story.

What a story it is! It begins with conception, with Creation, and moves on through life and death to Resurrection, and most of it is impossible in ordinary terms of provable fact. If I have to keep in the Bible only what can be proved, I'll be left with a book of very few pages.

TEMPORAL GROUNDWORK

AUGUST 5

C. S. Lewis points out that our roots are really elsewhere. True. But we do not get to that elsewhere except through our journey in this life on this planet. While we are here we must put down roots so that we will not be uprooted by a passing storm. The roots may reach down through earthly life to "elsewhere," but they have to go through the earth and our life on earth before getting to "elsewhere." What else does the Incarnation affirm? Jesus came not to deny life, but to offer life, and life more abundant. We are not to retreat from life, pinning our hopes on "elsewhere," but to know that we will come to that final destination best by living fully here and now, be it through joy, or pain, or a mix of both.

WHERE HOME IS FOUND

AUGUST 6

When we are truly *in love,* not in the sense of romantic, erotic love, but in the sense of God's love for all that the Power of Love created, then our homesickness is alleviated. When we are *in love* we are no longer homesick, for Love is home.

And where is this home that we long for? I lay in my hospital bed and wondered. Surely I was alive because of the skill and immediate care of fine doctors. But ultimately my life was beyond their skill. God calls on us to collaborate with the divine purpose. I believe that the Spirit can guide the doctors' minds and hands. I believe that I was called on to be willing to die, and then, to be willing to live, and that willingness included work, moving my bladder and my bowels on my own once the tubes were out, walking down the corridor, pushing my I.V. stand and, later, pushing a wheelchair to keep my balance. God urges us to collaborate. But we cannot do it ourselves. We need the everlasting love pushing, nudging, if not outright shoving.

So my question was: What, dear Lord, is your purpose for my life? Where, during the rest of my mortal years, is home? Ultimately it is with you, Lord, but meanwhile I believe that I am to make a home in the strange island of Manhattan for my granddaughters, who have been so good for me as they have been in college in New York, teaching me, pushing me, not allowing me to get into any kind of rut. I believe, too, that our home is to be an open one, so that friends who are called to be briefly in the city have a welcoming place to stay.

ANTICIPATING THE KINGDOM

Thy kingdom come. That is what co-creation with our Maker is all about, the coming of the kingdom. Our calling, our vocation, in all we do and are to try to do is to help in the furthering of the coming of the kingdom—a kingdom we do not know and cannot completely understand. We are given enough foretastes of the kingdom to have a reasonable expec-

AUGUST 7

tation. Being a loved and loving part of the body; praying together; singing together; forgiving and accepting forgiveness; eating together the good fruits of the earth; holding hands around the table as these fruits are blessed, in spontaneous joy and love, all these are foretastes.

RESTORATION THROUGH CONFESSION

Cardinal von Stromberg, a German priest, befriends Katherine and Justin Vigneras after Katherine's concert in Munich. He invites them to supper. To this point, Justin has been bitter and unforgiving toward Germans for breaking his hands in a concentration camp.

Justin accepted the cardinal's invitation to supper, murmuring to Katherine, "We can hardly blame him for the entire war." The stone house by the cathedral was half destroyed, but the great library had been untouched and they sat there, with wine and cheese and bread and pickles and whatever the cardinal could find in the larder, talking, talking as though they had known each other forever, as they talked first about music, and then about the war and its horrors, its scars which would never disappear. And then the cardinal turned to Justin, knelt on the marble floor and confessed, for confession was what it was, all the sins of omission of the Church during the years just past, during twenty centuries of sins of omission and commission. He wept over Justin's hands, and there was a strange power of healing in the tears. The broken hands would never be able to express the intricacies of a fugue, but they would be hands which, in their turn, held healing.

Justin, too, had wept, all politeness gone, tears of rage, of hatred, hatred for the Nazis, hatred for the cardinal whose food he had just eaten.

Von Stromberg, head bowed, murmured, "So slow I am to learn some of the meaning which infuses the psalms. You show me, for the first time, what it meant to cry out:

> Du Tochter Babels, du Verwüsterin,
> Heil dem, der dir vergilt,
> Was du uns angetan hast!
> Heil dem, der deine kleinen Kinder nimmt,
> und sie zerschmettert an dem Felsen!

But although your music makes that cry of hate, what ultimately it gives is healing and joy."

Katherine had looked at the two men, von Stromberg still on his knees, being helped up by Justin, so that the two of them stood together. She knew just enough German to understand that the cardinal had been quoting something about a daughter of Babylon, in misery, and something terrible about blessing those who took her children and threw them against the stones. What was there in those angry and anguished words to turn Justin's vengefulness into forgiveness? For, as the cardinal had confessed to Justin, so, then, Justin in turn confessed, telling Cardinal von Stromberg what they had vowed never to tell anybody, Justin's mutilation. Somehow Wolfi—and it was as though they had been calling him Wolfi forever—by dawn was able to bring healing to Justin, to—somehow—man him again.

He was a healer, the Grey Wolf.

FORGIVENESS IS A GIFT

And ultimately forgiveness is a gift of grace rather than an act of will. I have to be willing to forgive, but I cannot will myself to forgive. I can forgive with my mind, but forgiveness is finally a matter of the heart. And the forgiveness of the heart comes from God, not from me. My part in it is to be willing to accept it. One test which indicates whether or not forgiveness has really taken place is to look at whatever it is that needs to be forgiven and see if it still hurts. If it does, forgiveness has not yet happened. But I have also learned, and I have learned it through pain, that I must be patient with myself. Just as my body is going to need more time to complete its healing from the physical trauma of the accident, so my heart, my spirit, also need time, and I, ever impatient, must be patient with myself.

THE UNQUENCHABLE MERCY OF GOD

Zachary Gray, a friend of Polly O'Keefe, has a serious heart condition and has had a heart attack. Believing that he could be healed by a tribal leader, he has put Polly in danger. Bishop Colubra, who has gone through the time door with Polly and Zachary, speaks to Zachary.

Open your eyes." It was a stern command.
Zachary's eyelids flickered.
"Sit up," the bishop ordered. "You are not beyond redemption, Zachary."

Zachary moaned, "I was willing to let Polly die."

"But not when it came down to it, Zach!" Polly cried. "You tried to stop them."

"But it was too late." Tears gushed out.

"Look at me! I'm here! There will be no sacrifice!"

Now his terrified gaze met hers. "You're all right?"

"I'm fine."

He sat up. "I'll die if it will help you, I will, I will."

"You don't need to, Zach. There is peace now on both sides of the lake."

"But what I did—I can't be forgiven—" He looked wildly from Polly to Tynak to the bishop.

"Zachary." The bishop spoke softly but compellingly. "William Langland, writing around 1400, said, 'And all the wickedness in the world that man might work or think is no more to the mercy of God than a live coal in the sea.'"

GOD IS ON EVERYONE'S SIDE

Emma Wheaton, the protagonist of Certain Women, *and her husband, Nik, discuss the dispute between biblical characters David and Saul. This leads to the following conversation.*

I t bothers me." The fresh air of the street felt welcome as she breathed it in.

"What, hon?"

"Do you think the Lord chooses one side in a battle and helps that side to win?"

"I haven't the faintest idea."

Despite the tinge of impatience in his voice, Emma continued.

"But that's what's implied, isn't it? That when David fought, the Lord was with him, and so his enemies were defeated. And I know that there are people now who believe that God is on our side in this horrible war, and God doesn't care how many Germans or Italians or Japanese people are killed. And I hope God *is* on our side—I mean, this is not an equivocal war, I do believe that it has to be fought, and I don't want Adair or Etienne risking their lives in vain, but—"

"But?"

She looked down at her feet. The toes of her kid pumps were slightly scuffed. "But, Nik—there have to be people in Germany praying that God is on their side. And believing it."

"Probably. And presumably God, if there is a God, loves the Germans as much as he loves us. War between his children must be painful for God. It's not easy."

LIFE IS A GIFT

Emma and her father are both actors.

AUGUST 12 Emma went to the pilothouse to say good night to her father. He was drowsy but held out his arms to her. "Ah, Em, Em. Are you all right?"

"Yes, Papa, fine."

"They'll all be here tomorrow, all the available ones."

"Yes."

"I'll make my peace with Billy and Adair and Etienne later." She pressed his hand gently.

"Everard and Chantal. Good children. You'll say goodbye for me?"

"Yes, Papa. I will."

"Goodbyes are not easy, but I'm ready to move on. I'm not reluctant, Emma, not holding back. I don't have answers to the questions, at least not yet, but I have some good questions. I have loved life, and I believe that life is to be loved, because it is a gift."

Again, she pressed his hand.

"Love it, Emma."

"I do. Most of the time."

"You can love it even when you're in anguish."

"I know."

"When you're onstage, you love. We both love when we're onstage. You're better offstage than I've been. But I'm not beating my breast. I'm not saying what I want to. What I want is for you to be happy."

"I know, Papa. Thank you. Mostly I am. Good night."

"Emma, you don't have to make the mistakes I have made."

"I know."

"Good night, my sweet child."

There were tears in her eyes when she left him.

CHOOSE THE WEDDING

Norma is an old Indian friend of David Wheaton, the aged father of Emma Wheaton. Abby is one of David's ex-wives and Emma's godmother. She and David have remained friends in spite of their divorce. Sophie, another ex-wife, is present. She too has come to visit David before he dies. Nik, Emma's husband, is included in the conversation.

AUGUST 13

213

W e're at a crossroads," Sophie said softly, "and we must be careful which road we choose. I haven't always been careful."

Emma gasped, putting her hand to her mouth. At a crossroads. Surely a common expression, but it brought back uncommon memories. She looked around the table. "Do you remember Norma?"

"Sure," Sophie said. "That magnificent Indian woman. Has Davie seen her this summer?"

"Yes," Emma assured her. "We stopped at Norma's village and she and Papa had a good visit."

"Oh, I'm so glad. Norma's always been good for Davie. She's a tough old bird. No Indian's life is easy, thanks to us, I guess."

Abby looked at her godchild. "Is there something about Norma and a crossroads?"

Emma nodded gravely. "When Norma was young, she had a terrible time—she nearly died. I spent several days with her after—after a very bad time in my own life. Norma told me that when she was well and able to think again, the wise woman of her tribe told her that she was at a crossroads."

Sophie looked across the table inquiringly.

Emma smiled at Sophie. "The wise old woman said that one road led to a funeral and the other to a wedding. Norma said, 'I chose the wedding.'"

There were tears in Sophie's eyes. "Davie has always chosen the wedding. He's choosing it even now."

"You can say that, Sophie, after seeing Papa's depressions?" Emma asked.

"Davie's depressions weren't the real Davie. I know that now." She looked around the table. "Yes, we are all at a crossroads." She looked at Emma. At Nik.

"I have usually chosen the funeral," he said, "and this has been disaster for everybody I have loved. I can't blame it on the fact that my parents always chose the funeral. I made my own choices."

"And now?" Abby asked.

"I choose the wedding. No matter what"—he looked at Emma—"I will still choose the wedding. I've had too many funerals."

"But when Papa dies"—Louis's voice was choked—"how can we choose the wedding?"

Sophie laughed. "By giving him an enormous great grand glorious funeral at the Cathedral, a real show for all his family and friends and fans. And by going on living, living better because we've been part of his life than if we'd never known him."

NEVER GLORIFY WAR

The god of war has troubled me all my life because I have lived in a century of war, and I don't think that war is ever *right*. I don't know whether or not Desert Storm was necessary or not; it may have been. But it is not right to glorify it, to make heroes out of those who ordered more killing than was needed. When we kill civilians, women and children and old people, it may be because they were simply victims of bombs that were intended not for them but for the ending of the war, but it must never be glorified. And we have tended to do that, because if we can bask in glory it can obscure the fact that we killed, maimed, destroyed. We do what we have to do, prayerfully, and then we need to repent of the evil that has been done through us, not glorify it.

AUGUST 14

215

ELDER BROTHERS ALL

AUGUST 15

We are broken creatures, and yet this is not in itself a terrible thing. Refusing to admit it is what is terrible. *The sacrifices of God are a broken spirit. A broken and contrite heart, O God, you will not despise,* sang King David in Psalm 51. The younger son is usually considered by the older siblings to be so stupid that they feel he's a drag on them as they set off on the Quest, so they leave him alone in the darkest part of the forest, in order to get on with the business of the world. They expect to succeed and to succeed through their own power and control. And they are not generous. Many of Jesus' stories point this out. When the Prodigal Son returns, the elder brother is not pleased. He goes out and sulks because he does not want his father to give a party for this kid who has made such a mess of his life. The elder brothers in the parable of the workers in the vineyard are furious at the vineyard owner for paying those who worked for only an hour at the end of the day the same wages as the good elder brothers who worked all day in the heat of the sun. The elder brothers all scream for justice, fairness. And there is something in most of us that agrees. It isn't fair! we cry out. And it isn't. But God is not a God of fairness, but of Love.

SURRENDER INTO GOD

AUGUST 16

Meditation is the practise of death and resurrection. When we include meditation as part of our daily practise of prayer we are not dabbling in New Age-ism. We are simply letting go of that conscious control we hold so dear; we are opening ourselves up to the darkness between the galaxies which is the same as the great darkness in the spaces within our own hearts. Only if we have such faith in the reality of the happy ending can we let go of everything we think of as being ourselves, knowing that the Maker of the Universe who has Named us into being is there, waiting for us, calling us into deeper being. Occasionally those who meditate (the wise old women, male and female) are given the further gift of contemplation, which is beyond human thought. And until we can let go of our conscious, cognitive selves in this way, we are not ready for the happy ending.

If we look for the happy ending in this world and according to the standards of this world, we'll never find it. We can't earn it; we don't deserve it; there's no way we can acquire it, no matter how many merit badges we manage to pile up.

GOD'S ENCOMPASSING LOVE

And that's what it's all about: God's love. God's unmerited, unqualified love, waiting for us. We don't have to deserve that love which is ours, ours whether we want it or not. If we don't want it, that love can be terrible indeed. But if we reach out for God with love, God's love will surround us. God made us, made us in love, and that love will never falter. Wherever we are, whatever we do, God's love for us is there, firm, steadfast, forever, and shown us in the love that came to us in Jesus Christ, in whose resurrection we are all newly born and fully alive.

AUGUST 17

217

PEOPLE OF GOD DEPEND ON GOD

AUGUST 18   And so it goes. The people of God are not all good and moral people. They do terrible things. But they know that they are utterly dependent on God, and if they do anything that is good, it is because God pushes them into it and helps them every inch of the way. They do not feel that they have to protect God from other people; they know that they fail God but they pick themselves up (with God's help) out of the mud and try again. And they rejoice. David danced for God, leaping with joy around the ark.

PRICELESS FORGIVENESS

AUGUST 19   We were bought with a price, and what has cost God so much cannot be cheap for us.

God took a tremendous risk when he created creatures who could make mistakes and wrong choices. We do not pay for our mistakes by ourselves; God pays with us. Forgiving us is part of that payment. Over and over God forgave his stiff-necked people; over and over he forgives us and calls us to be part of that forgiveness.

Forgiveness requires healing grief. Forgiveness hurts, as all grief must, and if it hurts to forgive, it hurts equally to be forgiven. We can feel magnanimous when we forgive—in which case it isn't real forgiveness because it does not involve grief. True forgiveness involves fellow-feeling with the one forgiven. When we *accept* forgiveness we accept ourselves as sinners, which is not popular today, even in the church.

HEAVEN IS WHERE GOD IS

O*ur Father which art in heaven*. And where is heaven? It too is a word which has been abused. The good go to heaven and the bad go to hell. But who are the good and who are the bad? Only God knows that, and when we try to make such judgments we invariably blunder. It is God who is in heaven, who, perhaps, *is* heaven. Surely it is not a place that is either up or down. Heaven is wherever and whenever God is present; when he is present within us, then heaven is within us. If we do not begin to live in heaven now we will not be able to recognize it later—in fact, we may confuse it with hell. But trying to define heaven is like trying to define God. It is, I believe, that place where our souls continue to be taught to grow in love and wisdom, and how that teaching is to be done I do not know. Where is Hugh, now? Where is Tallis? God will not forget them; el holds them in the palm of the protecting hand.

AUGUST 20

WE MATTER, SO DO OTHERS

T o matter in the scheme of the cosmos: this is better theology than all our sociology. It is, in fact, all that God has promised to us: that we matter. That he cares. As far as I know, no great prophet has promised people that God will give them social justice, though he may have threatened doom and extinction if the people themselves don't do something about it. If God cares about us, we have to care about each other.

Sociology is rational. God is not.

God knows the very moment we are born.

AUGUST 21

REVOLVING INTO NEWNESS OF LIFE

What is the Establishment? What is revolution? They are not incompatible. Each is essential to the life of the other. If they are to live at all, they must live symbiotically, each taking nourishment from the other, each giving nourishment in return. The Establishment is not, thank God, the Pentagon, or corruption in the White House or governors' palaces or small-town halls. It is not church buildings of any denomination. It is not organized groups, political parties, hierarchies, synods, councils, or whatever. It is simply the company of people who acknowledge that we cannot live in isolation, or by our own virtue, but need community and mystery, expressed in the small family, and then the larger families of village, church, city, country, globe.

Because we are human, these communities tend to become rigid. They stop evolving, revolving, which is essential to their life, as is the revolution of the earth about the sun essential to the life of our planet, our full family and basic establishment. Hence, we must constantly be in a state of revolution, or we die. But revolution does not mean that the earth flings away from the sun into structureless chaos. As I understand the beauty of the earth's dance around the sun, so also do I understand the constant revolution of the community of the Son.

MOVING BETWEEN TWO TIMES

This summer I sit in the rocking chair and rock and sing with one or other of my granddaughters. I sing the same songs I sang all those years ago. It feels utterly right. Natural. The same.

But it isn't the same. I may be holding a baby just as I used to hold a baby, but chronology has done many things in the intervening years, to the world, to our country, to my children, to me. I may feel, rocking a small, loving body, no older than I felt rocking that body's mother. But I am older bodily; my energy span is not as long as it used to be; at night my limbs ache with fatigue; my eyes are even older than the rest of me. It is going to seem very early—it is going to *be* very early—when the babies wake up: Alan, Josephine, Cynthia, and I take turns getting up and going downstairs with them, giving them breakfast, making the coffee. Is it my turn again so quickly?

Chronology: the word about the measurable passage of time, although its duration varies: how long is a toothache? how long is standing in line at the supermarket? how long is a tramp through the fields with the dogs? or dinner with friends, or a sunset, or the birth of a baby?

Chronology, the time which changes things, makes them grow older, wears them out, and manages to dispose of them, chronologically, forever.

Thank God there is kairos, too: again the Greeks were wiser than we are. They had two words for time: *chronos* and *kairos*.

Kairos is not measurable. Kairos is ontological. In kairos we *are*, we are fully in isness, not negatively, as Sartre saw the isness of the oak tree, but fully, wholly, positively. Kairos can sometimes enter, penetrate, break through chronos: the child at play, the painter at his easel, Serkin playing the *Appassionata,* are in kairos. The saint at prayer, friends around the dinner table, the mother reaching out her arms for her newborn baby, are in kairos. The bush, the burning bush, is in kairos, not any burning bush, but the very particular burning bush before which Moses removed his shoes; the bush I pass on my way to the brook. In kairos that part of us which is not consumed in the burning is wholly awake. We too often let it fall asleep, not as the baby in my arms droops into sleepiness, but dully, bluntingly.

I sit in the rocking chair with a baby in my arms, and I am in both kairos and chronos. In chronos I may be nothing more than some cybernetic salad on the bottom left-hand corner of a check; or my social-security number; or my passport number. In kairos I am known by name: Madeleine.

The baby doesn't know about chronos yet.

COMMUNION AT CROSSWICKS

After Madeleine's mother's death, a house mass was held in the living room of Crosswicks.

AUGUST 24

This time out of time in the absolute familiarity of the living room is healing and redemptive for me. Tallis uses a chalice which he designed, setting it with stones which had belonged to his mother; this is the first time he has used it. He has us all sit around the living room as we usually do for our home services when there are too many of us for the Tower. And there in the living room is, for me, the Church, an eclectic group, Congregational, Roman Catholic, Jewish, agnostic, Anglican, atheist. The dogs and the babies wander around. Jo and I sit on the little sofa which Mother bought, and where she always sat. The only additions to the Prayer Book service are from the Orthodox liturgy: stark; terrible; glorious.

The most moving moment is when everybody receives the bread and wine, each person spontaneously holding out hands.

This is the Church which I affirm, and the mystery by which I live.

NEVER FORGOTTEN

Madeleine goes to Jacksonville to bury her mother.

The psalmist cries out his anguish: My sight faileth for very trouble; Lord, I have called daily upon thee, I have stretched forth my hands unto thee. Dost thou show wonders among the dead? or shall the dead rise up again, and praise thee? Shall thy loving-kindness be showed in the grave? or thy faithfulness in destruction? Shall thy wondrous works be known in the dark? and thy righteousness in the land where all things are forgotten?

AUGUST 25

O God. O God.

To the ancient Hebrew the ultimate hell consisted in being forgotten, erased from the memory of family and tribe, from the memory of God. If God forgets you, it is as though you have never existed. You have no meaning in the ultimate scheme of things. Your life, your being, your *ousia,* is of no value whatsoever. You are a tale told by an idiot; forgotten; annihilated.

I will never forget my mother.

THE INFINITE MEMORY OF GOD

Our memories are, at best, so limited, so finite, that it is impossible for us to envisage an unlimited, infinite memory, the memory of God. It is something I want to believe in: that no atom of creation is ever forgotten by him; always is; cared for; developing; loved.

AUGUST 26

My memory of Mother, which is the fullest memory of anybody living, is only fragmentary. I would like to believe that the creator I call God still remembers all of my mother, knows and cares for the *ousia* of her, and is still teaching her, and helping her to grow into the self he created her to be, her integrated, whole, redeemed self.

THE SHIFTING DANCE STEPS

It is now the summer after the death of Madeleine's mother.

AUGUST 27

The pattern has shifted; we have changed places in the dance. I am no longer anybody's child. I have become the Grandmother. It is going to take a while to get used to this unfamiliar role. It is not so much with my actual grandchildren, Léna and Charlotte, that I feel the difference, but one generation down, with Alan and Josephine; Peter and Maria; Bion. While they called my mother Grandmother, she held the position. Now it has suddenly become mine, and I don't want it, but I will have to accept it, not as matriarchy—our men are all far too dominant for any of us on the distaff side to assume the matriarchal role—but as a change of pattern, the steps of the dance shifting.

The rhythm of the fugue alters; the themes cross and recross. The melody seems unfamiliar to me, but I will learn it.

THE ONE UNBEARABLE THING

AUGUST 28

The children grow in all ways. Their vocabulary advances in leaps and bounds. I am no longer Madden or Gan-madlen. When they are formal with me, I am Grandmadeleine.

Mostly it is Gran. Occasionally Charlotte rushes up to me and flings her arms around me. "Granny, Granny, Granny."

One night I put them to bed, and after all the songs and stories they beg for two last songs. "*Long* ones."

So I start the *Ballad of Barbara Allen.* I have sung only a couple of verses when Charlotte says, her voice quivering slightly, "Gran, you *know* that's a bad one."

"What, Charlotte?"

"You *know* that's a bad one."

Both Barbara Allen and her young man are dead and buried at the end of the ballad; I ask, "Why, Charlotte? Because it's sad?"

"No! Because she didn't love *anybody.*"

Charlotte knows what it is all about. The refusal to love is the only unbearable thing.

THE INCREDIBLE BEGINNING
OF ALL THINGS

The discoveries made since the heart of the atom was opened have irrevocably changed our view of the universe and creation. Our great radio telescopes are picking up echoes of that primal act of creation which expanded to become all the stars in their courses. It would seem that the beginning of all things came from something so incredibly tiny as to be nothing, a sub-sub-atomic particle so infinitesimal that it is difficult even to imagine. So science brings us back to a God who created *ex nihilo.* And who then took that early primordial soup, that chaos, and made from it night and day and galaxies and solar systems and all creatures great and small.

AUGUST 29

There are many theories today which I find immensely exciting theologically, but I want to sit lightly enough on it all so that if something new and perhaps contradictory is revealed I won't be thrown off-center, as were Darwin's frightened opponents, but will go on being excited about the marvelousness of being—of snowflake and starfish and geranium and galaxy.

CONTEMPORARY MYSTICS

AUGUST 30 Science changed, irrevocably, with the splitting of the atom, and our perception of reality has not yet caught up with this change. We discovered that for every question we have answered, a hundred new questions have been uncovered. For all our knowledge, all our technical advances, we have learned to our chagrin (and sometimes delight) that we know practically nothing.

We are still in the process of tiptoeing over the sill of this new perception of the universe which is, strangely, far more like the universe in which Abraham and Sarah found themselves when they left home and went into a strange land, than it is like the exalted individualism of Renaissance man, or the technocratic smugness of the late nineteenth and early twentieth centuries.

Our contemporary mystics are the astrophysicists, the cellular biologists, the physicists who study quantum mechanics, for they are dealing with the nature of being itself. Like Abraham and Sarah they are continually discovering the extraordinary mystery of being, and the charting of the worlds within us as well as the worlds beyond us. And we, too, are being asked to leave our comfortable home and go out into the wilderness, like Abraham and Sarah, into the mysterious world of unknown spaces, where there may be famine, drought, hostile inhabitants.

TRUST THE PATTERN

The *symboles* by which I live are the answers to my questions, are themselves the questions, are the healers of our brokenness. When we deny our wholeness, when we repress part of ourselves, when we are afraid of our own darkness, then the dark turns against us, turns on us, becomes evil. Just as the intellect when it is not informed by the heart becomes vicious, so the intuition, the subconscious, when it is forcibly held below the surface, becomes wild, and until we look at it and call it by name, our own name, it can devour us.

AUGUST 31

Am I afraid to look down into the dark and acknowledge myself, and say: Madeleine! and know that this, too, is part of what I am meant to be? Yes, I am afraid sometimes, but I become less afraid as my trust in the pattern of the universe deepens. I, too, have my place, as do we all, with the greatest galaxies, the smallest particles. Perhaps it takes all of this, all of creation, to make the Body of Christ, and the bride.

SEPTEMBER

WHERE ARE THE ANGELS?

SEPTEMBER 1 What accounts for all the anger and horror in the world around us? Where are the angels? Can they come if we refuse to believe in them? What accounts for the darkness in human hearts as the world becomes more and more secular? Why are people turning to drugs for comfort rather than to the Light of Love? I don't know the answers to these questions. But I do know that wherever the light is, the darkness tries to snuff it out. Perhaps all the terrible things that are happening are, indeed, a sign that the Spirit of Love is abroad, that more and more of us are turning to this forbearing and yet ferocious power who pushes us into doing what we don't think we can do, who gives us courage we never dreamed we had.

I take the devil and his machinations seriously indeed. One thing which we can count on the devil to do is to take the original good which God created, and try to make something ugly out of it. Sometimes he succeeds—though that does not make the original good any less good. There are people today who play with the powers of love, who take them trivially, who seek easy answers.

There are no easy answers, but I think we need to be aware that if we deny the world beyond the world of technology and provable fact, we do so to our peril.

WALK IN THE LIGHT

SEPTEMBER 2 We are to be children of the light, and we are meant to walk in the light, and we have been groping along in the darkness. The creative act helps us to emerge into the light, that awful light which the disciples saw on the Mount of Transfiguration, and which the Hebrew children saw on the face of Moses when he had been talking with God on Mount Sinai.

If we are blind and foolish, so were the disciples. They simply failed to understand what the light was about—these three disciples who were closest to him. They wanted to trap Jesus, Elijah, and Moses in tabernacles, tame them, pigeonhole and label them, as all of us human beings have continued to do ever since.

FAMILY COMFORT

Meet the Austins begins with the death of a good family friend of the Austins whom the children call Uncle Hal. SEPTEMBER 3 *Uncle Hal's copilot, Maggy's father, also died. Maggy, whom the Austins have not previously met, has come to stay with the Austins temporarily and proves to be a disturbing presence in this peaceful family. After Maggy has gone to bed, Mrs. Austin invites the older children, Vicky and her brother John, to go with her to Hawk Mountain to watch the sky. They take blankets and the two dogs, hop into the station wagon, and take off. Once they have arrived and settled down a bit, the following conversation takes place.*

Mother said, "I know you're both very upset about Uncle Hal and Maggy's father. We all are. I thought maybe if we came and looked at the stars it would help us to talk about it a little."

Just then a shooting star flashed across the sky, and John said, "There's a shooting star and I don't know what to wish. I want to wish it back to before yesterday and that none of this would have happened, but I know it wouldn't work."

I said, "Mother, I don't understand it," and I began to shiver.

Mother said, "Sometimes it's very hard to see the hand of God instead of the blind finger of Chance. That's why I wanted to come out where we could see the stars."

"I talked to Aunt Elena for a while," John said, in a strained sort of voice, "when everybody else was busy. We took Mr. Rochester and Colette for a walk." Mr. Rochester came up to us then and lay down beside me with a thud, putting his heavy head across my knees. Colette was already cuddled up in Mother's lap. I looked toward John, and the lenses of his glasses glimmered in the starlight. "She said that she and Uncle Hal knew that they were living on borrowed time," John said. "They'd always hoped it would be longer than it was, but the way their lives were, they only lived together in snatches, anyhow. And she said she was grateful for every moment she'd ever had with him, and, even if it was all over, she wouldn't trade places with anybody in the world."

"She said that to you, John?" Mother asked.

"Yes," John said, and then another star shot across the sky, this time with a shower of sparks. We sat there, close, close, and it was as though we could feel the love we had for one another moving through our bodies as we sat there together, moving from me through Mother, from Mother to John, and back again. I could feel the love filling me, love for Mother and John, and for Daddy and Suzy and Rob, too. And I prayed, "Oh, God, keep us together, please keep us together, please keep us safe and well and together."

It was as though our thoughts were traveling to one another, too, because John said, "Oh, Mother, why do things have to change and be different!" He sounded quite violent. "I like us exactly the way we are, our family. Why do people have to die, and people grow up and get married, and everybody grow away from each other? I wish we could just go on being exactly the way we are!"

"But we can't," Mother said. "We can't stop on the road of Time. We have to keep on going. And growing up is all part of it, the exciting and wonderful business of being alive. We can't understand it, any of us, any more than we can understand why Uncle Hal and Maggy's father had to die. But being alive is a gift, the most wonderful and exciting gift in the world. And there'll undoubtedly be many other moments when you'll feel this same way, John, when you're grown up and have children of your own."

"I don't understand about anything," John said. "I don't understand about people dying, and I don't understand about families, about people being as close as we are, and then everybody growing up, and not having Rob a baby any more, and having to go off and live completely different lives."

"But look how close Grandfather and I still are," Mother said.

John shook his head. "I know. But it isn't the same thing. It's not like when you were little."

"No," Mother said. "But if I'd never grown up and met Daddy and married him you wouldn't be here, or Vicky or Suzy or Rob, and we wouldn't be sitting up here on Hawk Mountain shivering and looking at the stars. And we must have been here at least half an hour. Time to go home."

We went home and then we just stood outside for a while. The moon was sailing high now, and the sky was clear and white above the black pines at the horizon, with northern lights, which we hadn't seen up on Hawk at all, sending occasional rays darting high up into the sky. Daddy had heard us drive up, and he came out and stood with us, his arm about Mother. I'd never seen such a startlingly brilliant night, the fields and mountains washed in a flood of light. The shadows of trees and sunflowers were sharply black and stretched long and thin across the lawn. It was so beautiful that for the moment the beauty was all that mattered; it wasn't important that there were things we would never understand.

JESUS KNEW OUR PAIN

SEPTEMBER 4

I know I live and die by the assurance that *God so loved the world that he gave his one and only Son,* and in that Word's hour of need what pain must God have felt! Jesus was able to endure the agony of Holy Week and of the Cross only because he was never separate from the Source, and never doubted that he was loved or, at least, only for a fragment of a minute.

"My God, my God, why have you forsaken me?" For our sakes Jesus went through all the suffering we may ever have to endure, and because he cried out those words we may cry them out, too. The night I knew my husband was dying I turned, as usual at bedtime, to Evening Prayer. It was the fourth of the month, and the first psalm for the evening of the fourth day is Psalm 22, and I read, *"My God, my God, why have you forsaken me?"*

Don't confuse me by saying that Jesus was merely quoting David in the Psalms. Allow me to know that Jesus was willing to go through the same kind of anguish that sooner or later comes to us all.

This is the story that gives meaning to my life, that gave meaning to those draggingly difficult days in the hospital, and if it isn't story it doesn't work. The life-giving, life-saving story is true story that transcends facts.

THE IMAGE OF GOD IS LOVE

God reproves us whenever we decide that El is like us, or like our own particular group. There is only one criterion to use in deciding whether or not the image of God we are finding within us is really God's image, or a projection of ourselves. The one thing we know about God for certain is that *God is love*. Where there is not love, even if there is righteousness, or justice, it is not God.

SEPTEMBER 5

This is perhaps the most difficult lesson of all to learn. If we love God, then we must also love each other. Indeed it would be a good and joyful thing if all God's children could learn to dwell together in unity.

Can the heavenly kingdom come until this happens?

REVISIONING WORK

One problem with the word *work* is that it has come to be equated with drudgery, and is considered degrading. Now some work *is* drudgery, though it is not always degrading. Vacuuming the house or scrubbing out the refrigerator is drudgery for me, though I find it in no way degrading. And that it is drudgery is lack in me. I enjoy the results and so I should enjoy producing the results. I suspect that it is not the work itself which is the problem, but that it is taking me from

SEPTEMBER 6

other work, such as whatever manuscript I am currently working on. Drudgery is not what work is meant to be. Our work should be our play. If we watch a child at play for a few minutes, "seriously" at play, we see that all his energies are concentrated on it. He is working very hard at it. And that is how the artist works, although the artist may be conscious of discipline while the child simply experiences it.

THE MYSTERY OF LOVE

SEPTEMBER 7

As I observe and contemplate love, it is never self-righteous. It does not condemn. It is a sacrifice, a sacred and hallowed giving. I have received this love and been allowed to give it, and this is why, rather than by accident of birth, I am a Christian.

And Joseph, despite the pantheon of gods with which he was surrounded, was able to retain his faith in the One God of his people.

But such faith is a mystery. The phrase about God which means the most to me is the *mysterium tremendum et fascinans*. It doesn't translate well: the tremendous and fascinating mystery. It does better in Latin.

MERCY AND TRUTH HAVE KISSED

SEPTEMBER 8

All I have to know is that I do not have to know in limited, finite terms of provable fact that which I believe. Infallibility has led to schisms in the Church, to atheism, to deep misery. All I have to know is that God is love, and that love will not let us go, not any of us. When I say that I believe in the resurrection of the body, and I do, I am saying what I believe to be true, not literal, but true. Literalism and infallibility go hand in hand, but mercy and truth have kissed each other. To be human is to be fallible, but it is also to be capable of love and to be able to retain that childlike openness which enables us to go bravely into the darkness and towards that life of love and truth which will set us free.

GOD'S OPEN SYSTEM

What is our part in keeping this planet alive? Working toward stopping the folly and horror of atomic devastation? To say that nuclear war is inevitable is defeatism, not realism. As long as there is anybody to care, to pray, to turn to God, to be willing to be el's messenger even in unexpected ways, there is still hope.

SEPTEMBER 9

How can we have a wide view of the unity of the universe and of God without lapsing into a vague pantheism? If God created *all* of Creation, if God is the author of Buddhists and Hindhus and Jains as well as those who have "accepted Jesus Christ as Lord," how can we avoid a wishy-washy permissiveness?

Not by retreating back into a closed system. Not by saying: Only those who believe exactly as I do can be saved. Not by insisting that only those whose god fits into the same box as my god will go to heaven. Not by returning to polytheism and proclaiming that our god is greater than the gods of other cultures.

Paradoxically, it comes back to us, to our acceptance of ourselves as created by God, and loved by God, no matter how far we have fallen from God's image in us. It is not a self-satisfied, self-indulgent acceptance, but a humble, holy, and wondrous one.

HINTS OF HEAVEN

SEPTEMBER 10

In the Bible, heaven is described metaphorically, not literally. We are given some hints and clues, but it remains for us a realm of mystery.

When my father died when I was seventeen, I pondered heaven and God's plan for el's complex and contradictory children, and it seemed to me evident that nobody I knew, certainly including myself, was ready for heaven after this mortal life in which we are all, one way or another, bent and broken. There may be a handful of people who are prepared for the unveiled vision of God. But most of us are not, most of us still have a vast amount to learn. I don't know how God plans to teach me all that I need to know before I am ready for the Glory, but my faith is based on the belief that I don't have to know. I have to know only that the Maker is not going to abandon me when I die, is not going to make creatures who are able to ask questions which simply cannot be answered in this life, and then drop them with the questions still unanswered.

TAKE ANGELS SERIOUSLY!

SEPTEMBER 11

I believe in angels; guardian angels; the angels who came to Gideon and told a shy, not very brave young man that he was a man of valour who was going to free his people; the angels who came to Jesus in the agony of the Garden. And, what is less comforting, avenging angels, destroying angels, angels who come bringing terror when any part of God's creation becomes too rebellious, too full of pride to remember that they are God's creatures. And, most fearful of all, fallen angels, angels who have left God and followed Lucifer, and daily offer us their seductive and reasonable temptations. If we read the Bible, and if what we read has anything to do with what we believe, then we have no choice but to take angels seriously; and most artists do, from Milton to Doré to Shakespeare to. . . .

GOD COMES INTO OUR PLACES OF PAIN

I do not want ever to be indifferent to the joys and beauties of this life. For through these, as through pain, we are enabled to see purpose in randomness, pattern in chaos. We do not have to understand in order to believe that behind the mystery and the fascination there is love.

SEPTEMBER 12

In the midst of what we are going through this summer I have to hold on to this, to return to the eternal questions without demanding an answer. The questions worth asking are not answerable. Could we be fascinated by a Maker who was completely explained and understood? The mystery is tremendous, and the fascination that keeps me returning to the questions affirms that they are worth asking, and that any God worth believing in is the God not only of the immensities of the galaxies I rejoice in at night when I walk the dogs, but also the God of love who cares about the sufferings of us human beings and is here, with us, for us, in our pain and in our joy.

I come across four lines of Yeats and copy them down:

> But Love has pitched her mansion in
> The place of excrement;
> For nothing can be sole or whole
> That has not been rent.

The place of excrement. That is where we are this summer. How do we walk through excrement and keep clean in the heart? How do we become whole by being rent?

This summer is not the first time I have walked through the place of excrement and found love's mansion there. Indeed, we are more likely to find it in the place of excrement than in the sterile places. God comes where there is pain and brokenness, waiting to heal, even if the healing is not the physical one we hope for.

AFFIRMING THE WORTH
OF HUMAN BEINGS

How could I live, endure this summer, without imagination? How can anyone even begin to have an incarnational view of the universe without an incredible leap of the imagination? That God cares for us, every single one of us, so deeply that all power is willing to come to us, to be with us, takes all the imagination with which we have been endowed. And how could I get through this summer without affirming the worth and dignity of human beings? Isn't that what the incarnation was about? It is the message for me during these long weeks of Hugh's illness. During the interminable month of June when he was in the hospital I watched the doctors and nurses struggling with all their skill to affirm the dignity and worth of the patients. On the cancer floor this is no easy task. Hugh told of one of the nurses holding his head and the basin all through the night, while he retched and retched.

But to certain Christians it is un-Christian to affirm the dignity and worth of human beings. If that is so, then I cannot be a Christian. My husband, struggling to eat, to walk, to regain strength, sharing with me an article in the *Times* that caught his interest because of his concern for me, is an example of the dignity and worth of the human being in the place of excrement.

PRAY ACCORDING TO
THE NEEDS OF THE HEART

When I went to New Orleans (so short a time ago), I took a small paperback book a friend gave me over a year ago. *When Bad Things Happen to Good People*. It is a fine book by one who has gone through the fire. The writer watched his young son die of a dreadful disease in which a child grows into an old man and dies of old age—at fourteen, in the case of Rabbi Kushner's son. He asks all the hard questions and addresses them honestly. In two places I feel very differently from the way he does. He is a man, and a rabbi. I am a woman, struggling with an incarnational view of the universe.

SEPTEMBER 14

I write in my journal: "He writes that if a God of love allows terrible things to happen to innocent people, then God must be powerless. I can't believe that the power that started the glories of the galaxies ever loses power. But we human beings have free will, and disease is a result of our abuse of that free will throughout the centuries.

"He also writes that there are prayers that one is not allowed to pray, such as my 'Please, dear God, don't let it be cancer.' Rabbi Kushner says I can't pray that way, because right now either it is cancer or it is not.

"But I can't live with that. I think we *can* pray. I think the heart overrides the intellect and insists on praying."

If we don't pray according to the needs of the heart, we repress our deepest longings. Our prayers may not be rational, and we may be quite aware of that, but if we repress our needs, then those unsaid prayers will fester.

THE CRY OF FAITH

Who is this creator to whom I cry out, "Help!" How can I believe in a God who cares about individual lives or one small and unimportant planet? I don't know. I just don't know. But I cannot turn away from the hope and the mystery which can never be understood. I know only that when I cry out, "Help!" the fact that I am crying out affirms that somewhere in some part of me I hope that there is someone who hears, who cares. The One I cry out to is not limited by size or number, and can be glimpsed only in metaphor, that chief tool of imagery of the poet. And it is only in the high language of poetry that anything can be said about God. Hildegard of Bingen likened herself to "a feather on the breath of God." Lady Julian of Norwich saw the entire universe in a hazelnut.

WE ARE EACH PART
OF ONE ANOTHER

But I am grateful beyond words for the community which surrounds me. I am not alone, as so many people in today's society are alone. The family is staunchly with me. Here on this floor of the hospital I now know most of the nurses by name. When fruit juice or ginger ale is brought around for the patients, I am included. Charlie, the interim minister from our Congregational Church, comes faithfully to call, to sit and talk a real visit. There are cards and flowers from various members of the church, although Hugh and I are there only in the summer, unable to be the active members we used to be when we lived at Crosswicks year round. Prayers for Hugh and me continue to uphold and strengthen, and are an affirmation that what is going on in our lives matters. There is a feeling of being an interdependent part of the whole human predicament, a oneness with other patients, other anxious families, a oneness even with people's tragedies as we read about them in the paper.

This oneness is consistent with what we now know of the nature of creation as understood in terms of particle physics. We seem to have forgotten this oneness, this interdependence, with our different countries, languages, religions, factions within religions, with our nuclear families frequently isolated from grandparents, aunts, uncles. We desperately need to remember that we are each part of one another.

GALACTIC SETTING
FOR INDIVIDUAL PAIN

I f we human beings were truly aware that all creation is a unity, as two lovers are aware of unity, wouldn't we treat each other better? There have been many signs of a newly awakened caring in recent years, and I need to remember all the signs of goodness and hope, particularly after I look at the paper or listen to the news. We are one planet, a single organism. What happens on this floor makes a difference everywhere.

SEPTEMBER 17

For the entire universe with its countless galaxies is the setting for this pearl of pain.

JOURNEY TOWARD GOD

During my journey through life I have moved in and out of agnosticism and even atheism, as I become bewildered by what mankind has done to God; and so, too often, I see God in man's image, rather than the other way around. But I cannot live for long in this dead-end world, but return to the more open places of my child's intuitive love of God, where I know that all creatures are the concern of the God who created the galaxies, and who nevertheless notes the fall of each sparrow. And from the darkness I cry out: God!

And it is enough.

THE BUTTERFLY EFFECT

In a recent article on astrophysics I came across the beautiful and imaginative concept known as "the butterfly effect." If a butterfly winging over the fields around Crosswicks should be hurt, the effect would be felt in galaxies thousands of light years away. The interrelationship of all of Creation is sensitive in a way we are just beginning to understand. If a butterfly is hurt, we are hurt. If the bell tolls, it tolls for us. We can no longer even think of saying, "In the Name of the Lord will I destroy them." No wonder Jesus could say that not one sparrow could fall to the ground without the Father's knowledge.

Dr. Paul Brand points out that every cell in the body has its own specific job, in interdependence with every other cell. The only cells which insist on being independent and autonomous are cancer cells.

Surely that should be a lesson to us in the churches. Separation from each other, and from the rest of the world is not only disaster for us, but for everybody from whom we separate ourselves. We must be very careful lest in insisting on our independence we become malignant.

If we take the whole sweep of the story, rather than isolating passages out of context, this is the message of Scripture.

THE FALL OF EVEN
A SPARROW MATTERS

Adam Eddington, the protagonist of The Arm of the Starfish, *a novel set in Portugal, saves a girl named Kali from a shark. She has an evil father and has been responsible in part for betrayal and the death of a good friend of the O'Keefe family. Dr. O'Keefe has left to try to save Kali's partly severed arm using his new science. Canon Tallis, another friend of the O'Keefes, Polly O'Keefe, and Adam discuss the situation. Virbius is the village chief with whom Dr. O'Keefe has been working.*

SEPTEMBER 20

B ut why!" Polly demanded passionately. "*Why* did he have to go?"

Adam was silent while Temis came out and draped a softly woven robe about him. Then he said, heavily, "Because of Joshua."

"But she killed Joshua!" Polly cried. "Why should daddy help her now? I don't want to help her! Adam should have let the shark kill her!"

Adam was silent.

"Father!" Polly cried.

Canon Tallis said quietly, "Suppose it had been Adam the shark attacked?"

Tears began to roll down Polly's cheeks. "But Adam's good, and she's—"

Adam stood up, holding Temis' robe about his shoulders. He could not say what he had to say sitting down. "I killed Joshua, too."

"But—"

"Be quiet, Polly," Canon Tallis commanded.

Adam let the robe drop as he clenched and unclenched his fists. "If I hadn't used the knife, or if we didn't try to help Kali now, it would be justice, wouldn't it?"

Virbius nodded, saying the English word, "Justice," nodding again.

"But Joshua—" Adam said. "Joshua—" he broke off.

"It's Joshua I'm thinking about!" Polly cried.

"It was what he always said," Adam choked out, "about the sparrow. Even Kali would be a sparrow to Joshua. If you're going to care about the fall of the sparrow you can't pick and choose who's going to be the sparrow. It's everybody, and you're stuck with it." He sat down and put his arms about his knees and his head on his arms.

Virbius spoke. When he had finished there was silence until he spoke again, rather crossly, to Polly. She translated.

"He says it is not enough if you pray neither for nor against. He says he will go to his gods and pray. For."

IMMORTAL, INVISIBLE, GOD ONLY WISE

SEPTEMBER 21 I seek for God that he may find me because I have learned, empirically, that this is how it works. I seek: he finds. The continual seeking is the expression of the hope for a creator great enough to care for every particular atom and sub-atom of his creation, from the greatest galaxy to the smallest farandolae. Because of my particular background I see the coming together of macrocosm and microcosm in the Eucharist, and I call this Creator: God, Father; but no human being has ever called him by his real name, which is great and terrible and unknown, and not to be uttered by mortal man. If inadvertently my lips framed the mighty syllables, entire galaxies might explode.

As I read the Old and New Testaments I am struck by the awareness therein of our lives being connected with cosmic powers, angels and archangels, heavenly principalities and powers, and the groaning of creation. It's too radical, too uncontrolled for many of us, so we build churches which are the safest possible places in which to escape God. We pin him down, far more painfully than he was nailed to the cross, so that he is rational and comprehensible and like us, and even more unreal.

And that won't do. That will not get me through death and danger and pain, nor life and freedom and joy.

THE MYSTERY OF
THE WORD MADE FLESH III

I look at my husband's beloved body and I am very aware of the mystery of the Word made flesh, his flesh, the flesh of all of us, made potential when that first great Word was spoken that opened the tiny speck from which came all the galaxies, all the solar systems, all of us.

SEPTEMBER 22

That great beginning was probably a simpler action of the Word than that Word becoming incarnate, the ultimate unfathomable mystery of the Word made flesh.

We cannot explain the incarnation. It is understandably referred to as "the scandal of the particular." It takes every leap of the imagination to accept this amazing impossible gift of the Creator.

I have long felt that the sacrifice of the mystery of the Word made flesh was a far greater sacrifice than the crucifixion. That was bad, yes. Terrible, yes. But it was three hours on the cross, three hours. This summer I have seen in this hospital people dying in agony and by inches, week after week, month after month. Oh, I do not negate the agony on the cross. The abandonment of Jesus by his closest friends. The seeming failure of all for which he had become flesh. It was terrible.

But there are worse deaths. And these deaths make no sense at all unless the mystery of the Word made flesh is present in them too; death makes no sense at all if the God who is in it with us is not in the dying body of the young man down the hall; the people killed, burned, in the most recent air crash; in my husband, in me, our children.

I have come to the hospital this morning just after receiving what my friend Tallis calls "the holy mysteries," bread and wine which are bread and wine but are also more than bread and wine, since the bread and wine, like the stars, like the snow, like all of us, is made of the original substance of creation, that which Jesus put on as human flesh. It is by these holy mysteries that I live, that I am sustained.

GOD'S PROMISE OF CARE

SEPTEMBER 23

Charlotte's father enters her bedroom to say goodnight. He holds a glass of whiskey. He is widowed, drinks too much, and can't get his current books published. It is Christmas. Charlotte is twelve years old.

She thought of the words of the carol that they had sung every year but this year, that was one of his most favorite. *Of the Father's love begotten, Ere the worlds began to be.*

"You still pray, Cotty?" her father asked her. "You still say your prayers at night? The nuns see to that?"

"Yes, Father."

"You don't forget? Even when you're away from the convent?"

"No, Father."

"And what do you pray for, hah? Now that you're too old to ask for dolls and toys."

Her voice was low. "That we may be together for Christmas. That we may be happy."

"But that's not in it, Cotty. That's not part of the bargain. Pray all you like, ask anything you want, but don't forget that he never promised he'd say yes. He never guaranteed us anything. Not anything at all. Except one thing. Just one thing."

After a moment she asked, "What one thing, Father?"

"That he cares. Never forget that, Cotty. That is all. Nothing else. But it is enough. It is why I write what I write . . ." His voice faded. Then, "It is enough. Isn't it, Cotty?"

A LITTLE CHILD SHALL LEAD THEM I

Mrs. Austin comes upstairs to read to Vicky and her siblings and to put them to bed. Their Uncle Hal, a pilot who is a friend of the family, has been killed that day in a plane crash. Rob is Vicky's youngest brother; his character is based on Madeleine's own son.

SEPTEMBER 24

When Mother closed the book, we turned out the light and said prayers. We have a couple of family prayers and Our Father and then we each say our own God Bless. Rob is very personal about his God Bless. He puts in anything he feels like, and Mother and Daddy had to scold Suzy to stop her from teasing him about it. Last Christmas, for instance, in the middle of his God Bless, he said, "Oh, and God bless Santa Claus, and bless you, too, God." So I guess that night we were all waiting for him to say something about Uncle Hal. I was afraid maybe he wouldn't, and I wanted him to, badly.

"God bless Mother and Daddy and John and Vicky and Suzy," he said, "and Mr. Rochester and Colette and Grandfather and all the cats and Uncle Douglas and Aunt Elena and Uncle Hal and . . ." and then he stopped and said, "and all the cats and Uncle Douglas and Aunt Elena and Uncle Hal," and then he stopped again and said, "and especially Uncle Hal, God, and make his plane have taken him to another planet to live so he's all right because you can do that, God, John says you can, and we all want him to be all right, because we love him, and God bless me and make me a good boy, Amen."

LOVE LESSONS

SEPTEMBER 25

I know that when I am most monstrous, I am most in need of love. When my temper flares out of bounds it is usually set off by something unimportant which is on top of a series of events over which I have no control, which have made me helpless, and thus caused me anguish and frustration. I am not lovable when I am enraged, although it is when I most need love.

One of our children when he was two or three years old used to rush at me when he had been naughty, and beat against me, and what he wanted by this monstrous behavior was an affirmation of love. And I would put my arms around him and hold him very tight until the dragon was gone and the loving small boy had returned.

So God does with me. I strike against him in pain and fear and he holds me under the shadow of his wings. Sometimes he appears to me to be so unreasonable that I think I cannot live with him, but I know that I cannot live without him. He is my lover, father, mother, sister, brother, friend, paramour, companion, my love, my all.

EVERY LIFE IS CHERISHED

Vicky Austin writes this poem after the dolphin Ynid's baby dies.

The earth will never be the same again.
Rock, water, tree, iron, share this grief   SEPTEMBER 26
As distant stars participate in pain.
A candle snuffed, a falling star or leaf,
A dolphin death, O this particular loss
Is Heaven-mourned; for if no angel cried,
If this small one was tossed away as dross,
The very galaxies then would have lied.
How shall we sing our love's song now
In this strange land where all are born to die?
Each tree and leaf and star show how
The universe is part of this one cry,

That every life is noted and is cherished,
And nothing loved is ever lost or perished.

Did I believe that? I didn't know, but I had not, as it were, dictated the words, I had simply followed them where they wanted to lead.

And whether or not it was a passable sonnet I didn't know, nor whether or not I'd presume to show it to Dr. Nutteley or Adam.

But I felt the good kind of emptiness that comes when I've finished writing something.

FAITH—NO MAGIC CHARM

SEPTEMBER 27

Does enjoying my faith imply protection from the slings and arrows of outrageous fortune? No. It did not stop my husband from dying prematurely. It did not stop a careless truck driver from going through a red light and nearly killing me. My faith is not a magic charm, like garlic to chase away vampires. It is, instead, what sustains me in the midst of all the normal joys and tragedies of the ordinary human life. It is faith that helps my grief to be creative, not destructive. It is faith that kept me going through the pain at the very portals of death and pulled me, whether I would or no, back into life and whatever work still lies ahead.

GRIEF, GRACE, AND LOVE

SEPTEMBER 28

The search for grace, costly grace, involves the acceptance of pain and the creative grief which accompanies growth into maturity. Don't be afraid the pain will destroy the wholeness. It leads, instead, to the kind of wholeness that rejoices in Resurrection.

No one dares to grieve who does not dare to love, and love is always part of costly grace. It has been said that before we can give love we must first have received love, and indeed love is a response to love. To be a Christian and not to be a lover is impossible. We cannot grieve in any healthy way in total isolation—solitude, yes, but not isolation. Grief, like Christianity, is shared by the entire body. Nothing that affects one part of the body does not affect it all.

COSTLY GRACE

B ut in thinking about love and grief we must be careful not to confuse either with that sentimentality which is part of cheap grace. The kind of loving grief I'm talking about involves acceptance of the precariousness of life and that we will all die, but our wholeness is found in the quality rather than the quantity of our living. Real love, between man and woman, friend and friend, parent and child, is exemplified for us in the life, death and resurrection of Jesus Christ who offered us and still offers us the wholeness of that costly grace which gives us the courage for healthy grief.

SEPTEMBER 29

We live in a time where costly grace is what makes life bearable; more than bearable—joyful and creative, so that even our grief is part of our partnership in co-creation with God.

A TREMENDOUSLY EXCITING GOD

In A Winter's Love, *Virginia Bowen has just talked with her mother, Emily, about a poem she discovered in school that*

SEPTEMBER 30

autumn, *"The Hound of Heaven."* *This precipitates a shar-*
ing of a poem Virginia has written.

Virginia pulled a piece of paper out of the book of poetry.
"Well, this is one daddy liked. I sort of got the idea from
reading science fiction stories."

"Read it to me."

Virginia cleared her throat:

> "I am fashioned as a galaxy,
> Not as a solid substance but a mesh
> Of atoms in their far complexity
> Forming the pattern of my bone and flesh.

"I've been writing a lot of sonnets this winter," she said,
looking up from the slip of paper.

"Go on," Emily said.

> "Small solar systems are my eyes.
> Muscle and sinew are composed of air.
> Like comets flashing through the evening skies
> My blood runs, ordered, arrogant, and fair.

> Ten lifetimes distant is the nearest star,
> And yet within my body, firm as wood,
> Proton and electron separate are.
> Bone is more fluid than my coursing blood.
> What plan had God, so strict and so empassioned
> When He an island universe my body fashioned?"

"I like that, Vee," Emily said. "I like that very much. Your poetry has improved a lot this winter."

"We've been studying atoms in chemistry this year, too," Virginia said, "and they kind of fascinate me. And God. God is tremendously exciting, mother. He's so much bigger, so much more—more enormous—than most churches let Him be. When you look at the mountains—or when you look at the stars and think how many of them probably have planets with life on them—and maybe life entirely different from ours—Mother, *why* do people all the time try to pull God down so He's small enough to be understood?"

Emily stood up and put her hands on Virginia's shoulders. "I suppose because most people are afraid of what they can't understand."

"Mother, do you suppose I'll ever be able to write poetry that will give people gooseflesh the way 'The Hound of Heaven' does me?"

"Who knows?" Emily said. "The main thing is to be as aware as you can, every single minute. Never be bored by anything. Because everything, no matter how trivial, is grist to the poet's mill. And now, my sweet, 'The time has come, the Walrus said.' We're all starved and I'm going to dish out the stew. But I did like your sonnet very much."

OCTOBER

BEING TIME IS NEVER WASTED

OCTOBER 1 Perhaps one of the saddest things we can do is waste time, as Shakespeare knew when he had Richard the Second cry out, "I have wasted time, and now doth time waste me."

But *be*ing time is never wasted time. When we are *be*ing, not only are we collaborating with chronological time, but we are touching on *kairos,* and are freed from the normal restrictions of time. In moments of mystical illumination we may experience, in a few chronological seconds, years of transfigured love.

Canon Tallis says that his secretary does not understand that when he is thinking, he is working: she thinks he is wasting time. But thinking time is not wasted time. There are some obvious time-wasters, such as licentious living, drunkenness, adultery, all the things Paul warns us about. A more subtle time-waster is being bored. Jesus was never bored. If we allow our "high creativity" to remain alive, we will never be bored. We can pray, standing in line at the super market. Or we can be lost in awe at all the people around us, their lives full of glory and tragedy, and suddenly we will have the beginnings of a painting, a story, a song.

KAIROS—SACRED TIME

OCTOBER 2 Kairos. Real time. God's time. That time which breaks through chronos with a shock of joy, that time we do not recognize while we are experiencing it, but only afterwards, because kairos has nothing to do with chronological time. In kairos we are completely unselfconscious, and yet paradoxically far more real than we can ever be when we are constantly checking our watches for chronological time. The saint in contemplation, lost (discovered) to self in the mind of God is in kairos. The artist at work is in kairos. The child at play, totally thrown outside himself in the game, be it building a sand castle or making a daisy chain, is in kairos. In kairos we become what we are called to be as human beings, co-creators with God, touching on the wonder of creation. This calling should not be limited to artists—or saints—but it is a fearful calling. Mana, taboo. It can destroy as well as bring into being.

ALL SHALL BE WELL

The twins, Sandy and Dennys Murry, have been transported back to the time of Noah and find themselves involved in a biblical flood story. They have met Noah's daughter Yalith, who is not listed as a passenger on the ark. They know the flood is coming to the people they are visiting. In this episode, they are talking to the seraphim Alarid in an effort to figure out how to save Yalith when the flood comes.

OCTOBER 3

Alarid turned to the boy. "What is it?"

"You can't let Yalith drown in the flood."

"Why not?"

"Yalith is good. I mean, she is really *good.*"

Alarid bowed his head. "Goodness has never been a guarantee of safety."

"But you can't let her drown."

"I have nothing to say in the matter."

"I should have spoken to Aariel," Dennys said in frustration. "Aariel loves her."

"He has no more say than I." The seraph turned his head away.

Dennys realized that he had hurt Alarid, but he plunged ahead. "You're seraphim. You have powers."

"True. But, as I told you, it is dangerous to change things. We do not meddle with the pattern."

"But Yalith isn't *in* the pattern." Dennys's voice rose and cracked. "There's no Yalith in the story. Only Noah and his wife and his sons and their wives."

Alarid's wings quivered slightly.

"So, since she isn't in the story, it won't change anything if you prevent her from being drowned in the flood."

"What do you want me to do?" Alarid asked.

"You aren't going to be drowned, are you?" Dennys demanded. "You, and the other seraphim?"

"No."

"Then take her wherever it is you're going to escape the flood."

"We cannot do that," Alarid said sadly.

"Why not?"

"We cannot." Again, the seraph turned his face away.

"Where are you going, then?"

Alarid turned back to Dennys and smiled, but not in amusement. "We go to the sun."

No. Yalith could not go to the sun. Nor to the moon, which Dennys had been about to suggest. Yalith could not live where there was no atmosphere. But surely there was something to be done! He made a strangled noise of outrage. "We're not in the story, either, Sandy and I. But we're here. And Yalith is here."

"That is so."

"And if we drown, that is, if Sandy and I drown, that's going to change the story, isn't it? I mean, we're not going to be born in our own time if we get drowned now, and even if that makes only a tiny difference, it will make a difference to our family. If Sandy and I don't get born, maybe Charles Wallace won't get born. Maybe Meg will be an only child."

"Who?"

"Our older sister and our little brother. I mean, the story would be *changed*."

Alarid said, "You must go back to your own time."

"That's easier said than done. Anyhow, what I wanted to talk to you about is Yalith. Listen, it's a stupid story. Only the males have names. It's a chauvinist story. I mean, Matred has a name. She's a mother. And Elisheba and Anah and Oholibamah. They're real people, with names."

"That is true," Alarid agreed.

"The nephilim," Dennys went on. "They're like whoever wrote the silly ark story, seeing things only from their own point of view, *using* people. They don't give a hoot for Tiglah or Mahlah, for instance. They're just women, so they don't matter. They don't care if Yalith gets drowned. But you ought to care!"

Alarid asked gently, "Do you think I don't care?"

Dennys sighed. "Okay. I know you care. But are you just going to stand by and do nothing and then fly off to the sun?"

Again Alarid's wings quivered. "Part of doing something is listening. We are listening. To the sun. To the stars. To the wind."

Dennys felt chastened. He had not paused to listen, not for days. "They don't tell you anything?"

"To continue to listen."

The breeze lifted, washed over Dennys in a wave of sadness. "I don't like this story," he said. "I don't like it at all."

He left Alarid. Before he reached the oasis he paused, sat on a small rock. Tried to quiet himself so that he could listen. To the wind. How could he unscramble the words of the wind which came to him in overlapping wavelets?

He closed his eyes. Visioned stars exploding into life. Planets being birthed. Yalith had spoken of the violence of Mahlah's baby's birth. The birth of planets was no gentler. Violent swirlings of winds and waters. Land masses as fluid as water. Volcanoes spouting flame so high that it seemed to meet the outward flaming of the sun.

The earth was still in the process of being created. The stability of rock was no more than an illusion. Earthquake, hurricane, volcano, flood, all part of the continuing creation of the cosmos, groaning in travail.

The song of the wind softened, gentled. Behind the violence of the birthing of galaxies and stars and planets came a quiet and tender melody, a gentle love song. All the raging of creation, the continuing hydrogen explosions on the countless suns, the heaving of planetary bodies, all was enfolded in a patient, waiting love.

Dennys opened his eyes as the wind dropped, was silent. He raised his face to the stars, and their light felt against his cheeks like dew. They chimed at him softly. *Do not seek to comprehend. All shall be well. Wait. Patience. Wait. You do not always have to do something. Wait.*

Dennys put his head down on his knees, and a strange quiet flowed through him.

Above his head, the white wings of a pelican beat gently through the flowing streams of stars.

AND YALITH WAS NOT

As the first drops of rain fall, the seraphim lead Yalith, Sandy, and Dennys into the desert. The seraph named Aariel takes Yalith's hand and stands with her next to a monolith of silvery rock. The other seraphim take the boys' hands and form a circle around Yalith, Aariel, and the rock.

OCTOBER 4

Alarid said, "Yalith, child, you did not know your Great-great-grandfather Enoch."

Mutely, she shook her head.

"But you know of him?" Aariel asked.

"I know that he did not die like ordinary men. He walked with El, and then, according to Grandfather Lamech, he was not. That is, he was not with the people of the oasis. He was with El."

With a rush of hope, Sandy remembered his conversation with Noah and Grandfather Lamech and their recounting of this strange happening.

Aariel smiled down on Yalith. "El has told us to bring you, and in the same way."

She shrank back. "I don't understand."

Dennys moved as though to go to her, but Higgaion nudged him to stay still.

Aariel said, "There is no need to understand, little one. I will take you, and it will be all right. Do not fear."

She looked very small, very young. She asked, timidly, "Will it hurt?"

"No, little one. I think you will find it a rapturous experience."

She looked up at him, trustingly.

"Enoch, your forebear, will explain everything you need to know."

Adnarel's fingers held Sandy back. "You will tell Noah and Matred?"

"I will tell them," Sandy said. "I think they will be very happy."

Dennys, who had not heard the extraordinary story of Enoch, looked confused but hopeful. If Aariel was taking Yalith somewhere, she would not be drowned after all. The seraphim were to be trusted. He was certain of that. Aariel would not take Yalith to the sun, or to the moon, or anywhere that was not possible for her with her human limitations.

Aariel said, "It is time."

Yalith remembered the words Aariel had said to her when she had gone out to the desert in the heat of the day. "Many waters cannot quench love," she whispered. "Neither can the floods drown it. Oh, twins, dear twins, I love you."

Sandy and Dennys spoke together, their voices cracking. "Yalith. Oh, Yalith. I love you."

"Will you go back now, to where you came from?"

The twins glanced at each other.

"We will try," Sandy said.

"We think the seraphim will help us," Dennys added.

"If we had been older—" Sandy started.

Dennys laughed. "If we had been older, it would have been very complicated, wouldn't it?"

Yalith, too, laughed. "Oh, I love you both! I love you both!"

Aariel urged, gently, "Come, Yalith."

"I can't say goodbye to my parents? To Japheth and Oholibamah?"

"It is best this way," Aariel said, "without goodbyes, as it was for your forebear Enoch."

Yalith nodded, then reached up to Sandy and kissed him on the lips. Then Dennys. Full, long kisses.

Aariel wrapped her in his creamy wings, glittering with gold at their tips. Then he held her only with his arms, lifted and spread the wings, beat with them softly, and then rose into the air, up, up.

They watched until all they saw was a speck of light in the sky, as though from a new star.

GOD—WHO WAS HUMAN

To be a Christian is to believe in the impossible.

Jesus was God. Jesus was human.

OCTOBER 5

This is what Scripture affirms. Yet theologians and philosophers and ordinary people have argued about it for nearly two thousand years. How could Jesus be both human and divine? That he was both is the basic affirmation of the Christian faith.

We human beings seem quite capable of accepting that light is a particle, and light is a wave. So why should it be more difficult for us to comprehend that Jesus was completely God and Jesus was completely human? Of course it takes imagination, but so does it take imagination for us to understand as we watch a glorious sunset, that it is the planet earth that is turning, not the sun that is setting.

Those are the wonderful things that are beyond ordinariness—like love—that make life worth living.

Even for Jesus, the human being, his understanding of his Godness did not come all at once. There was a glimmer when he was a boy of twelve and talked with the elders in the Temple. But full understanding did not come until he was a young man and was baptized by his cousin John: John, who, years before, had recognized Jesus in the womb when pregnant Mary had visited Elizabeth.

John was reluctant to baptize Jesus, saying that he was not worthy even to lace up his sandals; but Jesus insisted, and as John baptized him in the River Jordan, the Holy Spirit came upon Jesus from above, and a thunder came from Heaven, and out of the thunder Jesus heard a voice saying: "This is my beloved son in whom I am well pleased."

And then Jesus knew who he was: a human being who was God. God who was human. A most Glorious Impossible!

WHERE GOD IS, IS HEAVEN

OCTOBER 6   I remember one night at the dinner table when two college students asked, rather condescendingly, if I really needed God in order to be happy (blessed). And I said, "Yes. I do. I cannot do it on my own." Simply acknowledging my lack of ability to be in control of the vast technological complex in which my life is set helps free me from its steel net.

Okay, they agreed. So we know we can't control traffic jams and sanitation-department strikes and flu epidemics, but certainly you can't believe in heaven, can you? All that pie-in-the-sky stuff?

Certainly not pie-in-the-sky. Whoever dreamed that one up didn't have much imagination. But the Beatitudes tell me that *Blessed are the poor in spirit: for theirs is the kingdom of heaven.* That's the very first one. I may hold off on heaven till the last of the Beatitudes because it's going to take a steady look at all of them to get me ready. All I know for now is that wherever God is, heaven is, and if I don't have glimpses of it here and now, I'm not going to know it anywhere else.

A LITTLE CHILD SHALL LEAD THEM II

But the happiness offered us by the Beatitudes is not material; it is more spiritual than physical, internal than external; and there is an implication which I find very exciting that the circle of blessing is completed only when man blesses God, that God's blessing does not return to him empty. This completing of the circle is difficult for adults to comprehend, but is understood intuitively by children. Our youngest child, when he was a little boy, used to have intimate, leisurely, and long conversations with God. Bedtime was my most special and privileged time with my children; we read aloud; we sang; and then we had prayers, and although I knew that the prayers were often extended to inordinate lengths in order to prolong

OCTOBER 7

bedtimes, that was all right, too. It's not a bad thing to extend conversation with God, no matter what the reason.

This little boy's conversations with God were spontaneous, loving, and sometimes dictatorial. Many of them I recorded in my journal, so that I would not forget them—such as the prayer one rainy autumn evening when he paused in his God-blesses and said, "O God, I love to listen to the rain; I love to listen to you talk." Another evening he paused again and said severely, "And God: remember to be the Lord." This was during one of the many times when the adults had huddled by the radio during a world crisis; but it took a four-year-old to remind me in my own praying that God is the Lord who is in charge of the universe no matter what we do to mess it up.

And one night this little boy, when he had asked God to bless family and friends and animals, said, "And God! God bless you, too."

THE WONDER OF WORDS

OCTOBER 8

The English language, despite what we have done to it with all our jargons, is still extraordinarily rich and powerful in quality, though not in quantity, of words. Both the Greeks and the Hebrews used many words where we have been satisfied with one. As there are many words for our one *love,* so with *mercy.* The Hebrew *chesed* is seen over and over again in the Psalms, and Coverdale frequently translates it as *loving kindness,* that continued forbearance shown by God even when his chosen people are slow to keep his commandments and swift to turn to foreign gods.

Another Hebrew word for mercy is *rachamim,* which has to do with tender compassion, the care of the shepherd for the stray lamb, the pity shown to the weak and helpless. And there is *chaninah,* a joyful, generous mercy, loving and kind.

So mercy, as all the other Beatitudes, is a Christ-like word, and I must look for understanding of it in the small and daily events of my own living, because if I do not recognize it in little things I will not see it in the great.

THE MIXED BLESSING OF AN EDUCATION

My faith in a loving Creator of the galaxies, so loving that the very hairs of my head are counted, is stronger in my work than in my life, and often it is the work that pulls me back from the precipice of faithlessness. It is not necessarily an unmixed blessing to be a well-educated person in a secular society. A man whose name is unknown to me, but whose words I copied out years ago, wrote, "God must be very great to have created a world which carries so many arguments against his existence."

OCTOBER 9

THE COMFORT OF A SIMPLE VIEW OF GOD

Simon Renier, the protagonist of Dragons in the Waters, *is traveling by ship to Venezuela with a man he thinks is his cousin. He is oblivious to an attack on his life, from which someone has just saved him while he was deep in thought.*

OCTOBER 10

Simon had heard nothing. He reached across the ocean to the woman who had given him life as much as if she had borne him.

"I'm a very old woman, Simon, and in the nature of things I don't have a great deal longer to live. But I've already so far outlived normal life expectancy, and I'm so fascinated by the extraordinary behavior of the world around me and the more ordered behavior of the heavens above, that I don't dwell overmuch on death. And I'm still part of a simpler world than yours, a world in which it was easier to believe in God."

"Why was it easier?"

"Despite Darwin and the later prophets of science, I grew up in a world in which my elders taught me that the planet Earth was the chief purpose of the Creator, and that all the stars in the heavens were put there entirely for our benefit, and that humankind is God's only real interest in the universe. It didn't take as much imagination and courage then as it does now to believe that God has time to be present at a deathbed, to believe that human suffering does concern him, to believe that he loves every atom of his creation, no matter how insignificant."

SCAR TISSUE

OCTOBER 11

In A House Like a Lotus, *Polly O'Keefe is eating dinner with a middle-aged artist, Max Horne, who is a friend of the family. Ursula Heschel, who shares Max's house with her, is out of town. Nettie is the servant.*

When Nettie had withdrawn to the kitchen quarters, Max said, "Don't be sorry for me, Polly. I've had a good life. I'm not a great painter, but I'm a good one, and I've had more than my fair share of success. I have few regrets. Not many people can say that." We were silent for a while, listening to the evening sounds around us. A tiny lizard skittered up the screen. Summer insects were making their double-bass rumblings. "There isn't anything that happens that can't teach us something," she said, "that can't be turned into something positive. One can't undo what's been done, but one can use it creatively." She looked at me and her eyes were sea-silver. "I'm glad I had the experience of having a baby. I wouldn't undo it, have it not have happened. The only thing is to accept, and let the scar heal. Scar tissue is the strongest tissue in the body. Did you know that?"

"No."

"So, I shouldn't be surprised if it's the strongest part of the soul."

SCARS ON THE SOUL

Aunt Olivia is telling Stella Renier, the protagonist of The Other Side of the Sun, *about a tragedy that befell her brother, Theron, during the Civil War. He was a doctor and was shot as a traitor to the Confederacy. Therro, the father of Stella's husband, was a young boy when his father was murdered. Mado is Theron's widow. Honoria is a magnificent black woman and Mado's best friend. The day after Theron was buried, the Renier home is set on fire.*

OCTOBER 12

Therro helped carry stretchers—we got all the wounded men out safely and into the old slave quarters—and his hands were badly burned; he carried the scars until he died. The two baby girls, Olivia and Lucy, and their nurse, were trapped upstairs. Clive's brother died trying to get them out. Mado—she had baby Jamie in her arms, but it was only Clive's

271

holding her that kept her from rushing back in after the little girls. Stella, Stella, we have known so much pain and grief together. If Therro bore the scars on his hands, there were other scars that did not show, no matter how wildly he tried to forget them. And Mado—Mado had scars, too, not physical ones, but scars of the heart. No: scars of the soul. And yet I was the one to rage and rebel and deny God. Mado was never bitter nor resentful, never."

Honoria turned from her contemplation of the ocean. "Never, Miss Livia? Miss Mado, she got through the darkness. She knowed love has to work itself all the way through the dark feelings; you can't go round them; they has to be gone through, all the way through."

"Only on love's terrible other side," Aunt Olivia said softly, "is found the place where lion and lamb abide." She reached one small, gloved hand towards Honoria. "They did well, didn't they, Honoria? The people we have loved. They were lights to lighten the darkness. And I—I cannot sleep at night without leaving a candle burning."

THE AWESOMENESS OF LOVE

Stella Renier narrates. Clive is Honoria's husband.

OCTOBER 13 I went out to the kitchen where Clive was washing up, his sleeves rolled up, his hands deep in soapy water. "Is Honoria all right?"

"She praying, Miss Stella."

"How can—how can God help her?"

"With love, Miss Stella. Ain't no other way." He wiped his
hands, took the little cross I had given him out of his pocket
and put it on the table in front of me.

"Are you on the other side, Clive?" I asked. "The way Mado
said—only on love's terrible other side—is it very terrible,
Clive?"

"Terror is not fear, Miss Stella. It is right and proper that we
should feel terror before the power of the Lord."

"Is love terrible, Clive?"

"Yes, Miss Stella."

MOVING THROUGH PAIN

*Polly O'Keefe has dinner with Ursula, Max's housemate and
a surgeon. Over dinner, Ursula tells Polly about a woman
she knows who has had a series of benign brain tumors removed and has been disfigured by the surgeries.*   OCTOBER 14

A few days ago another tumor was removed, and several
more smaller ones were discovered. I agreed with the decision not to do further surgery. She said that she is looking
with her mind's eye at the tumors, willing them to shrink, *seeing* them shrink. And she quoted Benjamin Franklin to me:
Those things that hurt, instruct. An extraordinary woman. A
holy woman. She looks at her devastated face in the mirror
and, she says, she still does not recognize herself. But there is
no bitterness in her. She sails, and as soon as she gets out of
the hospital she plans to sail, solo, to Bermuda. At sea, what
she looks like is a matter of complete indifference. My patients

teach me, Polly. Old Ben knew what he was talking about, and it's completely counter to general thinking today, where we're taught to avoid pain and seek pleasure. Pain needs to be moved through, not avoided."

Ursula was referring to her own pain, I thought. And Max's. And mine.

"Why is hurting part of growing up?" I demanded.

"It's part of being human. I've been watching you move through it with amazingly mature compassion."

THERE ARE WORSE THINGS
THAN DYING

Polly is remembering when she discovered that Max is dying of a rare tropical disease.

OCTOBER 15

Not many people have the privilege of being given time to prepare for death. I can't say that I'm ready to die—I'm still *in media res* and I have things I'd like to paint . . . things I'd like to do—but I'm beyond the denial and the rage. I don't like the pain."

"Oh, Max—" I looked helplessly at Ursula.

Urs glanced at Max, rose, picked up the journal, and dropped it in the swing. "I'm off to the kitchen. Come and join me in a few minutes, Polly."

"Little one," Max said. "There are worse things than dying. Losing one's sense of compassion, for instance; being inured to suffering. Losing the wonder and the sadness of it all. That's a worse death than the death of the body."

WOUNDS AS MIDWIVES
OF LOVELINESS

In a conversation with a friend, Madeleine said:

I think God wants us to be whole, too. But maybe some- times the only way he can make us whole is to teach us things we can learn only by being not whole." And I remember reading *The Limitations of Science*, by J. W. N. Sullivan, the only book which made sense to me during my dark agnostic period, and the book he wrote on Beethoven, in which he said that Beethoven's deafness was necessary for his full genius. As I think over Beethoven's work chronologically, this seems to be indisputable. How amazing to think that the paeon of joy in the great Ninth Symphony was written when Beethoven was totally shut off from any external sound. And Milton wrote *Paradise Lost* after he was blind.

INTERCONNECTEDNESS

Polly O'Keefe is the protagonist. This is a conversation with her friend Max, which Polly is remembering while she is in *Greece. The excerpt is taken from* A House Like a Lotus.

Pol, listen to this," Max said. "It's by a physicist, A. J. Wheeler. He says: 'Nothing is more important about the quantum principle than this, that it destroys the concept of the world as "sitting out there," with the observer safely separated from it by a 20-centimeter slab of plate glass. Even to observe so minuscule an object as an electron, we must shatter the glass.'" She made a movement with her hand as though breaking through glass, and her face was bright with interest as she looked up from the book, blinking silver eyes against the light of the candles in the hurricane globes. "We cannot separate ourselves from anything in the universe. Not from other creatures. Not from each other."

RE-MEMBERING
THE ORIGINAL ONENESS

OCTOBER 18

The thought of the Original Oneness which preceded the big bang keeps returning to me, the Original Oneness which preceded galaxies and stars and planets and Adam and Eve and you and me. Was that the primordial fall? Are the stars in their courses singing the Lord's song in a strange land?

There was war in heaven: Michael and his angels fought against the dragon; and the dragon fought, and his angels, and prevailed not; neither was their place found any more in heaven. And the great dragon was cast out, that old serpent called the Devil, and Satan, who deceives the whole world; he was cast out into the earth, and his angels with him . . .

So goes the old song, and what does it mean?

The dragon and his angels did not want to be One; they wanted independence and individuation and autonomy, and they broke wholeness into fragments . . .

When will we once again be one?

Perhaps galaxy by galaxy, solar system by solar system, planet by planet, all creation must be redeemed.

Where were we when the morning stars sang together, and all the sons of God shouted for joy?

THE ANCIENT HARMONIES

In this fantasy, A Swiftly Tilting Planet, *Charles Wallace is on the back of the unicorn Gaudior. They are time traveling. Charles Wallace is tired from an encounter with the evil ones, the Echthroi. Gaudior tells him he must stay awake. Charles Wallace is not sure he can.*

OCTOBER 19

Sing, then," Gaudior commanded. "Sing to keep yourself awake." The unicorn opened his powerful jaws and music streamed out in full and magnificent harmony. Charles Wallace's voice was barely changing from a pure treble to a warm tenor. Now it was the treble, sweet as a flute, which joined Gaudior's mighty organ tones. He was singing a melody he did not know, and yet the notes poured from his throat with all the assurance of long familiarity.

They moved through the time-spinning reaches of a far galaxy, and he realized that the galaxy itself was part of a mighty orchestra, and each star and planet within the galaxy added its own instrument to the music of the spheres. As long as the ancient harmonies were sung, the universe would not entirely lose its joy.

He was hardly aware when Gaudior's hoofs struck ground and the melody dimmed until it was only a pervasive beauty of background. With a deep sigh Gaudior stopped his mighty song and folded his wings into his flanks.

FIREFLY BALLET

OCTOBER 20

The boy Charles Wallace is "within" Chuck Maddox (a person in Charles Wallace's past). Chuck's sister is Beezie. The boy and the girl have a special relationship. The smell in the house is death.

One evening after supper Beezie said, "Let's go see if the fireflies are back." It was Friday, and no school in the morning, so they could go to bed when they chose.

Chuck felt an overwhelming desire to get out of the house, away from the smell, which nearly made him retch. "Let's go."

It was still twilight when they reached the flat rock. They sat, and the stone still held the warmth of the day's sun. At first there were only occasional sparkles, but as it got darker Chuck was lost in a daze of delight as a galaxy of fireflies twinkled on and off, flinging upward in a blaze of light, dropping earthward like falling stars, moving in continuous effervescent dance.

"Oh, Beezie!" he cried. "I'm dazzled with gorgeousness."

Behind them the woods were dark with shadows. There was no moon, and a thin veil of clouds hid the stars. "If it were a clear night," Beezie remarked, "the fireflies wouldn't be as bright. I've never seen them this beautiful." She lay back on the rock, looking up at the shadowed sky, then closing her eyes. Chuck followed suit.

"Let's feel the twirling of the earth," Beezie said. "That's part of the dance the fireflies are dancing, too. Can you feel it?"

Chuck squeezed his eyelids tightly closed. He gave a little gasp. "Oh, Beezie! I felt as though the earth had tilted!" He sat up, clutching at the rock. "It made me dizzy."

She gave her bubbling little giggle. "It can be a bit scary, being part of earth and stars and fireflies and clouds and rocks. Lie down again. You won't fall off, I promise."

THE MUSIC OF THE SPHERES

OCTOBER 21

Calvin O'Keefe, Meg Murry, and Charles Wallace are travel-ing through space with three angelic beings. One of the be-ings, Mrs. Whatsit, turns into a winged, Greek, centaurlike creature. They are on the planet Uriel. Calvin kneels.

N o," Mrs. Whatsit said, though her voice was not Mrs. Whatsit's voice. "Not to me, Calvin. Never to me. Stand up."

The children are instructed to get on the marvelous beast's back. They fly off, over a field in which they see many beasts similar to Mrs. Whatsit. The beasts are singing, making music that comes from the movement of their throats as well as the movement of their wings. When Meg asks what they are singing, she is told that there is no way to put their music into human words. Charles Wallace, who has gifts of ex-trasensory perception, is asked to see if he can understand the words. He has some success, but not enough. So Mrs. Whatsit says she will try to put the song into their words.

"Listen, then," Mrs. Whatsit said. The resonant voice rose and the words seemed to be all around them so that Meg felt that she could almost reach out and touch them: "*Sing unto the Lord a new song, and his praise from the end of the earth, ye that go down to the sea, and all that is therein; the isles,*

279

and the inhabitants thereof. Let the wilderness and the cities thereof lift their voice; let the inhabitants of the rock sing, let them shout from the top of the mountains. Let them give glory unto the Lord!"

Throughout her entire body Meg felt a pulse of joy such as she had never known before. Calvin's hand reached out; he did not clasp her hand in his; he moved his fingers so that they were barely touching hers, but joy flowed through them, back and forth between them, around them and about them and inside them.

When Mrs. Whatsit sighed it seemed completely incomprehensible that through this bliss could come the faintest whisper of doubt.

THE DANCE OF LIFE

OCTOBER 22

Sandy and Dennys Murry, twins from the twentieth century who have been transported back to the time of Noah, are with Noah and his sons as they bury Noah's father, Lamech.

The grave was dug.

As the son and grandsons picked the old man up to place him in the grave, Dennys sensed, rather than heard, presences behind them, and turned to see the golden bodies of seraphim standing in a half circle. Once again, he could hear clearly the singing of the moon and the stars.

Aariel called, "Yalith!"

Startled, she let out a small cry.

Aariel raised arms and wings skyward, and the song increased in intensity. "Sing for Grandfather Lamech."

Obediently, Yalith raised her head and sang, a wordless melody, achingly lovely. Above her, the stars and the moon sang with her, and behind her the seraphim joined in great organ tones of harmony.

Japheth took Oholibamah's hands and drew her out onto the clear sands, and they began to dance in rhythm with the song. They were joined by Ham and Anah, and the four of them wove patterns under the stars, touching hands, moving apart, twirling, touching, leaping. Shem and Elisheba joined in, then Noah and Matred and the older daughters and their husbands, and then Yalith took Dennys's hands and drew him into the kaleidoscope of moving bodies, an alleluia of joy and grief and wonder, until Dennys forgot Sandy, forgot that Grandfather Lamech would never be in his tent again, forgot his longing to go home. The crimson flush at the horizon turned a soft ash-rose, then mauve, then blue, as more and more stars brightened, and the harmony of the spheres and the dance of the galaxies interwove in radiance. Slowly the dancers moved apart, stopped. Dennys closed his eyes in a combination of joy and fierce grief, opening them only when the requiem was over. The sky was brilliant with the light of the moon and the stars. The seraphim were gone. Yalith stood beside him, tears streaming down her cheeks.

Noah and his sons tamped down the earth over Grandfather Lamech's grave.

THE STUFF OF THE STARS

This past Sunday when I knelt at the altar in church, the minister put the bread into my hands, and I took it into OCTOBER 23

281

my mouth. That morsel of bread, my hands, the minister's hands on my head as he prayed for me, all the other people in church, in other churches, on the streets, alone, all, all, are made of the same stuff as the stars, that original stuff with which Jesus clothed himself when he came to live with us. I ate the bread, took the cup, and with it all the truth of the stories that tell us about ourselves as human beings. And I was as close to Joseph as I was to the people on either side of me.

After church I went home for lunch with a few of the people who had shared communion with me. I had made a mess of pottage, that mixture of lentils, onions, and rice, which Joseph's father, Jacob, sold to Esau for his birthright. It wasn't nice of Jacob to sell it and defraud his brother, but the pottage was a tempting dish. Friends, food, the love of God, all calling us to be human—not infallible, but human.

THE UNIVERSE IS GOD'S

OCTOBER 24 A while ago when I was at Berea College in Kentucky I was asked the usual earnest questions about creationism vs. evolution.

I laughed and said that I really couldn't get very excited about it. The only question worth asking is whether or not the universe is God's. If the answer is YES! then why get so excited about *how*? The important thing is that we are God's, created in love. And what about those seven days? In whose time are they? Eastern Standard Time? My daughter in San Francisco lives in a time zone three hours earlier than mine. In Australia, what time is it? Did God create in human time? Solar time? Galactic time? What about God's time? What matter if the first day took a few billennia in our time, and the second day a few billennia more?

I told the student at Berea that some form of evolution seems consistent with our present knowledge, and that I didn't think that God put the fossil skeletons of fish in the mountains of Nepal to test our faith, as some creationists teach. But if I should find out tomorrow that God's method of creation was something quite different from either creationism or evolution, that would in no way shake my faith, because that is not where my faith is centered.

EVERYTHING IS CONTAINED IN THE MIND OF GOD

Thank God. If my faith were based on anything so fragile, how would I have lived through my husband's dying and death? How would I continue to live a full and loving life? My faith is based on the wonder that everything is contained in the mind of God, all that we can see, all that we cannot see, all that is visible and all that—like sub-atomic particles—is invisible. All the laughter, all the pain, all the birthing and living and dying and glory, all our stories, without exception, are given dignity by God's awareness and concern.

OCTOBER 25

But we get frightened, and we begin to wonder if all this explosion of knowledge doesn't make us so tiny and insignificant that we don't even count in the vastness of Creation. In the enormity of existence, we ask, Is there really a point to it all?

That there is, indeed, a point is something that all who believe in Christ affirm. We may not always know what the point is, but we base our lives on *God's* knowing. When we say that

Christ is Lord we are affirming that God cares so much that we get the point, that the Second Person of the Trinity came to live with us, to be one of us, just to show us the point.

NO SMALL PARTS

OCTOBER 26

For the Christian, the Trinity is the true metaphor for family, but in the churches nowadays we seem to be skipping over the Trinity, or dispensing with it altogether, and this may be because we are also skipping over and dispensing with family, forgetting the joys of unity in diversity.

A metaphor of unity in diversity is the world of the theatre, where I was always a very small part of the making of a play. But, as Stanislavski reminds us, "There are no small parts; there are only small actors," and I rejoiced in being a part of this Oneness. No one was expendable; everyone was needed to make the play work. Another metaphor is the orchestra, where the lowly tuba may be as important as the first violin. All the instruments have to play together to make unity, a symphony, a concerto, or an orchestral suite.

EVERYONE IS CALLED

OCTOBER 27

We are not all called to go to El Salvador, or Moscow, or Calcutta, or even the slums of New York, but none of us will escape the moment when we have to decide whether to withdraw, to play it safe, or to act upon what we prayerfully believe to be right, knowing that with all our prayers we may be wrong, and knowing that we will probably be punished by those who do not want universe-disturbers to stand up and be counted.

Perhaps what we are called to do may not seem like much, but the butterfly is a small creature to affect galaxies thousands of light years away.

LOVING OBEDIENCE

And God's will, no matter how fervent our prayers, is not always done. We human creatures abuse our free will, set it over against God's will. Sometimes when we may truly be doing God's will, it is thwarted because of the abuse of free will by others. My faith is that ultimately God's will *will* be done, and I know to my rue that when I am willful I am obstructing that will. At my occasional best, I am lovingly obedient to what I pray is the will of God. Loving obedience should never be difficult; we are not being coerced, or manipulated. Loving obedience is doing the Lord's will with enthusiasm— doing the Lord's will filled with the Spirit of God.

OCTOBER 28

A DEFINITION OF SIN

Why are we so afraid to be human, depending on legalism and moralism and dogmatism instead? Jesus came to us as a truly human being, to show us how to be human, and we were so afraid of this humanness that we crucified it, thinking it could be killed. And today we are still afraid to be human, struggling instead with a perfectionism which is crippling, or which in some cases can lead to a complete moral breakdown.

OCTOBER 29

We are not perfect. Only God is perfect. And God does not ask us to be perfect; God asks us to be human. This means to know at all times that we are God's children, never to lose our connection with our Creator. Jesus was sinless not because he didn't do wrong things: he broke the law, picking corn, for instance, on the Sabbath. He was sinless because he was never for a moment separated from the Source.

SIN IS SEPARATION FROM GOD

OCTOBER 30

One of the bits of dogma that used to concern me was that Jesus is exactly like us—except he's sinless. Well, of course if he's sinless he's not exactly like us; he's not like us at all. And then I arrived at a totally different definition of sin. Sin is not child abuse or rape or murder, terrible though these may be. Sin is separation from God, and Jesus was never separate from the Source. Of course if we were close to our Source, if we were not separated from God, it would be impossible for us to commit child abuse or rape or murder. But when we are separated from God, that sin makes all sins possible.

THE WILD WONDER OF GOD'S LOVE

OCTOBER 31

For Christians, Hallowe'en is fulfilled in the gift of the birth of Jesus far more than in the death of Jesus. What a magnificent mystery of the Word Made Flesh! Christ, the power that created the universe, relinquished all power to come to us as one of us, mortal, human, walking the short road from the womb to the tomb. Often we stumble along, not knowing where we're going, but understanding that the journey is worth it because Jesus took it for us, shared it with us. Because the immortal God became mortal, we all share in the immortality as well as the mortality. And how can we begin to understand our immortality until we accept our mortality?

What I believe is so magnificent, so glorious, that it is beyond finite comprehension. To believe that the universe was created by a purposeful, benign Creator is one thing. To believe that this Creator took on human vesture, accepted death and mortality, was tempted, betrayed, broken, and all for love of us, defies reason. It is so wild that it terrifies some Christians who try to dogmatize their fear by lashing out at other Christians, because a tidy Christianity with all answers given is easier than one which reaches out to the wild wonder of God's love, a love we don't even have to earn.

NOVEMBER

SAINT SHINRAN

When I walk my dog at night, the route on the way home takes me past a Buddhist temple with a terrace on which stands a huge statue of Saint Shinran Shunin, a Buddhist saint of the twelfth century. This particular statue was in Hiroshima when the bomb fell, and was sent by the Buddhists of that city to the Buddhists in New York as a symbol of forgiveness and hope. Each night as my dog and I walk by the great statue, the huge bulk of metal wearing a patina I have never seen on another statue, I say, "Good night, Saint Shinran. Forgive us, and help us," and for me, at that moment, Saint Shinran is one of God's angels. Am I worshipping a pagan saint? A lifeless hunk of metal? No! It is an attitude of heart, a part of turning to Christ.

I rejoiced to read in William Johnston's *The Inner Eye of Love* that Saint Shinran rebelled against legalism and proclaimed "the pre-eminence of faith and grace," and that "he has been frequently compared to Luther."

NOTHING IS SECULAR . . .

The *St. Matthew Passion* is an icon of the highest quality for me, an open door into the realm of the numinous. Bach, of course, was a man of deep and profound religious faith, a faith which shines through his most secular music. As a matter of fact, the melody of his moving chorale, *O sacred head now wounded*, was the melody of a popular street song of the day, but Bach's religious genius was so great that it is now recognized as one of the most superb pieces of religious music ever written.

There is nothing so secular that it cannot be sacred, and that is one of the deepest messages of the Incarnation.

NEW EVERY MORNING

Bach is, for me, the Christian artist *par excellence,* and if I ask myself why, I think it has something to do with his sense of newness. I've been working on his C Minor Tocatta and Fugue since college, and I find something new in it every day. And perhaps this is because God was new for Bach every day, was never taken for granted. Too often we do take God for granted. I'm accustomed to being a Christian. I was born of Christian parents who were born of Christian parents who were. . . .

That's all right, when one is a child, this comfortable familiarity with being Christian, because to the child . . . everything is wonderful and new, even familiarity. The edge has not been taken off the glory of God's creation. But later on there comes a time when this very familiarity can become one of those corrupting devices. We learn this early, in our attachment to certain bedtime routines of bath and story and prayer and teddy bear and glass of water and good-night kiss—and the routine must never be varied, because this is security in what the child learns early is an insecure world.

HOLINESS AS GIFT

Along with reawakening the sense of newness, Bach's music points me to wholeness, a wholeness of body, mind, and spirit, which we seldom glimpse, but which we are intended to know. It is no coincidence that the root word of whole, health, heal, holy, is hale (as in *hale and hearty*). If we are healed, we become whole; we are hale and hearty; we are holy.

The marvellous thing is that this holiness is nothing we can earn. We don't become holy by acquiring merit badges and Brownie points. It has nothing to do with virtue or job descriptions or morality. It is nothing we can *do,* in this do-it-yourself world. It is gift, sheer gift, waiting there to be recognized and received. We do not have to be qualified to be holy. We do not have to be qualified to be whole, or healed.

APPOINTED TO SERVE

NOVEMBER 5

Moses wasn't qualified (as I run over my favourite characters in both Old and New Testaments, I can't find one who was in any worldly way qualified to do the job which was nevertheless accomplished); Moses was past middle age when God called him to lead his children out of Egypt, and he spoke with a stutter. He was reluctant and unwilling and he couldn't control his temper. But he saw the bush that burned and was not consumed. He spoke with God in the cloud on Mount Sinai, and afterwards his face glowed with such brilliant light that the people could not bear to look at him.

In a very real sense not one of us is qualified, but it seems that God continually chooses the most unqualified to do his work, to bear his glory. If we are qualified, we tend to think that we have done the job ourselves. If we are forced to accept our evident lack of qualification, then there's no danger that we will confuse God's work with our own, or God's glory with our own.

THE "PRICE" OF THE GIFT

To trust, to be truly whole, is also to let go whatever we may consider our qualifications. There's a paradox here, and a trap for the lazy. I do not need to be "qualified" to play a Bach fugue on the piano (and playing a Bach fugue is for me an exercise in wholeness). But I cannot play that Bach fugue at all if I do not play the piano daily, if I do not practice my finger exercises. There are equivalents of finger exercises in the writing of books, the painting of portraits, the composing of a song. We do not need to be qualified; the gift is free; and yet we have to pay for it.

NOVEMBER 6

TOO GOOD TO BE TRUE

Isaiah knew himself to be mortal and flawed, but he had the child's courage to say to the Lord, "Here I am. Send me." And he understood the freedom which the Spirit can give us from ordinary restrictions when he wrote, "When you pass through deep waters I am with you; when you pass through rivers, they will not sweep you away; walk through fire and you will not be scorched, through flames and they will not burn you." He may not have had this understanding before he wrote those words, for such understanding is a gift which comes when we let go, and listen. I think I looked up this passage because I dreamed that a friend reached into the fireplace and drew out a living coal and held it in his hand, looking at its radiance, and I wondered at him because he was not burned.

NOVEMBER 7

It may be that we have lost our ability to hold a blazing coal, to move unfettered through time, to walk on water, because we have been taught that such things have to be earned; we should deserve them; we must be qualified. We are suspicious of grace. We are afraid of the very lavishness of the gift.

But a child rejoices in presents!

CALLED TO BE HUMAN

NOVEMBER 8

We make a terrible error when we think that to be human means to be perfect, some kind of unerring Christian model that cannot exist in reality. Only God is perfect. To be human is to be able to laugh, to cry, to live fully, to be aware of our lives as we are living them. We are the creatures *who know that we know,* unlike insects who live by unthinking instinct. That ability to think, to know, to reflect, to question, marks us as human beings. And our humanness includes an awareness that we are mortal. To be a human being is to be born, to live, to die. We have a life span. George MacDonald reminds us that Jesus came to us in a human body not so that he would be like us, but so that we would be like Jesus. Jesus died to his human life, and what he demands of us is equally hard, never sentimental or easy, and it is always part of that call to be human.

EXPLORING THE MEANING OF *PERFECT*

NOVEMBER 9

What about the mandate to *be perfect as your Father in heaven is perfect?* The word *perfect* comes from the Latin and means *to do thoroughly.* So, if we understand the word that way, we might say that it means to be human, perfectly human, and perhaps that is what we are meant to understand by this command which is on the surface a contradiction to Jesus' emphasis that only his Father was good, only his Father was perfect. We human beings are to be human—to be perfectly human, not indefectible or impeccable or faultless or superhuman, but complete, right, with integrity undivided.

STORIES DISCLOSE HUMAN BEING

We tell stories, listen to stories, go to plays, to be amused, to be edified, but mostly so that we can understand what it means to be a human being. Jesus was a story-teller. Indeed, according to Matthew, he taught entirely by telling stories. One of the great triumphs of Satan has been to lead us to believe that "story" isn't true. I don't know if all the facts of the story of Joseph are true, but it is a true story. That is very important to understand. Jesus did not tell his parables in order to give us facts and information, but to show us *truth*. What is the truth of the story of the man with the great plank in his eye? Doesn't it tell us very clearly that we must not judge others more stringently than ourselves?

And Joseph's story tells us much about what it means to be human. More important than whether or not Potiphar's wife actually tried to seduce him is the truth of his integrity in refusing to betray his master. Story is the closest we human beings can come to truth. God is truth. God is beyond the realm of provable fact. We can neither prove nor disprove God. God is for faith.

NOVEMBER 10

TRUTH—BEYOND AND THROUGH PARADOX

NOVEMBER 11 The image of God in ourselves is often obscured, and we surely don't find it in the bathroom mirror. Better mirrors are our friends, those we love and trust most deeply. That image is never found in competition with our neighbours or colleagues; rather, in not wanting to let down those who believe in us and in God's image in us. Each one of us is probably as varied as the Jesus in *The Acts of John,* and which aspect is the more true? Probably the whole bundle together.

Certainly the more human we are, the more varied and contradictory we are. And that is as it should be. God often reveals the infinite Presence to us through paradox and contradiction, and Scripture is full of both. Through paradox and contradiction we are enabled to sift for truth, that truth which will set us free, that truth which is not limited by literalism. What confuses many people about Scripture is that some of it is history, and some of it is story. The story of Joseph may be part history, and part story, but it is *true.*

CREATURES WHO KNOW THEY DON'T KNOW

NOVEMBER 12 To be human is, yes, to be fallible. We are the creatures who *know,* and we know that we know. We are also the creatures who know that we don't know. When I was a child, I used to think that being grown up meant that you would know. Grown-ups had the answers. This is an illusion that a

lot of people don't lose when they grow up. But our very fallibility is one of our human glories. If we are fallible we are free
to grow and develop. If we are infallible we are rigid, stuck in
one position, as immobile as those who could not let go the
idea that planet earth is the centre of all things.

RECOGNIZING THE PARADOX
OF HUMAN BEING

Part of our inheritance from our Puritan ancestors is a feeling that we "ought" to be good. Certainly it is not a bad
thing to want to be good. The daily problem is that what my finite, conscious mind tells me I ought to do, and what the untamed, submerged, larger part of me makes me do are often in
direct conflict. But this is no surprise for the Christian. Two
thousand years ago Paul of Tarsus admitted quite openly that
the things he wanted to do were the very things he didn't do,
and the things he didn't want to do were the very things he did.
And yet Paul did not despair, nor drop out. He was even able to
accept the reality that he had cheered on the stoning of Stephen
and had been one of the most successful persecutors of the
early Christians. And yet when God took him by the scruff of
the neck and shook him, he was able to let go, to let go of himself and his control of himself, and instead trust God, and experience a total reversal of his life. Alan Jones points out that
before his conversion on the Damascus Road, Paul was suffering from *paranoia*, was out of his right mind. And afterwards
he was in a state of *metanoia*—and metanoia means being
turned around, repentance, being in a healthy state of mind.

NOVEMBER 13

297

MIND AND HEART
BELONG TOGETHER

In prayer, in the creative process, these two parts of ourselves, the mind and the heart, the intellect and the intuition, the conscious and the subconscious mind, stop fighting each other and collaborate. Theophan the Recluse advised those who came to him for counsel to "pray with the mind in the heart," and surely this is how the artist works. When mind and heart work together, they *know* each other as two people who love each other know; and as the love of two people is a gift, a totally unmerited, incomprehensible gift, so is the union of mind and heart. David cried out to God, "Unite my heart to fear thy Name." It is my prayer, too.

"KNOWING"—REVISITED

But how do we *know*? We've lost much of the richness of that word. Nowadays, to know means to know with the intellect. But it is a much deeper word than that. Adam *knew* Eve. To know deeply is far more than to know consciously. In the realm of faith I *know* far more than I can believe with my finite mind. I *know* that a loving God will not abandon what he creates. I *know* that the human calling is co-creation with this power of love. I *know* that neither death, nor life, nor angels, nor principalities, nor powers, nor things present, nor things to come, nor height, nor depth, nor any other creature, shall be able to separate us from the love of God, which is in Jesus Christ our Lord.

INTENTIAL IDENTIFICATION

The problem of pain, of war and the horror of war, of poverty and disease is always confronting us. But a God who allows no pain, no grief, also allows no choice. There is little unfairness in a colony of ants, but there is also little freedom. We human beings have been given the terrible gift of free will, and this ability to make choices, to help write our own story, is what makes us human, even when we make the wrong choices, abusing our freedom and the freedom of others. The weary and war-torn world around us bears witness to the wrongness of many of our choices. But lest I stumble into despair I remember, too, seeing the white, pinched-faced little children coming to the pediatric floor of a city hospital for open-heart surgery, and seeing them, two days later, with colour in their cheeks, while the nurses tried to slow down their wheel-chair races. I remember, too, that there is now a preventative for trachoma, still the chief cause of blindness in the world. And I remember that today few mothers die in childbirth, and our graveyards no longer contain the mute witness of five little stones in a row, five children of one family, dead in a week of scarlet fever or diptheria.

NOVEMBER 16

George MacDonald gives me renewed strength during times of trouble—times when I have seen people tempted to deny God—when he says, "The Son of God suffered unto death, not that men might not suffer, but that their suffering might be like his."

DYING RITE

Vicky Austin's grandfather, who has leukemia, has taken a turn for the worse. He has just returned from the hospital where he was given a blood transfusion. His son-in-law expresses the desire to rent a hospital bed.

Grandfather's hand stroked Ned and the purr came louder. "During my lifetime I've learned a good bit about dying. In Alaska, for instance, an old man or woman would prepare to die, and would call the family for instructions and farewells. And when they had done what they wanted to do, wound up their affairs as we might say, they died. It was a conscious decision, a letting go which involved an understanding of the body that we've lost. And I thought then and I think now that it's far better than our way of treating death. But what I didn't realize when I was watching someone's sons and daughters standing around the deathbed, sometimes stolid, sometimes weeping, always moving deeply into acceptance of grief and separation, was that I do not have the strength of my Eskimo friends. It hurts me too much to see you being hurt."

Daddy took his hand. "It's a part of it, Father, you know that."

Grandfather looked at me. "I know. But the look in my daughter's eyes this afternoon . . . "

Grandfather was looking at me but he was seeing Mother.

"Perhaps I'd be better off in the hospital. Perhaps you shouldn't have brought me home . . . I thought I could die with you around me, and I did not realize how much it would hurt you and that I cannot stand that hurt."

"Perhaps," Daddy suggested, "you ought not to deprive us of that hurt?"

I knelt by Grandfather, and Rochester leaned against me, almost knocking me over. "I think the Eskimos are right, Grandfather, and I know you're just as strong as anybody else in the world."

He looked at me and blinked, as though clearing his vision. "Vicky?"

"Yes, Grandfather. We don't want you off in the hospital where you're a number and a case history. We want you to be strong enough to let us be with you." I bit my lip because tears were beginning to well up in my eyes.

PAIN, PRELUDE TO JOY

Vicky Austin talks with her terminally ill grandfather about the deeper meanings of things.

"Grandfather, you told us once that if we aren't capable of being hurt we aren't capable of feeling joy."

NOVEMBER 18

"Yes . . . yes . . ."

"You were with Gram when she died."

He continued to pat my hand absent-mindedly. "That is different. Caro and I were one. This—"

"It's a different kind of oneness. It's a deep but dazzling darkness."

Now he took my hand in his. "Poetry does illuminate, doesn't it? Bless you for understanding that, and for remembering."

THE PROMISE OF LIFE

I don't need faith to know that if a poem has fourteen lines, a specific rhyme scheme, and is in iambic pentameter, it is a sonnet; it may not be a good sonnet, but it will be a sonnet. I don't need faith to know that if I take flour and butter and milk and seasonings and heat them in a double boiler, the mix will thicken and become white sauce. Faith is for that which lies on the *other* side of reason. Faith is what makes life bearable, with all its tragedies and ambiguities and sudden, startling joys. Surely it wasn't reasonable of the Lord of the Universe to come and walk this earth with us and love us enough to die for us and then show us everlasting life? We will all grow old, and sooner or later we will die, like the old trees in the orchard. But we have been promised that this is not the end. We have been promised life.

FREEDOM WITHIN THE PATTERN

Mrs. Whatsit is an angelic being summoned to help Meg Murry rescue her brother, Charles Wallace, from the power of IT. Meg's father and her friend Calvin O'Keefe know Meg must go alone. Mrs. Whatsit explains that she cannot see into the future. The Happy Medium is someone Meg, Charles Wallace, and Calvin met on their way to the planet Camazotz, where Charles Wallace is being held prisoner.

If we knew ahead of time what was going to happen we'd be—we'd be like the people on Camazotz, with no lives of our own, with everything all planned and done for us. How can I explain it to you? Oh, I know. In your language you have a form of poetry called the sonnet."

"Yes, yes," Calvin said impatiently. "What's that got to do with the Happy Medium?"

"Kindly pay me the courtesy of listening to me." Mrs. Whatsit's voice was stern, and for a moment Calvin stopped pawing the ground like a nervous colt. "It is a very strict form of poetry, is it not?"

"Yes."

"There are fourteen lines, I believe, all in iambic pentameter. That's a very strict rhythm or meter, yes?"

"Yes." Calvin nodded.

"And each line has to end with a rigid rhyme pattern. And if the poet does not do it exactly this way, it is not a sonnet, is it?"

"No."

"But within this strict form the poet has complete freedom to say whatever he wants, doesn't he?"

"Yes." Calvin nodded again.

"So," Mrs. Whatsit said.

"So what?"

"Oh, do not be stupid, boy!" Mrs. Whatsit scolded. "You know perfectly well what I am driving at!"

"You mean you're comparing our lives to a sonnet? A strict form, but freedom within it?"

"Yes," Mrs. Whatsit said. "You're given the form, but you have to write the sonnet yourself. What you say is completely up to you."

THROUGH A GLASS DARKLY

All institutions resist change, and whenever anything happens to alter what the institution has decided is the right picture of God and the universe—not only the right picture but the only picture—they resist. It is frightening to be told that the "truth" that the institution has been teaching is not the "truth" after all. But it isn't the truth that changes, only our knowledge. Truth is eternal, but our knowledge is always flawed and partial.

The way we look at the making of the universe is inevitably an *image,* an *icon.* Joseph, standing out in the desert at night and looking at the sun sliding down behind the western horizon, turning to see the moon coming up in the east, understandably saw the sun and the moon as heavenly bodies that revolved around the earth. That, indeed, is how it looks to all of us. We may know that it is not the sun that is setting, but rather our planet that is turning, nevertheless the evidence of our eyes is that *the sun sets.*

As our knowledge changes, our images, our icons, must change, too, or they become idols. Our understanding of the universe today is very different from Joseph's understanding, but we, too, must be willing to allow our understanding to change and grow as we learn more about God's glorious work. We still tend to cling to our own ideas, or what we have been taught, or told, and to feel threatened if anything new is revealed. What we know now is probably as far from the way God really created as the patriarch's limited vision and version. How do we stay open to revelation?

CHERISHING THE WONDER OF CHOICE

The God I believe in is greater than anything I or anybody else can conceive. But part of my faith is that the Creator NOVEMBER 22 who made human beings with at least an iota of free will does not diminish that marvelous and terrible gift by manipulating us. God is not a Great Dictator. Every once in a while when life seems nearly unbearable I might long, fleetingly, for such a God who has already, as it were, written the story, but I do not want to be part of a tale that has already been told. God calls us to work with our Maker on the fulfilling of Creation. What we do either moves us towards the Second Coming, the reconciliation of all things, or holds us back.

Yes, each of us is that important, and this can be very frightening. With our abuse of free will we have increased the ravages of disease; our polluted planet is causing more people to die of cancer than when the skies and seas and earth were clean. But this does not mean that we have to throw out the idea of a God who loves and cares.

What kind of a God of love can we believe in at this point in the human endeavor? How do we reconcile God's love and the strange gift of free will?

PRAYING INCLUSIVELY

God be in my thoughts, and in my heart. In my left hand and in my right hand. Atone me. At-one me with you and NOVEMBER 23 your love. Help me to pray for those I fear as well as those I love, knowing that you can take my most ungracious prayers and give them grace. Whenever we pray, we are tapping the power of creation, and that's a mighty power. There are a lot of battle lines to cross in order for us to pray with each other, and with the rest of the world, with those who do not agree with us, with those who worship God in ways we do not understand. But that is all right. We do not have to understand. We do have to try to turn to love, to know that the Lord who created all, also loves all that which was made.

PRAYER PRELIMINARIES

NOVEMBER 24

Before I can listen to God in prayer, I must fumble through the prayers of words, of willful demands, the prayers of childish "Gimmies," of "Help mes," of "I want. . . ." Until I tell God what I want, I have no way of knowing whether or not I truly want it. Unless I ask God for something, I do not know whether or not it is something for which I ought to ask, and I cannot add, "But if this is not your will for me, then your will is what I want, not mine." The prayers of words cannot be eliminated. And I must pray them daily, whether I feel like praying or not. Otherwise, when God has something to say to me, I will not know how to listen. Until I have worked through self, I will not be enabled to get out of the way.

KYTHING AS INTERCESSORY PRAYER

NOVEMBER 25

We do not exist in isolation. We are part of a vast web of relationships and interrelationships which sing themselves in the ancient harmonies. Nor can we be studied objectively, because to look at us is to change us. And for us to look at anything is to change not only what we are looking at, but ourselves, too.

And our deepest messages of love are often conveyed without words. In my writing I have used the word *kything,* found in an old Scottish dictionary of my grandfather's, to express this communication without words, where there is "neither speech nor language." To kythe is to open yourself to someone. It is, for me, a form of intercessory prayer, for it is to be utterly vulnerable.

NEW PERSPECTIVES
ON THE HOLY GOOD

We can recognize the holy good even while we are achingly, fearfully aware of all that has been done to it through greed and lust for power and blind stupidity. We forget the original good of all creation because of our own destructiveness. The ugly fact that evil can be willed for people by other people, and that the evil comes to pass, does not take away our capacity to will good. There may be many spirits abroad other than the Holy Spirit (the Gospels warn us of them), but they do not make the Holy Spirit less holy. Our paradoxes and contradictions expand; our openness to God's revelations to us must also be capable of expansion. Our religion must always be subject to change without notice—our religion, not our faith, but the patterns in which we understand and express our faith. Surely we would feel ill at ease today with people who had family morning prayers and Scripture readings daily, and yet kept slaves?

NOVEMBER 26

THANKS AND PRAISE—
PART OF THE PATTERN

I will have nothing to do with a God who cares only occasionally. I need a God who is with us always, everywhere, in the deepest depths as well as the highest heights. It is when things go wrong, when the good things do not happen, when our prayers seem to have been lost, that God is most present. We do not need the sheltering wings when things go smoothly. We are closest to God in the darkness, stumbling along blindly.

Yet even here I live with contradiction. Whenever anyone in the family is driving, I pray for a safe journey. And when I hear the car door slam and know that whoever it is is safely home, I breathe out, "Oh, God, thank you."

But I think there is a difference between offering a deep sigh of thanks and assuming that "the Lord was surely with me."

We need to say "Thank you" whenever possible, even if we are not able to reconcile the human creature's free will with the Maker's working out of the pattern. Thanks and praise are, I believe, some of the threads with which the pattern is woven.

There are many times when the idea that there is indeed a pattern seems absurd wishful thinking. Random events abound. There is much in life that seems meaningless. And then, when I can see no evidence of meaning, some glimpse is given which reveals the strange weaving of purposefulness and beauty.

The world of science lives fairly comfortable with paradox. We know that light is a wave, and also that light is a particle. The discoveries made in the infinitely small world of particle physics indicate randomness and chance, and I do not find it any more difficult to live with the paradox of a universe of randomness and chance and a universe of pattern and purpose than I do with light as a wave and light as a particle. Living with contradiction is nothing new to the human being.

FROM ST. LUKE'S HOSPITAL (1)

To my guardian angel

Beauty and form's singular absence
Has embarrassed me before the Power
Who made all loveliness. In the hour

NOVEMBER 28

When the Fall's result, dark ugliness,
Shakes my body, you, Angel, come,
Solid and familiar as a nanny in the room.

Thank you, Angel, for your presence
During all the vile indignities
That accompany body's dis-ease.

You hold the beauty of the images
Which make of all creation sacrament,
Even this. Now there is no embarrassment.

Sustained by your stern confidence
In the holiness of all created things
I rest within the comfort of your wings.

THE INSISTENCE OF CHRONOLOGY

During our mortal lives, however, *chronos* is not merely illusion. My body is aging according to human chronology, not nucleon or galactic chronology. My knees creak. My vision is variable. My energy span is shorter than I think it ought to be. There is nothing I can do to stop the passage of this kind of time in which we human beings are set. I can work with it rather than against it, but I cannot stop it. I do not like what it is doing to my body. If I live as long as many of my forbears, these outward diminishments will get worse, not better. But these are the outward signs of chronology, and there is another Madeleine who is untouched by them, the part of me that lives forever in *kairos* and bears God's image.

FIRST COMING

He did not wait till the world was ready,
till men and nations were at peace.
He came when the Heavens were unsteady,
and prisoners cried out for release.

He did not wait for the perfect time.
He came when the need was deep and great.
He dined with sinners in all their grime,
turned water into wine. He did not wait

till hearts were pure. In joy he came
to a tarnished world of sin and doubt.
To a world like ours, of anguished shame
he came, and his Light would not go out.

He came to a world which did not mesh,
to heal its tangles, shield its scorn.
In the mystery of the Word made Flesh
the Maker of the stars was born.

We cannot wait till the world is sane
to raise our songs with joyful voice,
for to share our grief, to touch our pain,
He came with Love: Rejoice! Rejoice!

DECEMBER

$E = MC^2$

In the fascinating study of modern physics we learn that energy and matter are interchangeable. So the sheer energy of Christ, for love of us, put on the matter of Jesus—ordinary human matter. What love! It is beyond all our puny efforts in clay, or stone, or music, or paint, or ink, but that love is behind our artistic endeavors, no matter how insignificant.

The Incarnation hallows our human lives. We've heard the story of Jesus so often that our ears have become blunted. Story reawakens us to truth, the truth that will set us free. Jesus, the Story, taught by telling stories, quite a few of which on the surface would appear to be pretty secular, but all of which lead us, if we will listen, to a deeper truth than we have been willing to hear before.

POINT THE CHILDREN TOWARD THE LIGHT

If we are not going to deny our children the darker side of life, we owe it to them to show them that there is also this wild brilliance, this light of the sun: although we cannot look at it directly, it is nevertheless by the light of the sun that we see. If we are to turn towards the sunlight, we must also turn away from the cult of the common man and return to the uncommon man, to the hero. We all need heroes, and here again we can learn from the child's acceptance of the fact that he needs someone beyond himself to look up to.

LIGHT A CANDLE FOR THE CHILDREN

To be responsible means precisely what the word implies: to be capable of giving a response. It isn't only the Flower Children or Hell's Angels who are opting out of society. A writer who writes a story which has no response to what is going on in the world is not only copping out himself but helping others to be irresponsible, too. I mentioned that all of us on the Children's Book Committee *do* give our response to the world around us in our books, even if only by implication. I brought up several books written by the members of the committee, books which are perfect examples of the kind of responsibility I am talking about, and added, "You're my friends, and you've read *The Young Unicorns* [it had recently been published]; you know there's more than just the story. If what I have to say is right, or if it is wrong, I'm responsible for it, and I can't pretend that I'm not, just because it's difficult."

DECEMBER 3

To refuse to respond is in itself a response. Those of us who write are responsible for the effect of our books. Those who teach, who suggest books to either children or adults, are responsible for their choices. Like it or not, we either add to the darkness of indifference and out-and-out evil which surround us or we light a candle to see by.

LOVED AND FREED TO LOVE

In chapter five of Romans Paul assures us that *God has poured out his love into our hearts by the Holy Spirit, whom*

DECEMBER 4

he has given us—our Trinitarian God, Father, Son, and Holy Spirit, all there since the beginning, all here, all now, loving us.

In John's first epistle he commands us, *Since God so loved us, we also ought to love one another. . . . If we love one another, God lives in us and his love is made complete in us.* And John tells us not just to *say* that we love, but to show our love in all that we do. Yes, because God loves us, we are to love each other, and we can love, as long as we are certain of God's love for each one of us. It is much easier for me to love someone who is being difficult when I remember that God loves me even when I am at my worst, at my most unlovable.

THE LIVING WORD

K arl Barth said, "I take the Bible far too seriously to take it
literally." The Bible is a book which urges us to keep our

DECEMBER 5

concept of God open, to let our understanding grow and develop as we are illuminated by new discoveries. If we stopped where Scripture leaves us, in the New Testament as well as the Old, we could still, with clear consciences, keep slaves. The apostle Paul exhorts masters to treat their slaves well, and slaves to be obedient, with no hint that slave-owning may not be a good thing in the eyes of God. According to the law, a woman taken in adultery was to be stoned. To death. Not men. If we stopped, literally, with Scripture, we could keep on justifying going into any country we wanted, when we needed extra living space, and slaughtering the heathen natives, because God is on our side, and will help get rid of the pagans for us, so we can have their country.

Who are the pagans? A child, asked this question in Sunday school, replied, "The pagans are the people that don't quarrel about God."

It is terrifying to realize that we can prove almost anything we want to prove if we take fragments of the Bible out of context. Those who believe in the righteousness of apartheid believe that this is scriptural. I turn to the Bible in fear and trembling, trying to see it whole, not using it for my own purposes, but letting its ongoing message of love direct me.

SHE KNOWS THE SHEPHERD

There's a true story I love about a house party in one of the big English country houses. Often after dinner at these parties people give recitations, sing, and use whatever talent they have to entertain the company. One year a famous actor was among the guests. I've been told he might have been Charles Laughton. When it came his turn to perform, he recited the Twenty-third Psalm, perhaps the most beloved psalm in the Psalter. *The Lord is my shepherd, I shall not want.* His rendition was magnificent, and there was much applause. At the end of the evening someone noticed a little old great aunt dozing in the corner. She was deaf as a post and had missed most of what was going on, but she was urged to get up and recite something. In those days people used to memorize a lot of poetry! So she stood up, and in her quavery old voice she started, *The Lord is my shepherd,* and went on to the end of the psalm. When she had finished there were tears in many eyes. Later one of the guests approached the famous actor.

DECEMBER 6

"You recited that psalm absolutely superbly. It was incomparable. So why were we so moved by that funny, little old lady?"

He replied, "I know the psalm. She knows the shepherd."

GOD'S LOVE OUTLASTS OUR REBELLION

DECEMBER 7
If we read Scripture from the first verse of Genesis through to the last line of John's Revelation with a big pad, and set down the angry passages on one side, and the loving and forgiving passages on the other, the love and forgiveness far outweigh the anger. Over and over God calls us to say, "I'm sorry, Daddy, I want to come home," and then the door is flung open.

I have been asked, and many times, "But can't we choose to exclude ourselves?" Of course. Haven't we, as children, haven't our own children flung out of the room in anger? And haven't we waited for them to come back? We have not slammed the door in their faces. We have welcomed them home. Jesus said, *"If you . . . know how to give good gifts to your children, how much more will your Father in heaven give good gifts to those who ask him!"*

STORY AS VEHICLE FOR TRUTH

DECEMBER 8
People have always told stories as they searched for truth. As our ancient ancestors sat around the campfire in front of their caves, they told the stories of their day in order to try to understand what their day had meant, what the truth of the mammoth hunt was, or the roar of the cave lion, or the falling

318

in love of two young people. Bards and troubadours throughout the centuries have sung stories in order to give meaning to
the events of human life. We read novels, go to the movies,
watch television, in order to find out more about the human
endeavor. As a child I read avidly and in stories I found truths
which were not available in history or geography or social
studies.

BEYOND BIBLICAL LITERALISM

The Bible is not objective. Its stories are passionate, searching for truth (rather than fact), and searching most deeply
in story. The story of David is one of the most complex and
fascinating in the Bible, with its many prefigurings of Jesus. In
working on *Certain Women* I discovered many more contradictions than I had remembered—two different ways of bringing David himself into the story, two different versions of
Saul's death, for instance. But what the biblical narrator is trying to do is tell us the truth about King David, and the truth is
more important than facts.

DECEMBER 9

THE PARABLES ARE TRUE

Jesus, the storyteller, told of a man who had a plank of wood
in his eye and yet criticized another man for having a speck
of dust in his eye. *"You hypocrite,"* he said, *"first take the plank
out of your own eye, and then you will see clearly to remove
the speck from your brother's eye."* This parable, like most
of Jesus' stories, is true. Why must it be factual? Are we supposed to think that a man actually had a large plank of wood

DECEMBER 10

in his eye? The parable is, instead, a true story about our unwillingness to see our own enormous faults, and our eagerness to point out much smaller faults in other people. However, it's a lot easier to see this story as factual rather than true. If we can make ourselves believe that the man had a beam of wood in his eye, literally, then we don't have to look at our own faults, be challenged by Jesus' story, or maybe even feel that we have to do something about our faults. Literalism is a terrible crippler, but it does tend to let us off the hook. Or do I mean the cross?

SOUL FOOD

DECEMBER 11

The stories in the Bible have nourished me all my life, as has the poetry, the long lists of laws, the history, and even the begats. (In my little play *The Journey with Jonah,* I named the three little rats on the sinking ship Huz, Buz, and Hazo, out of the begats!) During my morning and evening reading of Scripture I do not skip. If it's there, it's there for a reason, and I read it all, every bit of it. If we read Leviticus with an open heart we will see that the message is not to burden people with an overwhelming number of laws, but to call us to be God's holy people. The laws are there to help us, not to hinder.

GOD'S WAYS ARE NOT OUR WAYS

DECEMBER 12

But it's the stories that have always drawn me. When I was a child (as now) there were stories I found difficult, such as that of the workers in the vineyard, where those who had worked only an hour were paid as much as those who had worked all day in the heat of the sun. It wasn't fair! Like most children, I wanted things to be fair, even though life had already taught me that unfairness abounds. I think many of us still feel like the child stamping and crying out, "It's not fair!" Those who have worked all day long should certainly be paid more than those who came in at the last minute! But Jesus is constantly trying to make us understand that God's ways are not our ways, and that God's love is far less selective and far greater than ours. "Is thine eye evil because I am good?" God asks in Matthew's Gospel after he has finished paying all the workers the same wage. When God blesses those we deem unworthy, does our jealousy make our eye become evil? Are we, like the elder brother, like Jonah, upset at God's forgiveness? Daily I need a deep and penitent awareness of how much greater God's love is than my own.

JESUS' STORIES ARE TRUE

O ne of the wonders of story is that it is alive, not static. A story that meant one thing to me when I was forty may mean something quite different to me today. Certainly I understand Sarah better now than I did when I was a child, or even when I was a child-bearing woman, having my babies during the normal age-span. We bring our own preoccupations and preconceptions to story, our own wounds, our own joys, and therefore our responses are going to vary. That does not invalidate them. The stories of Jesus' healing are particularly poignant to me right now, while I am still in the midst of my own healing. I was not able to reach out and touch the hem of Jesus' garment, but those who loved me touched it for me.

DECEMBER 13

EMBODYING THE GOSPEL

DECEMBER 14

We hear a lot about evangelism today and how the church must pay more attention to evangelism. But mostly evangelism is not what we tell people, unless what we tell is totally consistent with who we are. It is who we are that is going to make the difference. It is who we are that is going to show the love that brought us all into being, that cares for us all, now, and forever. If we do not have love in our hearts, our words of love will have little meaning. If we do not truly enjoy our faith, nobody is going to catch the fire of enjoyment from us. If our lives are not totally centered on Christ, we will not be Christ-bearers for others, no matter how pious our words.

THE LONELY LORD

DECEMBER 15

God's tough love did not stop with the birth in Bethlehem. It shone all through the life of Jesus. The Gospels show him as a strong and uninhibited man who enjoyed his friends, most of whom weren't "the right people"; he enjoyed his great gift of healing; he turned water into wine at a wedding feast; and he enjoyed his faith, even when no one understood him or why he was on this earth or what he was offering us. How terrible it must have been for him that no one understood him—not the disciples, not his friends, not Mary of Magdala, or Mary of Bethany. No one. And he kept on loving, even in his time of total abandonment.

The story of Jesus is indeed a great story, but it goes far, far beyond the realm of provable fact and into the realm of mystery and marvel.

JUST AS I AM, WITHOUT ONE PLEA

One of the many things the Bible stories have taught me is that God loves me, just as I am. I don't have to struggle for some kind of moral perfection impossible to attain. It is the biblical protagonists who, like us, far from perfect, show us how to be truly human. I don't believe that God deliberately made me with one leg considerably longer than the other, but that is how I am, and I am loved that way, resultant clumsiness and all. I knew that God loves me as I am, so I was able to accept the wondrous truth that my husband did too—one result of enjoying my faith! For we cannot give love if we cannot accept it.

DECEMBER 16

GET THE WHOLE STORY

Let's recover our story because we'll die without it. It's a life-giving story—this magnificent narrative we find in Scripture—if we are willing to read openly and to read all of Scripture, not just passages selected to help us prove our point. The God of Scripture can sometimes seem brutal, seen through the eyes of the early biblical narrator, who is looking at the Creator through crudely primitive eyes. But the God of Scripture is also the God who refused to nuke Nineveh, even though that's what Jonah wanted; who forgave David for a really staggering list of wrongdoings; who wants only for us stiff-necked people to repent and come home; who goes out into the stormy night for the one lost black sheep; who throws a party when the Prodigal Son returns; who loves us so much that God did indeed send his only begotten son to come live with us, as one of us, to help us understand our stories—each one unique, infinitely valuable, irreplaceable.

DECEMBER 17

GOD'S STORYBOOK

God is a great storyteller, and the Bible is the greatest of all storybooks. The early protagonists of the biblical stories had a directness in their encounters with God that was, perhaps, simpler in their simpler world than it is for us in our far more complex universe. Abraham dared to correct God: "Shall not the Master of the Universe do right?" he demanded. Moses talked with the God of light so intimately that it was contagious—his face shone. And Moses, like many of us, wanted to know what God looks like and was bold enough to ask to see God. God informed Moses that no one can look at the Lord of the Universe and live, and in one of the most extraordinary passages in Scripture, he put Moses in the cleft of a rock and protected him with his hand, and out of the corner of his eye Moses glimpsed God's "hindquarters" as he passed by.

I do not believe that we're meant to take this passage literally. It does emphasize the fact that we human beings with our human limitations cannot see, with our finite eyes, what the infinite Creator looks like. The God whom Moses ultimately saw with Resurrection eyes was different from the God whose hindquarters he saw as God passed by.

THE WORD OF THE LORD

God's story is true. We know that God's story is true because God gave us his Word—that Word who came to us, as one of us, and died for us, and descended into hell for us, and rose again from the dead for us, and ascended into heaven for us. The Word became the living truth for us, the only truth that can make us free. Part of that freedom is mortification. Part of that freedom is the Cross, for without the Cross there can be no Resurrection.

When was the last time anybody asked you, "Do I have your word?" Or when was the last time anybody said to you, "I give you my word," and you knew that you could trust that word, absolutely? How many times in the last few decades have we watched and listened to a political figure on television and heard him say, "I give you my word . . ." and shortly thereafter that word has been proven false. In the past year alone, how many people have perjured themselves publicly? Sworn on the Bible, given their word, and that word has been a lie? Words of honor are broken casually today, as though they don't matter.

Small wonder that when God tells us, "I give you my Word," few people take him seriously.

"I give you my Word," said God, and the Word became flesh, and dwelt among us, full of grace and truth.

AVOID IDOLATRY

The message of the Incarnation underlines the message that is all through Scripture: God cares about Creation. God is in it with us. If we hurt, God hurts. DECEMBER 20

If we abuse our free will, we hurt God. If we really cared about God and Creation, how could we continue to cut down the rain forests? to tear apart the ozone layer? to forget that our grandchildren will suffer from the results of our greed? What is happening to us human beings? Have all our icons become idols?

An icon is the opposite of an idol. An icon is an open window to the love of God. An idol is a closed door in the face of God's love. We must be sure that our symbols remain icons, rather than walls, like the Berlin Wall, or the Maginot Line, or the Iron Curtain—all of which have shown their fallibility.

THE TRUTH OF SCRIPTURE

DECEMBER 21

So what do I believe about Scripture? I believe that it is true. What is true is alive and capable of movement and growth. Scripture is full of paradox and contradiction, but it is true, and if we fallible human creatures look regularly and humbly at the great pages and people of Scripture, if we are willing to accept truth rather than rigidly infallible statements, we will be given life, and life more abundantly. And we, like Joseph, will make progress towards becoming human.

NAMING OVERCOMES EVIL

Meg Murry is discussing Naming with the cherub Proginoskes, who is more experienced in these things than she is.

DECEMBER 22

Progo! You said we were Namers. I still don't *know*: what *is* a Namer?"

"I've *told* you. A Namer has to know who people are, and who they are meant to be. I don't know why I should have been shocked at finding Echthroi on your planet."

"Why are they here?"

"Echthroi are always about when there's a war. They start all war."

"Progo, I saw all that awfulness you took me to see, that tearing of the sky, and all, but you still haven't told me exactly what Echthroi are."

Proginoskes probed into her mind, searching for words she could understand. "I think your mythology would call them fallen angels. War and hate are their business, and one of their chief weapons is un-Naming—making people not know who they are. If someone knows who he is, really knows, then he doesn't need to hate. That's why we still need Namers, because there are places throughout the universe like your planet Earth. When everyone is really and truly Named, then the Echthroi will be vanquished."

LOVE IS A FOUR-LETTER WORD

Meg's conversation with the cherub Proginoskes continues as they discuss the tests they face. Mr. Jenkins is the school principal. The evil Echthroi have created two false Mr. Jenkinses. Blajeny is the cosmic Teacher who has brought the cherub on his mission.

DECEMBER 23

B ut what—"
"Oh, earthling, earthling, why do you think Blajeny called for you? There is war in heaven, and we need all the help we can get. The Echthroi are spreading through the universe. Every time a star goes out another Echthros has won a battle. A star or a child or a farandola—size doesn't matter, Meg.

The Echthroi are after Charles Wallace and the balance of the entire universe can be altered by the outcome."

"But Progo, what does this have to do with our test—and with three Mr. Jenkinses—it's insane."

Proginoskes responded coldly and quietly. "Precisely."

Into the cold and quiet came the sound of the school buses arriving, doors opening, children rushing out and into the school building.

Charles Wallace was one of those children.

Proginoskes moved quietly in her mind through the roar. "Don't misunderstand me, Meg. It is the ways of the Echthroi which are insane. The ways of the Teachers are often strange, but they are never haphazard. I know that Mr. Jenkins has to have something to do with it, something important, or we wouldn't be here."

Meg said, unhappily, "If I hate Mr. Jenkins whenever I think of him, am I Naming him?"

Proginoskes shifted his wings. "You're Xing him, just like the Echthroi."

"Progo!"

"Meg, when people don't know who they are, they are open either to being Xed, or Named."

"And you think I'm supposed to Name Mr. Jenkins?" It was a ridiculous idea; no matter how many Mr. Jenkinses there were, he was Mr. Jenkins. That's all.

But Proginoskes was most definite. "Yes."

Meg cried rebelliously, "Well, I think it's a silly kind of test."

"What you think is not the point. What you do is what's going to count."

"How can it possibly help Charles?"

"I don't know. We don't have to know everything at once. We just do one thing at a time, as it is given us to do."

"But how do I do it? How do I Name Mr. Jenkins when all I think of when I see him is how awful he is?"

Proginoskes sighed and flung several wings heavenwards so violently that he lifted several feet, materialized, and came down with a thud. "There's a word—but if I say it you'll just misunderstand."

"You have to say it."

"It's a four-letter word. Aren't four-letter words considered the bad ones on your planet?"

"Come on. I've seen all the four-letter words on the walls of the washroom at school."

Proginoskes let out a small puff. "Luff."

"What?"

"Love. That's what makes persons know who they are."

GOD'S HUMBLE ACT OF LOVE

When we take ourselves too seriously, as the chief or only object of God's interest, then we fail to understand the magnitude of his love and concern for us. Artist and saint alike grope in awe to comprehend the incomprehensible disproportion of the glory of God and the humility of the Incarnation: the Master of the Universe, become of the earth, earthy, in order to be one with his creatures, so that we may be one with him.

DECEMBER 24

THE RISK OF BIRTH, CHRISTMAS, 1973

This is no time for a child to be born,
With the earth betrayed by war & hate
And a comet slashing the sky to warn
That time runs out & the sun burns late.

That was no time for a child to be born,
In a land in the crushing grip of Rome;
Honour & truth were trampled by scorn—
Yet here did the Saviour make his home.

When is the time for love to be born?
The inn is full on the planet earth,
And by a comet the sky is torn—
Yet Love still takes the risk of birth.

IMMANUEL!

And so he was born, this gloriously impossible baby, in a stable in Bethlehem. Mary and Joseph had to leave home because of the general census ordered by Rome; so Joseph took his young, pregnant wife to register in Bethlehem, because he was of the house of David.

Little Bethlehem was crowded, overcrowded with people coming to register. There was no room in the inn, no place for Joseph to take Mary, whose labor was beginning. How terrifying for Mary to be wracked with pain while Joseph tried helplessly to find someplace for them to stay. Finally they were guided to a cave where animals were lodged. There Mary gave birth to the infant Jesus, surrounded by lowing cattle, by donkeys and oxen. Exhausted, but filled with joy, she laid him in a manger.

Nearby, some shepherds were out in a field with their flocks when suddenly an angel of the Lord appeared before them and the glory of the Lord shone brilliantly all around them. And they were terrified.

"FEAR NOT!" the angel cried, and told them of the birth of the child who would bring joy to all people. They were told that they would find this holy child wrapped in linen cloths and lying in a manger.

Suddenly the angel was surrounded by a host of heavenly angels, singing in a mighty chorus to the glory of God.

When the angels left and the shepherds were able to speak, they hurried to Bethlehem. There they found Mary and Joseph, just as the angel had said, and the baby lying in a manger. They told Mary and Joseph about the angels, and Mary listened and treasured their words. Gently the shepherds placed the simple gifts—a lamb, a woolen wrap, a ball—by the baby and then Mary and Joseph were left alone with the child, marveling.

Holding the child in her arms, rocking, singing, Mary wondered what was going to happen to him, this sweet innocent creature who had been conceived by the incredible love of God and who had been born as all human babies are born.

God, come to be one of us.

GOD'S LOVE LETTER

I t is enjoyment in an ultimate victory that can be expressed only in the high language of poetry, not the low language of fact. What can we prove about Christ's coming in glory? Nothing. It is far beyond the language of limited proof. Indeed,

DECEMBER 27

our entire faith rests on a joyous acceptance of the factually impossible. When we celebrate Christmas we are celebrating that amazing time when the Word that shouted all the galaxies into being, limited all power, and for love of us came to us in the powerless body of a human baby. My faith is based on this incredible act of love, and if my faith is real it will be expressed in how I live my life, but it is outside the realm of laboratory or scientific proof. God—the holy and magnificent Creator of all the galaxies and solar systems and planets and oceans and forests and living creatures—came to live with us, not because we are good and morally virtuous and what God's creation ought to be, but precisely for the opposite reason, because we are stiff-necked and arrogant and sinful and stupid. We have indeed strayed from God's ways like lost sheep.

God still loves us so much that Christ, the second person of the Trinity, the Word, came to live with us as one of us, and all for love.

LIKE EVERY NEWBORN

DECEMBER 28

"The Lord is King, and hath put on glorious apparel; the Lord hath put on his apparel, and girded himself with strength:"

Like every newborn, he has come from very far.
His eyes are closed against the brilliance of the
star.
So glorious is he, he goes to this immoderate length
To show his love for us, discarding power and
strength.

Girded for war, humility his mighty dress,
He moves into the battle wholly weaponless.

CRYSTAL WITNESS

There is an ice storm, the electricity is out, and it is cold.
Vicky Austin narrates.

I don't know how long we'd been asleep when I felt someone shaking me, and I opened my eyes and it was Mother, DECEMBER 29
holding a flashlight. "Put something warm on, Vicky," she said,
"and come downstairs and see fairyland."

I put on my bathrobe and fuzzy slippers and wrapped a
blanket around myself and ran downstairs, and so did everybody else. Daddy had Rob rolled up in a blanket and was carrying him, which pleased Rob very much. We looked outdoors
and the moon was high and full and it streamed through the
trees and every single tiny twig was cased in ice and shimmered like diamonds. And the ground shimmered, too, because it was covered with spangles of ice. The two birches
were twin shining arcs of ice that seemed to be spraying off
rays of light. As the wind shook the trees tiny bits of ice would
break off and catch the moonlight as they fell to the ground.
Little clouds scudded across the moon, and it made the moon
look as though it were flying across the sky; and then the trees
made long delicate shadows that came and went along the icy
ground. It was so beautiful we couldn't speak, any of us. We
just stood there and looked and looked. And suddenly I was
so happy I felt as though my happiness were flying all about
me, like sparkles of moonlight off the ice. And I wanted to

hug everybody, and tell how much I loved everybody and how happy I was, but it seemed as though I were under a spell, as though I couldn't move or speak, and I just stood there, with joy streaming out of me, until Mother and Daddy sent us up to bed.

INFUSED WITH THE WONDER OF GOD'S LOVE

DECEMBER 30

What about the love? What about the love?

That's what! It's the Mysterium Tremendum et Fascinans. It's the energy of Christ informing mortal matter. It's the believing that permeates our being.

If we are infused, enthused with this joy and this wonder, then it will be infectious, far more infectious than answers to unanswerable questions. God loves us! We are not worthy—God save us from the worthy. We are saved by grace and bathed with love, and if we remember that with sheer, hilarious joy, then our numbers will stop dwindling (and numbers are something else we should stop worrying about).

Remember: "Our Lord said Feed my sheep, not count them!"

Grace is what it's all about, Lord of Lords in human vesture, Christ come to us as the mortal Jesus.

MARANATHA!

DECEMBER 31

We have much to be judged on when he comes, slums and battlefields and insane asylums, but these are the symptoms of our illness, and the result of our failures in love. In the evening of life we shall be judged on love, and not one of us is going to come off very well, and were it not for my absolute faith in the loving forgiveness of my Lord I could not call on him to come.

But his love is greater than all our hate, and he will not rest until Judas has turned to him, until Satan has turned to him, until the dark has turned to him; until we can all, all of us without exception, freely return his look of love with love in our own eyes and hearts. And then, healed, whole, complete but not finished, we will know the joy of being co-creators with the one to whom we call.

Amen. Even so, come Lord Jesus.

BOOKS BY MADELEINE L'ENGLE

Fiction

An Acceptable Time. New York: Farrar, Straus & Giroux, 1989; New York: Dell Publishing, 1990.

And Both Were Young. New York: Delacorte Press, 1949; New York: Dell Publishing, 1983.

The Arm of the Starfish. New York: Farrar, Straus & Giroux, 1965; New York: Dell Publishing, 1980.

Camilla. Reissuing in 1965 by Crowell of *Camilla Dickinson*, first published by Simon & Schuster, 1951; New York: Dell Publishing, 1983.

Certain Women. New York: Farrar, Straus & Giroux, 1992; San Francisco: HarperCollins, 1993.

Dragons in the Waters. New York: Farrar, Straus & Giroux, 1976; New York: Dell Publishing, 1982.

A House Like a Lotus. New York: Farrar, Straus & Giroux, 1984; New York: Dell Publishing, 1985.

A Live Coal in the Sea. New York: Farrar, Straus & Giroux, 1996.

Love Letters. New York: Farrar, Straus & Giroux, 1966; New York: Ballantine Books, 1983.

Many Waters. New York: Farrar, Straus & Giroux, 1986; New York: Dell Publishing, 1987.

Meet the Austins. New York: The Vanguard Press, 1960; New York: Dell Publishing, 1981.

The Moon by Night. New York: Farrar, Straus & Giroux, 1963; New York: Dell Publishing, 1981.

The Other Side of the Sun. New York: Farrar, Straus & Giroux, 1971; New York: Bantam Books, 1972; New York: Ballantine Books, 1983.

A Ring of Endless Light. New York: Farrar, Straus & Giroux, 1980; New York: Dell Publishing, 1981.

A Severed Wasp. New York: Farrar, Straus & Giroux, 1982.

The Small Rain. New York: Vanguard Press, 1945; New York: Farrar, Straus & Giroux, 1984. First section reissued as *Prelude* by Vanguard Press in 1968.

A Swiftly Tilting Planet. New York: Farrar, Straus & Giroux, 1978; New York: Dell Publishing, 1979.

Troubling a Star. New York: Farrar, Straus & Giroux, 1994; New York: Dell Publishing, 1995.

A Wind in the Door. New York: Farrar, Straus & Giroux, 1973; New York: Dell Publishing, 1976.

A Winter's Love. Philadelphia: Lippincott, 1957; New York: Ballantine Books, 1983.

A Wrinkle in Time. New York: Farrar, Straus & Giroux, 1962; New York: Dell Publishing, 1962.

The Young Unicorns. New York: Farrar, Straus & Giroux, 1968; New York: Dell Publishing, 1980.

Autobiographical

A Circle of Quiet. New York: Farrar, Straus & Giroux, 1972; San Francisco: Harper & Row, 1977.

The Irrational Season. New York: The Seabury Press, 1977; San Francisco: Harper & Row, 1983; New York: Farrar, Straus & Giroux, 1987.

The Summer of the Great-Grandmother. New York: Farrar, Straus & Giroux, 1974.

Two-Part Invention: The Story of a Marriage. New York: Farrar, Straus & Giroux, 1988; San Francisco: Harper & Row, 1989.

Personal Commentary on Scripture

And It Was Good: Reflections on Beginnings. Wheaton, IL: Harold
    Shaw Publishers, 1983.
Dance in the Desert. New York: Farrar, Straus & Giroux, 1969.
The Glorious Impossible. New York: Simon & Schuster, 1990.
The Journey with Jonah. Illustrations by Leonard Everett Fisher.
    New York: Farrar, Straus & Giroux, 1967. Reissued, 1991.
Ladder of Angels. New York: Seabury Press, 1979; New York: Pen-
    guin, 1980.
Penguins and Golden Calves: Icons and Idols. Wheaton, IL: Harold
    Shaw Publishers, 1996.
The Rock That Is Higher: Story as Truth. Wheaton, IL: Harold
    Shaw Publishers, 1993.
Sold into Egypt: Joseph's Journey into Human Being. Wheaton, IL:
    Harold Shaw Publishers, 1989.
A Stone for a Pillow: Journeys with Jacob. Wheaton, IL: Harold
    Shaw Publishers, 1986.

Poetry

A Cry Like a Bell. Wheaton, IL: Harold Shaw Publishers, 1987.
Lines Scribbled on an Envelope. New York: Farrar, Straus &
    Giroux, 1969.
The Weather of the Heart. Wheaton, IL: Harold Shaw Publishers,
    1978; New York: Farrar, Straus & Giroux, 1995.

Other

Anytime Prayers. Photos by Maria Rooney. Wheaton, IL: Harold
    Shaw Publishers, 1994.

Everyday Prayers. Illustrated by Lucile Butel. New York: Morehouse-Barlow, 1974.

Prayers for Sunday. New York: Morehouse-Barlow, 1974.

The Sphinx at Dawn. New York: Seabury Press, 1982.

The Twenty-Four Days Before Christmas. New York: Farrar, Straus & Giroux, 1964; Wheaton, IL: Harold Shaw Publishers, 1984.

Walking on Water: Reflections on Faith & Art. Wheaton, IL: Harold Shaw Publishers, 1980.

Recent Articles

"Epiphany: The Child Reconciles Us if We Will." *Episcopal Life* (January 1993), 20

"Good Friday: A Day When the Universe Shuddered." *Episcopal Life* (March 1993), 21.

"L'Engle Speaks of How Stories Capture Human Truths." *Language Arts* (February 1993), 137.

"Pentecost: We See Anew that the Spirit Always Was." *Episcopal Life* (May 23, 1993), 28.

"Tell Me a Story." *Victoria Magazine* (April 1995), 32–33.

"Too Obvious to Forget." *Victoria Magazine*. (June 1995), 26, 28.

Books Written with Others

"George MacDonald: Nourishment for a Private World." In *Reality and the Vision: 18 Contemporary Writers Tell Who They Read and Why,* edited by Philip Yancey. Dallas: Word Publishing, 1990.

Trailing Clouds of Glory: Spiritual Values in Children's Literature, edited with Avery Brook. Philadelphia: Westminster Press, 1985.

SOURCES BY BOOK

The Weather of the Heart (WOH), January 7, February 13, March
    22, April 2, April 6, April 25, November 28, December 25,
    December 28

A Wind in the Door (WID), March 1–3, December 22–23

A Winter's Love (WL), September 30

A Wrinkle in Time (WIT), January 25–26, February 17–18,
    October 21, November 20

SOURCES BY DAY

January

1 IS, 19–20
2 COQ, 206–7
3 IS, 2
4 COQ, 243
5 RTIH, 216
6 EL, January 1993, 20
7 WOH, 96
8 SOGG, 150–51
9 SFAP, 15
10 SFAP, 16–17
11 SFAP, 17
12 SFAP, 17–18
13 SFAP, 22
14 AIWG, 16–17
15 AIWG, 19
16 AIWG, 19–20
17 AIWG, 25
18 AIWG, 29–30
19 AIWG, 82
20 COQ, 10–11
21 COQ, 204–5
22 COQ, 174
23 AIWG, 31–32
24 AIWG, 32–33
25 WIT, 201–3
26 WIT, 206–8
27 TPI, 104
28 IS, 139–40
29 MW, 101–3
30 WOW, 133
31 WOW, 134

February

1 LL, 90–91
2 IS, 137
3 AIWG, 51
4 AIWG, 82–83
5 AIWG, 116–17
6 AIWG, 145–46
7 AIWG, 199
8 TPI, 151–52
9 COQ, 8
10 SFAP, 59
11 SFAP, 90
12 RTIH, 289
13 WOH, 20
14 LL, 72–73
15 LL, 73–74
16 AIWG, 21–22
17 WIT, 180–82
18 WIT, 184–86
19 RTIH, 56
20 RTIH, 96
21 RTIH, 100
22 RTIH, 173–74
23 SIE, 23
24 C, 59–61
25 C, 249–50
26 C, 92

27 ASW, 52–53
28 COQ, 174–75
29 SFAP, 124–25

March

1 WID, 178
2 WID, 178–79
3 WID, 190
4 AIWG, 61
5 RTIH, 89
6 RTIH, 40–41
7 RTIH, 149
8 IS, 94
9 COQ, 179
10 SFAP, 41–42
11 SFAP, 140–41
12 SFAP, 202–3
13 SFAP, 208–9
14 RTIH, 92–93
15 WOW, 45–46
16 RTIH, 145
17 RTIH, 147
18 COQ, 132
19 COQ, 132
20 COQ, 134
21 COQ, 194
22 WOH, 9
23 RTIH, 217
24 RTIH, 19–20
25 IS, 20
26 RTIH, 211–12
27 SFAP, 22–23

28 EL, March 1993, 21
29 IS, 17–18
30 SFAP, 209
31 RTIH, 174

April

1 RTIH, 260
2 WOH, 38
3 ROEL, 43–45
4 ROEL, 58–60
5 SIE, 213
6 WOH, 80
7 SFAP, 42–43
8 SFAP, 98
9 SFAP, 99
10 TS, 146
11 TS, 157–58
12 TPI, 194–95
13 SIE, 211
14 SFAP, 130–31
15 SFAP, 167
16 RTIH, 170
17 SFAP, 140
18 DIW, 267–68
19 DIW, 276–78
20 DIW, 328–29
21 SIE, 70–71
22 AT, 218–19
23 AT, 45–46
24 LL, 70–71
25 WOH, 44–45
26 WOW, 82

27 SOGG, 17–18
28 WOW, 88–89
29 WOW, 90–91
30 WOW, 91

May

1 SFAP, 84
2 SFAP, 154–55
3 SFAP, 168–69
4 SFAP, 174
5 SFAP, 175–76
6 SFAP, 201
7 SFAP, 211
8 PGC, 107–8
9 RTIH, 176
10 RTIH, 181
11 SFAP, 194
12 TSR, 298–99
13 TSR, 321
14 WOW, 13
15 WOW, 170
16 WOW, 19
17 WOW, 19
18 EL, May 1993, 28
19 CLAB, 80
20 COQ, 63
21 COQ, 63–64
22 ROEL, 288–89
23 ROEL, 317–18
24 ROEL, 322–24
25 PGC, 211–12
26 COQ, 34

27 COQ, 130
28 IS, 159
29 AT, 236–37
30 AIWG, 42–43
31 COQ, 180–81

June

1 IS, 156–57
2 ROEL, 61–62
3 ROEL, 72
4 RAV, 113
5 AIWG, 83–84
6 IS, 114
7 SFAP, 82
8 AIWG, 156
9 COQ, 178–79
10 WOW, 31
11 COQ, 99–100
12 COQ, 110–11
13 COQ, 124–25
14 CW, 93–94
15 CW, 326
16 ASW, 58
17 ASW, 126–27
18 ASW, 199–200
19 ASW, 202–3
20 ROEL, 144–45
21 ROEL, 146
22 ROEL, 149
23 COQ, 6–7
24 COQ, 11
25 COQ, 12–13

26 COQ, 32
27 COQ, 32–33
28 IS, 158
29 RTIH, 205
30 SFAP, 174–75

July

1 MBN 141–42
2 MBN, 144–45
3 SFAP, 47
4 WOW, 103
5 WOW, 104
6 SOGG, 48
7 SOGG, 72
8 SOGG, 126–27
9 ROEL, 156–57
10 ROEL, 160–64
11 SOGG, 53–54
12 C, 250–52
13 C, 98
14 ROEL, 236–37
15 ROEL, 268–70
16 SIE, 214
17 SIE, 60
18 SIE, 60–61
19 COQ, 243–44
20 COQ, 235
21 SOGG, 71
22 SOGG, 71
23 SFAP, 31
24 SFAP, 46
25 SFAP, 58–59

26 SFAP, 123–24
27 COQ, 41
28 COQ, 45
29 COQ, 97–98
30 SOGG, 134
31 SOGG, 142

August

1 ROEL, 202–3
2 ROEL, 218–19
3 RTIH, 21
4 RTIH, 22
5 RTIH, 25
6 RTIH, 30
7 RTIH, 145
8 ASW, 163–64
9 RTIH, 81–82
10 AT, 330–31
11 CW, 145
12 CW, 332–33
13 CW, 344–46
14 RTIH, 67
15 RTIH, 235
16 RTIH, 263
17 RTIH, 88
18 RTIH, 126
19 RTIH, 272–73
20 RTIH, 142
21 COQ, 111–12
22 COQ, 131
23 COQ, 244–45
24 SOGG, 233

25 SOGG, 234–35

26 SOGG, 235

27 SOGG, 243

28 SOGG, 243–44

29 SIE, 92–93

30 AIWG, 54

31 IS, 213

September

1 RAV, 120–21

2 WOW, 112

3 MTA, 39–41

4 RTIH, 20

5 SIE, 28–29

6 SIE, 99–100

7 SIE, 135–36

8 SIE, 205–6

9 SFAP, 89

10 SFAP, 165

11 WOW, 21

12 TPI, 123–24

13 TPI, 145

14 TPI, 94

15 TPI, 168

16 TPI, 166–67

17 TPI, 167–68

18 IS, 10–11

19 SFAP, 42

20 AOS, 242

21 IS, 171

22 TPI, 193–94

23 LL, 36

24 MTA, 20–21

25 IS, 153–54

26 ROEL, 166

27 RTIH, 176

28 RTIH, 276–77

29 RTIH, 277

30 WL, 152–53

October

1 WOW, 97

2 WOW, 98

3 MW, 277–80

4 MW, 295–97

5 GI, 17

6 IS, 58–59

7 IS, 60–61

8 IS, 77–78

9 WOW, 149

10 DIW, 132–33

11 HLL, 174

12 OTOS, 146

13 OTOS, 320

14 HLL, 154

15 HLL, 157

16 IS, 133–34

17 HLL, 40

18 IS, 10

19 STP, 72

20 STP, 183–84

21 WIT, 65, 67–68

22 MW, 224–25

23 SIE, 231

24 SIE, 64–65
25 SIE, 65
26 RTIH, 57
27 SFAP, 97
28 RTIH, 147–48
29 SIE, 20
30 SIE, 205
31 PGC, 35–36

November

1 SFAP, 101
2 WOW, 50
3 WOW, 55–56
4 WOW, 57
5 WOW, 62
6 WOW, 71
7 WOW, 71–72
8 SIE, 158–59
9 SIE, 163–64
10 SIE, 164
11 SIE, 165
12 SIE, 200
13 WOW, 129–30
14 WOW, 162
15 WOW, 181
16 WOW, 25–26
17 ROEL, 117–18
18 ROEL, 119
19 WOW, 22
20 WIT, 198–99
21 SIE, 59
22 SIE, 61

23 SFAP, 179
24 WOW, 24
25 AIWG, 20–21
26 AIWG, 209
27 TPI, 124–25
28 WOH, 37
29 SFAP, 198
30 CLAB, 57

December

1 RTIH, 218–19
2 COQ, 179
3 COQ, 98–99
4 RTIH, 69
5 SFAP, 65–66
6 RTIH, 64–65
7 RTIH, 71–72
8 RTIH, 90
9 RTIH, 93
10 RTIH, 94–95
11 RTIH, 127–28
12 RTIH, 128
13 RTIH, 131
14 RTIH, 166
15 RTIH, 174–75
16 RTIH, 175–76
17 RTIH, 217–18
18 RTIH, 293–94
19 RTIH, 294–95
20 SIE, 62
21 SIE, 201
22 WID, 97–98

23 WID, 98–99
24 WOW, 132
25 WOH, 47
26 GI, 5
27 RTIH, 172–73
28 WOH, 46
29 MTA, 133–34
30 PGC, 40–41
31 IS, 214–15

INDEX BY TITLE

ABOUT THE AUTHOR

Madeleine L'Engle is a world-famous author whose career spans more than fifty years and forty books, fiction and non-fiction, adventure stories, family dramas, autobiography, religious commentary, and intriguing points of intersection among those genres. *A Wrinkle in Time,* her Newbery Medal–winning book about a determined group of youngsters in search of a father, has defied easy categorization since its publication in 1962 and has sold over two million copies. She divides her time between New York City and rural Connecticut. A complete listing of her books can be found on pages 337–38 of this book.

ABOUT THE EDITOR

Carole F. Chase has a master's degree in Bible from the Presbyterian School of Christian Education, a doctorate in Christian Ethics from Duke University, and is an ordained Presbyterian minister. She currently works as a professor in the religious studies department at Elon College in North Carolina, where she teaches a course on the religious dimensions of Madeleine L'Engle's writings. In 1989, at Carole's invitation, Madeleine came to Elon College and gave a lecture series. Carole is the author of *Madeleine L'Engle, Suncatcher: Spiritual Vision of a Storyteller.*